FAITH

Other works by
Dr. Jay Worth Allen

A Brief History of Redemption

Bless His Holy Name: God's Pattern For Worship

*And many other writings, booklets and pamphlets,
currently being used throughout the body of Christ
expounding the Holy Writ and proclaiming
the gospel of Christ Jesus to the lost.*

FAITH
- the articles -

Dr. Jay Worth Allen

AIR QUOTE PUBLISHING
Bolivar, Nashville
2012

Faith - The Articles

Copyright © 2012, Dr. Jay & Miss Diana Ministries, Inc.

Published by Air Quote Publishing, Bolivar, Tennessee, exclusively for:

Dr. Jay & Miss Diana Ministries, Inc.

at the bequest & on behalf of

Darrell Teubner *and* The County Journal Newspaper

All rights reserved. No part of this publication may be reproduced, stored in a retrieval system or transmitted in any form by any means electronic, mechanical, photocopying, recording or otherwise, except brief extracts for the purpose of review, or educational purposes without permission of the publisher and copyright owner.

Compiler & Editor:	Diana Leigh Allen
Cover design:	Joco & Lily®
Book design, Layout, and Interior:	In-house
Photography on back cover:	Karan Simpson, Mimosa Arts Studio
	www.mimosaarts.com

All service and trademarks are the property of their owners, including, The County Journal.

Scripture quotations taken from The Holy Bible, New International Version®, NIV®. Copyright © 1973, 1978, 1984 by Biblica US, Inc.®. Used by permission.

Scripture quotations taken from the King James Bible (KJV) are in the public domain outside of the United Kingdom. Within the U.K., the rights to the KJV are vested in the Crown. The text commonly available now is that of the 1769 revision, of the original 1611.

Scripture quotations taken from The Message Bible, The Green Bible and etc., fall under the fair use doctrine, codified by the Copyright Act of 1976 under 17 U.S.C. Section 107.

The prayer given by Kansas minister, Joe Wright, was delivered before an October 2000 session of the Kansas state Senate, and is a matter of public record.

Other sources not specifically referenced here fall under the fair use doctrine, codified by the Copyright Act of 1976 under 17 U.S.C. Section 107.

Air Quote Publishing is an imprint of Dr. Jay & Miss Diana, Inc.

ISBN-13: 978-0-9851160-2-6

Printed in accordance with the U.S. Department of Agriculture's Lacey Act of 1900, as amended in May 2008, to insure proper handling of all paper products used in the manufacture of this book.

Printed in the United State of America.

10 9 8 7 6 5 4 3 2 1

To Daisy Laybourn who is no longer with us . . .
And to Diana, Brooke & Alison who are.

FAITH - *the articles* -

Contents

Publisher's Note 1
Author's Note 3
Mankind's Holy Grail 5
A Living Book / A Three Part Series
    God-breathed 9
    Inspiration & Revelation 12
    A Living, Organic Whole 15
The Biblical Gospel 19
The Doctrines of Grace / A Nine Part Series
    The Doctrines of Grace / Part 1 23
        God is Sovereign / *An introduction into the Doctrines of Grace*
    The Doctrines of Grace / Part 2 26
        Eternal Security of the Believer / *Some History: Jacobus Arminius, John Calvin, and the Apostle Paul*
    The Doctrines of Grace / Part 3 29
        Practical Application of the Teaching of Scripture / *Kerygma, John Calvin's T.U.L.I.P., and the D.A.I.S.Y.*
    The Doctrines of Grace / Part 4 32
        Total Depravity / *The Righteousness of God is all that God demands.*
    The Doctrines of Grace / Part 5 35
        Unconditional Election / *"Salvation is of the Lord" Jonah 2:9*
    The Doctrines of Grace / Part 6 38
        Limited Atonement (Particular Redemption) / *"God Loves Everyone."*
    The Doctrines of Grace / Part 7 41
        Limited Atonement / *For whom did Christ die?*
    The Doctrines of Grace / Part 8 44
        Irresistible Grace & Perseverance of the Saints / *God will not be disappointed.*

FAITH - *the articles* -

The Doctrines of Grace / Part 9 47
    The Gospel of the Apostle Paul / *God is Sovereign and He does what He pleases.*

One Baptism / *A Five Part Series*
   One Baptism / Part 1 51
      Terms / *Baptism is plural*
   One Baptism / Part 2 54
      The Baptism of the Father by the Holy Spirit into the Body of Christ
   One Baptism / Part 3 57
      The Baptism of the Son with the Holy Spirit and with fire
   One Baptism / Part 4 60
      The Baptism of the Holy Spirit / *Water Baptism*
   One Baptism / Part 5 63
      Conclusion

Revival In The Land 67

Sin & Redemption 71

People Without The Law 75

A Handful of Articles About Our Savior
   Two Doors 79
      John 10 / *Access & Fellowship*
   The Vine & The Branches 83
      The Vine & The Branches are One
   Spirit & Fire 87
      A Jesus' Baptism / *A short discourse on the baptism of the Holy Spirit*
   The Lord's Supper 91
      *excerpt from "Since You've Asked . . ."
   Broken For You 93

God's Love Perfected 97

Love One For Another 101

Wrong Response To His Cross 103

Have You Really come To Christ? 105

Not After The Flesh 109

The Meaning of Sincerity 113

" . . . to the obedience of Christ" 115

Three American Holidays
   The Thanksgiving Story 119

TABLE OF CONTENTS

Christ was born on 123
The Incredible, Eatable Easter Egg 127
Easter & The Equinox 131
I Hate Easter! 135
400 Years & Counting! 139
    The 400th Anniversary of The King James Bible
Right Judging 143
    Responsible "sons"
The End-Times Apostate Church / A Four Part Series
    Best-Selling Snake Oil 147
    Lucifer's Gospel 150
    Silencing The Elect 154
    Rebels Without A Clue 157
Truly Just & Truly Fair 161
Without Controversy 165
Starvation of the Lambs 167
Preach The Gospel 171
The Biblical Church / A Brief Series
    The Real McCoy vs. McChurch 175
    Welcome To The Revolution 178
Ruling Piety & Devotion 181
    includes opening prayer for the Kansas Senate in October 2000,
    by Kansas minister, Joe Wright
Wrapping The Cross With Ole Glory 185
Don't Worry, Everything's Under Control 191
The Trial Of Your Faith 195
Thorns 199
After This Manner Pray 203
    *published in part by The County Journal as "A Conspicuous Omission of Prayer"
Doubt 209
Puritan's Progress 215
    A personal testimony of faith.
God In Everything! 219

FAITH - *the articles* -

So, You Wanna Be A Preacher . . ." 221

Islam / A Multi-Part Series

  Wake Up Church! Islam's A Comin' 225
  Introduction By Example

  One If By Land! Two If By Sea! 227

  Don't Burn Books! 230

Islam / A Multi-Part Series (continued)

  Qur'an 101 232

  The Ladies Of Islam 235

  The Fruit Of Muhammad's Loins 238

  Israel: The Land That God Promised 241
  A Historical Thumbnail

  Eradicating Christianity 251
  Current Events

God Judges To Restore 255

Joshua Judges Ruth / A Six Part Series

  Joshua Judges Ruth / Part 1 261
  "Jehovah is a man of war" (Exodus 15:3).

  Joshua Judges Ruth / Part 2 264
  "The just shall live by faith" (Habakkuk 2:4).

  Joshua Judges Ruth / Part 3 267
  "Righteousness exalts a nation, but sin is a reproach to any people" & *"Jehovah executes righteous acts, and judgments for all that are oppressed"* (Psalms 103:6).

  Joshua Judges Ruth / Part 4 270
  How God's deliverance was shaped by the right man, to the right issue. / *"Every man did that which was right in his own eyes"* (Judges 21:5).

  Joshua Judges Ruth / Part 5 273
  Boaz, the Hebrew, and Ruth, the Moabitess, in union, became the highway for God's ultimate realization of His purpose.

  Joshua Judges Ruth / Part 6 276
  The Kinsman-Redeemer - Christ Jesus!

Go Show Yourself To Ahab / A Ten Part Series

  Go Show Yourself To Ahab / Part 1 279
  1 Kings 17 / Elijah, the Tishbite

  Go Show Yourself To Ahab / Part 2 282
  Elijah & Ahab

  Go Show Yourself To Ahab / Part 3 285
  "Make me first a cake." So she did.

TABLE OF CONTENTS

Go Show Yourself To Ahab / Part 4 287
    Elijah shows himself to Ahab.
Go Show Yourself To Ahab / Part 5 290
    Elijah repairs the alter of the LORD.
Go Show Yourself To Ahab / Part 6 293
    There came a still, small voice.
Go Show Yourself To Ahab / Part 7 296
    God puts Elijah back to work
Go Show Yourself To Ahab / Part 8 299
    "And there came a man of God."

Go Show Yourself To Ahab / A Ten Part Series (continued)

Go Show Yourself To Ahab / Part 9 302
    Elijah gives Ahab a final word.
Go Show Yourself To Ahab / Part 10 305
    Why would God commission a lying spiri?

What Makes A Man? 309
    A Brief Autobiography

More Reading 313
    Read more by the author on the subjects in this book.

FAITH *- the articles -*

Publisher's Note

During the process of compiling the following articles from Dr. Jay's weekly Faith column into book form, it became apparent that the best introduction would be to simply introduce the reader to the articles themselves. But which one should go first? "Mankind's Holy Grail" stood out above all as the most articulate rendering of Dr. Jay's heart for all people. It will introduce you, not only to his fearless, unabashed writing style, but more importantly, to the common theme that runs through all of these articles: the deep desire to see "all men live Free."

The book has been structured in such a way as to render the reader's experience, as much as possible, to that of the original printing in *The County Journal: The Weekly Newspaper of Hardeman County*. The publication dates have been inserted directly under each article, for those of you, who, like myself, are curious about such things.

The first article published by *The County Journal* was on July 15, 2010, entitled: "Don't Worry, Everything's Okay!" Soon after, Dr. Jay began writing articles for the opinion section, in addition to his weekly faith column. This has afforded him the opportunity to relate biblical teaching to the world in which we all live. Though unplanned, each week, his opinion articles coincide with his faith articles, supporting his biblical teachings - revealing the practical application of scripture for us who live "in the world," but are "not of it." As a result, several of the articles originally published under the opinion section have been included due to their biblical relevance.

In addition to *The County Journal*, Dr. Jay writes for a variety of physical & online publications. Some of these works have been included, given the larger scope of a book, and to offer the reader a broader understanding of the subjects in hand.

Finally, in keeping with the fact that within a writer's own words, the writer, himself, is revealed, "What Makes A Man?' has found its place as the last article in this book. Autobiographical in nature, it seemed best to place it there, reiterating the joy, hope and love you, the reader, will experience as you journey through this collection.

The Publisher

FAITH *- the articles -*

Author's Note

It is no accident that this book and these articles, first published in weekly newspaper form, are entitled FAITH. That is what's called a "Standing Head" in the arcane jargon of journalism, and it will not change anytime soon. Faith can, like other subjects, be written from any number of points of view. "Faith," states the writer of Hebrews, "is the substance of things hoped for, the evidence of things not seen." We are "justified by Faith," "we have access by Faith," "Faith comes by hearing," and "what is not of Faith is sin." Simple, eh? For everyone, except the most learned seminary professor, Faith must be considered obscure, esoteric, mysterious, mystifying, deep, profound and to the mere human, completely unfathomable. And, if anyone thinks that I am foolhardy enough to attempt to convey the true nuance of Faith within a thousand-words-or-less weekly newspaper column, giving sense & explanation to each and every ear, each and every week, I can only say that I agree. When Darrell Teubner, the kindly (and Christian) publisher of The County Journal, asked me to write a FAITH column for his weekly newspaper, I had no such idea in mind. I had been writing for years, and the idea of telling the story of our Glorious God and Savior to any and all who would read, sounded, to me, like the greatest thing since sliced-bread. However, when presented with the idea, I did have the customary reservations about the whole conception. But in the end I said, "Yes!" and I did, as I always do with any chore set before me, I simply followed the admirable advice of the King of Hearts in *Alice in Wonderland*, "Begin at the beginning, and go on until you come to the end: then stop." The results are these articles of FAITH.

The articles themselves are essentially theological, doctrinal, and, hopefully, relate to the ordinary Christian citizen and their concerns. There are unavoidable moments, from time to time, when basic matters of modern culture must be addressed - in order to explain heresy, schisms & differences in opinion or belief within the Body of Christ. But as far as possible, I have tried to steer clear of anything relating to rank & status in today's society, a subject which I am, in most cases, utterly unqualified to articulate, or to even get my tongue around. In doing so, I have, in the plainest manner possible, unambiguously followed the footsteps of many of the Old and New Testament Saints . . . I have tried to tell the Gospel story as it was told to me. The apostle Paul wrote, "Whatsoever things were written aforetime were written for our learning, that through patience and through comfort of the scriptures we might have hope" (Romans 15:4 KJV). So what you hold in your hands is my process of dialectical reasoning, as revealed in the Holy Scripture that you, upon reading, might have "hope." And with that "hope," an increased Faith. Hopefully I have succeeded.

So sit back, relax, and (hopefully) enjoy this short journey of FAITH, as seen through the innocent eyes of a writer.

Dr. Jay

Mankind's Holy Grail

My most frequently asked question is, Why it is that most people cannot see Truth, even when they're smacked in the face with it? After many conversations with friends who ask the same question, I've come to the conclusion that most People, just don't want to see truth.

There are extremely depraved men and women who make up the world's Power-Elite, both economically and ecclesiastically, who have cultivated pastures of lush-looking green grass for the Populace to graze upon. Fine and dandy. But why is it that hardly any of the Populace bother to look up from where they're grazing to notice the tags stapled to their ears. And why does that same Populace tend to view those of us - who see past the pasture into the parlor of the Feudal Lord's castle - as Insane?

Is it that the Populace simply "Doesn't want to see?" Or is it that they can't see what's happening because there is something blocking their view? Closed Doors: Doors, which open to Freedom. Doors, which must be Opened if mankind is ever to progress past Servant-Hood - if we are ever to be Free. Mankind's Holy Grail is not simply to live, but to live Free! There are Doors, which we must Open - Open with a turn of a knob, or a swift kick with a Boot!

There are approximately six billion people on the planet. Most of them will live and die without having seriously contemplated anything other than what it takes to Live on this earth.

Ten percent of the Populace will eventually Open a Door, which will begin to explain to them the History of this world. They will begin seeing the relationship between man and government and the meaning of God-Given, self-government. Sadly, ninety percent of the Populace in this group will live and die without Opening any other Door.

But, ten percent of that Populace will Open another Door to find that the resources of the world, including people - slave and free (Revelation 18:13), are controlled by extremely wealthy and powerful families, whose incorporated old-world assets have, with modern extortion strategies, become the foundation upon which the world's economy is currently indebted. Ninety percent of the Populace in this group will live and die without Opening any other Door.

Ten percent of that Populace will Open one more Door to discover that there exists The Elite aggregate of people who are fashionable, wealthy, and influential. These are Pop societies that perpetuate the generational transfers of arcane knowledge that is used to keep the ordinary people in political, economic and spiritual bondage. Ninety percent of the Populace in this group will live and die staring at the next Door.

Ten percent of that Populace will Open one more Door and discover that the Apostle John was right. The Dragon, Demons and Beast we thought were the fictional monsters of childhood literature, are real and are the controlling forces behind the World's societies.

> "And the great Dragon was cast out, that old Serpent, called the Devil and Satan, who deceives the whole world; he was cast out into the earth, and his angles were cast out with him" (Revelation 12:9).

Ninety percent of the Populace in this group will live and die without Opening another Door.

What's behind the next Door? I think it's where your spirit, soul and body has evolved to the point you can exist totally Free on earth, like the Apostle Paul or Peter, or one of the women who first discovered the Lord's empty tomb - people who are so in touch with God that they brighten the world around them no matter what.

The one Door all mankind must Open - since all men will eventually die, and if they are to ever enter Heaven's Door, which reveals God and the Life Force in all living things - is, as I understand it from John chapter 10, the Lord Jesus Himself: "I am the Door." Most of humanity will live and die without ever Opening that Door.

Now, if you do the math, there are only a handful people on the planet who have Opened more than two or three Doors. The irony is incredible. Those who are stuck behind whichever Door they find themselves, have little choice but to view the people who have Opened Doors beyond them as Insane. With each Opened Door, exponentially shrinking numbers of increasingly enlightened people are deemed Insane by exponentially increasing masses of decreasingly enlightened people. Adding to the irony, the harder a Door Opener tries to explain what he is able to see to those who can't, the more Insane he appears to them.

The great majority of people on the planet will never bother to Open any Door. These people are tools of the Feudal Lords: the gullible

Populace, whose ignorance justifies the actions of slapdash politicians and irreverent preachers, and whose station in life is to believe that the self-serving Machines of the Elite are matters worth dying for.

Those who do begin to Open Doors are an increasing liability to the Feudal Lords' Land, because of their decreasing ability to be used as Tools to consolidate power and wealth of the many into the hands of the Elite. It is common for these Door Openers to sacrifice their relationships with friends and family, their professional careers and personal freedoms, more and more, with each Door they Open.

Albert Jay Nock (1870-1945), author of Our Enemy, the State, said: "What was the best that the state could find to do with an actual Socrates and an actual Jesus when it had them? Merely to poison one and crucify the other, for no reason but that they were too intolerably embarrassing to be allowed to live any longer."

The Doors are there. Open them if you will.

3 March 2011

FAITH - *the articles* -

A Living Book
A Three Part Series

A man must have God's Word as the basis of his ministry. He also must possess the Holy Spirit to interpret that Word. He must have God's revelation and God's Spirit concerning God's Word. Without that revelation and that Spirit, he is not a minister of God's word.

A Living Book
Part One

God-breathed

When God created man out of the dust of the earth, man was not alive. Man was not made a living soul until God breathed His living breath into him. Congruently, the Bible would have been just another book, without God breathing His life upon every Word. Therefore, the Bible is a living book - written by men, yet God's breath is upon every word (2 Peter 1:21), which is the meaning of "all Scripture" being God's inspiration (2 Timothy 3:16).

What makes the Bible so unique is its dual character. On the one hand, there is the outward, physical shell. On the other hand, there is the spiritual, God-breathed, dimension. As far as its outward shell is concerned, it was written from man's memory and can be retained in man's memory. It issued from man's mouth and is heard by man's ears. It is written in human language and understood by human understanding. The truths contained in the Bible can be retained in man's memory, understood by man's mind, and passed on from one man to another - when one only deals with its outward shell. This is the physical aspect of the Bible. Doctrines and creeds can be included in this category, because they are elements that can be grasped, understood and comprehended by man's intellect.

But, there's another dimension. The Lord Jesus said, "The words which I have spoken to you are spirit and are life" (John 6:63). This dimension involves Spirit and Life. In this dimension, God speaks His word within man. It is God's speaking and God's breath - which is not something a clever man can understand or a man with a good memory can grasp. It is not something that an intelligent man can fathom. This requires another Being. Physical ears, eyes, and mind cannot see nor understand this dimension of God's word, because it is related, completely, to the Holy Spirit; it is God's speaking and God's breath.

So we understand the Bible, not by its physical dimension, but rather, by its spiritual dimension. Those who only touch its physical dimension are not ministers of God's word. If the Bible didn't have its physical side, there would be no mistake - a man would either be a minister of God's word or not.

But the Bible does have its physical element. In this aspect, the Bible can readily be understood and accepted by man.

This is where the danger lies.

A man can preach the physical, human elements in the Bible by the power of his own faculties, and presume that he is a minister of the word. He can present all of its human elements and presume that he is serving the Church. He can presume that the truths he preaches are scriptural truths and that they conform orthodox into pure faith. But he deceives himself because his teachings have nothing to do with the spiritual aspect of the Bible; they are from another realm. We may think that because we understand Greek, we understand God's word. But many men who understand Greek, know very little of God's word. We may understand Hebrew, but not necessarily understand the Old Testament, because, the Bible contains words which are beyond Hebrew and Greek. It is one thing to understand a language, it is another thing to know God's word.

It is a common misconception that the more we study God's word, the more we can be a minister of His word. The matter is not if we study the Bible, but how we study it. God has to speak His word into us before it can become God's word to us. We must know God's voice. Only God can speak God's word. We must know God's voice, and God has to speak to us before we can become ministers of God's word.

In preaching the gospel, we do not preach the basis of the gospel, we preach the gospel, itself. The Bible is the basis of the gospel - it is the basis of God's speaking. However, we cannot say that this is what God is speaking to us today. God has spoken through His Bible. Yes, indeed! Without a doubt, God spoke those words at one time. But, God must breathe His breath into those words before they become living to us today. We still need God's revelation, God's breath, today. The Bible is not just God speaking in the past, it is His speaking today. His past speaking was His word, but today He must breathe His breath, afresh, once again upon His word to bring life.

We must realize that there are two realms to God's word. One is the written Word: doctrines, knowledge, teachings, prophecies, and truths. But this is only the visible realm. We may read that Abraham believed God and God reckoned him righteous. But God's justification of those who believe, may be nothing more than an outward, physical teaching to us. Anyone with a strong physical intellect can preach justification by faith and believe he is preaching God's word, but actually, he may merely be preaching the superficial aspect of the word.

The Bible is the ministry of God's word by His servants in the past. Romans was Paul's past ministry. At one time God spoke - breathed upon - those words to and through Paul. But, today, He must breath upon those words or we may only be touching the surface, the physical, outward side of Romans. It is not enough for God to breathe His breath just once. He has to breathe once again before we can touch His word and live.

4 August 2011

A Living Book
Part Two

Inspiration & Revelation

What is inspiration? Simply, God's breath upon His book. The Bible is God's inspiration. It is God-breathed. Without God's inspiration, the Bible could not be called the Bible. Inspiration is the basis of the Bible. It was through God's inspiration, His breath, that Paul wrote Romans.

What is revelation? It is God's breathing upon the book of Romans once again, 2000 years later. Through revelation we touch God's original inspiration. Inspiration is a once-for-all event, but revelation is a repeated experience. When God breathes His breath afresh upon His word today, we see what Paul saw yesterday - we have revelation. Revelation means that God is reviving today what He once gave through His inspiration.

God's Spirit revives His word in such a way that it becomes as living as when it was first written. When God wrote Romans through Paul, God's life was vibrant in both the writer and the writing. Today that life can be released once again. God can fill His word with the Holy Spirit once again. And when this happens, the word becomes as powerful, enlightening, and life-giving as it was at the first. This is revelation. Without revelation it is useless to merely study the Bible. Without revelation, we can study the Bible from the first page to the last without hearing a single word from God. Yes, the Bible is the word of God. At one time God spoke those words. But if you want those words to be God's words today, you have to ask God to speak, to refresh those words through His Holy Spirit once again. His refreshing, His revelation, will bring His words to life again. Without revelation, the Bible remains a closed book.

Picture a man preaching God's word. Suddenly, God begins speaking through him. Now, not everyone will hear God's word. Everyone will hear the sound and the words, and some will hear God's speaking, but others won't. Some will hear the doctrine, the truth, the message conveyed through the sounds and the words. Some may be able to recite those words over and over, but they may not have heard God's speaking at all. God's word is not just a doctrine or a teaching. Of course we need to hear doctrine and teaching, but we also need to hear something else. We need to hear God's personal speaking also. Then and only then can we say, "I've heard Your word Lord." Only then have we touched something Real. And that Real has touches us.

Suppose that same man is preaching the gospel to one-hundred people. Ninety-nine may hear and understand the doctrine and the truth. They may nod their heads and say, "Amen." All ninety-nine may know and hear these things, but it is possible that only one of the hundred, the one apart from the ninety-nine, receives a teaching beyond the teaching that the others receive, hears a voice beyond the voice the others hear, and grasps a word beyond the word the others grasp. This one hears God's speaking in addition to hearing the preacher, and he bows his head and confesses, "I'm a sinner. O God, save me." Such a man has heard God's word. The ninety-nine may have only touched things related to the human and physical aspect of the word, and as a consequence, not heard God's word. There is a fundamental difference between the two.

The same is true when reading the Bible. The Bible is God's word. At one time God spoke to Paul, Peter, John, et alii . . . But God's word is more than just words, expressions, doctrines, truths, and teachings on a page. It is God's speaking in addition to man's speaking. One is the realm of doctrines, truths, teachings, language, and expressions. In this realm anyone who is diligent and intelligent, who has a good mind and a sharp memory, can get by pretty well. But in the other realm, God has to reiterate His word to men. This is revelation. Do we know the difference? God spoke, and His words are recorded verbatim in the Bible. But God can, and must speak to us a second time through the written words of His Bible. This is God's speaking today. Afresh. This is revelation. God must speak to us again, through the same words He once spoke. He must enlighten us. He must grant us fresh revelation from within His established inspiration.

Many of us have been used by God to speak for Him. Nothing dramatic, just a fruitful word to a fellow's need. A couple of months may go by and we encounter a similar situation. Now, we may think that what we said before is appropriate for this similar situation today, so we repeat the same words and guess what . . . they fall flat. But why? Because there was no revelation, no refreshing from the Holy Spirit -

even though we said the same words. God's revelation brings forth fruit. We need to recognize the distinction.

We can repeat God's word, but we cannot repeat God's revelation. Revelation is in God's hand.

A man may come to us, today. If we speak John 3:16, he may readily confess that he's a sinner and believe. A little later, another man may come along. We may be in the same room and quote the same John 3:16, but the Holy Spirit may not speak, and the second man may not believe. John 3:16 has not changed. The seeming contradiction is whether or not the revelation of the Holy Spirit was present in our speaking - not God's inspiration.

It's not how much of the Scriptures we understand, or how many verses we can quote. We need another ingredient. We need revelation. Without God's revelation, God's inspiration will have little, or no effect.

11 August 2011

A Living Book
Part Three

A Living, Organic Whole

Our spoken words cannot be independent from those that are found in the Bible. All of God's subsequent Words are based on His original Words. All of the Words of the New Testament are based on the Words of the Old Testament. Hence, our speaking today must be based on the Words of the Old & New Testaments. God's Word is one living and organic whole.

But our spoken words must not only have God's original Word as its foundation; God Himself must open and explain that Word to us, as well. Therefore, not everyone who bases his speaking on God's Word is a true expounder of His Word. Neither can a person claim to be a preacher of God's Word simply because he has equipped himself with that Word. Many disciples were well-versed in the Old Testament, but that didn't condition them to write the New Testament. In the same way, just because a man is well versed in the Old & New Testaments, ordained & licensed, doesn't mean he is a teacher of the Word today. The Bible must be the foundation, but God must also furnish the explanation. We cannot trust our minds, memory, or diligence in speaking the Word. We cannot take God's previously spoken Word as it is, and make it God's speaking today.

A man who memorizes all 150 psalms may not be able to expound the Psalms. A man cannot interpret Isaiah simply because he's memorized it, or explain Daniel's prophecies just because he's spent fifty years studying it. Those who do not base their speaking on God's previously spoken Word cannot be His spokesmen; but those who do, are not necessarily His mouthpieces either. Those who speak without the basis of God's written Word are immediately disqualified. But this doesn't mean that those who speak with such a basis are accepted either. There were many scribes and Pharisees who were very familiar with the Old Testament, but none were His spokesmen. Just because someone has studied the Bible very thoroughly, doesn't mean that he's qualified to teach the Bible. God's true spokesmen are those who are familiar with

God's written Word and those to whom God has explained and opened up that Word. God's spokesmen must first possess a proper foundation, but he also must have the proper interpretation.

How does God interpret His word? There are at least three ways: through prophecies, history, and synthesis[1]. And all three require revelation by the Holy Spirit.

The Holy Spirit took full control of Matthew when he related the story of the Prophecy of the Lord Jesus. "Behold, the virgin shall be with child and shall bear a son, and they shall call His name Emmanuel" (Matthew 1:23). This was Matthew's quotation of Isaiah 7:14. While Matthew was writing his Gospel, the Holy Spirit enlightened him, showing him that Isaiah referred to the birth of the Lord Jesus. That's revelation. "Emmanuel" - God is with us. Prior to that day, God was not with us in quite the same way. Now God is with us through the Lord's appearance on earth. This was revealed to Matthew by the Holy Spirit. We, as Matthew, must be familiar with God's past speaking, but we also must have the interpretation, the revelation of the Holy Spirit to His past speaking. Only the Holy Spirit can ascertain the meaning of the Word for us today.

Paul speaks of the History of Adam and Eve. "For Adam was formed first, then Eve; and Adam was not deceived; but the woman, having been deceived, was in the transgression" (1 Timothy 2:13,14). Satan didn't deceive Adam directly, his deception was aimed at Eve. He tempted Eve first, and then Eve tempted Adam. Eve fell as a result of Satan's deception, and then Adam fell as a result of Eve's temptation. In the Old Testament we only have the record of this fact. But in the New Testament, the Holy Spirit opened up this fact to reveal to us that a woman should not be the head in the church - she should not dominate over the man. A pattern is shown, and a basic principle is established. Whenever the woman assumes any headship, sin is brought into the world. This is part of the History of Adam and Eve. Yet, when this is opened up, it becomes the basis of the Word today.

On the day of Pentecost Peter, utilized Synthesis and spoke from three passages: Joel 2, Psalm 16, and Psalm 110. His ministry of the word at Pentecost consisted of three parts of the Scripture. The Holy Spirit combined three passages together and reveled the meaning behind them. With a Synthesis interpretation, we receive New light from the Word today.

---

[1] The word synthesis, was first used in 1611 in the King James Bible, meaning, to put together.

We do not receive isolated, unrelated, revelation all at once. Rather, we build upon God's past speaking. This was the way with Paul, Peter, and et alii. This is the Lord's way, today. There were men before Paul, and before us, there are the apostles, and God's written Word. Today's revelation must match our predecessors. Today's light and Word must match that of our forbearers. Paul needed the Spirit's revelation before he could preach or write the Word. If we want to be spokesmen of the Word today, we also need that same revelation of the Holy Spirit. God's Word is handed down from generation to generation. The second person sees more than the first, the third person more than the second, ad infinitum. As time moves on, more is revealed. God's Word continues to grow. In order to see more, we have to see what our predecessors saw. If God is merciful and gracious to us and opens our eyes to what He has spoken in the past, we will have a basis upon which to serve as true spokesmen of His Word today.

18 August 2011

FAITH *- the articles -*

The Biblical Gospel

Few churches today seem to be preaching the biblical Gospel. They announce a Savior from hell, rather than a Savior from sin, which is why so many are fatally deceived. For there are multitudes who wish to escape the Lake of fire, who have no desire to be delivered from their carnality and worldliness.

The Gospel is not "God loves you and has a wonderful plan for your life," nor is it "God gives you meaning for life." The Gospel is good news for bad people. It is objective, not subjective. The Gospel is the good news of Jesus Christ, the Son of God, being born under the law, as a human, living a perfect life by the aid of the Holy Spirit, and giving His life as a substitutionary sacrifice for others. But it doesn't stop there. By the power of the Holy Spirit, Christ Jesus was raised from the dead, ascended into heaven, and promises to return to consummate His kingdom.

It is by faith alone - *sola fide* - that we are justified. His righteousness is imputed to us and appropriated to us by faith alone. However this biblical Gospel is not being faithfully preached in many churches. Christianity for many is just a subjective affair between the individual and his own construct of God. Christians today are shifting from a historic faith towards a more amorphous spirituality - epitomized by the trivializing of God, our human condition, and the salvation wrought by God in Christ for us. We need to sort out the true gospel from the gimmickry or many will continue to be led away by the promise of "peace, peace" where there is none.

Natural-born man is so self-confident and self-sufficient that he deems himself quite competent to determine his own destiny. But over all his fancied efficiency, God has written, "without strength" (Romans 5:6) - not without physical, mental, or moral strength but, without spiritual strength, fallen man is spiritually dead. Therefore he is utterly unable to perform a spiritual act in a spiritual way or form a spiritual principle. Fallen, natural-born man is devoid of any spiritual desire or aspiration - though he may be very devout in the world's concept of "religion," he is dead, "without strength" God-ward.

But who believes this today. Who teaches this today? Few indeed, and fewer still have confirmed it by actual experience. The boast of Christendom today is: "I am rich, and increased with goods, and have need of nothing" - ignorant of her true condition, for the divine judge says to His Church, "you are wretched, and miserable, and poor, and blind, and naked" (Revelation 3:17). Nothing but God's great power can subdue the workings of such pride. Nothing but God's great power can bring the sinner as a humble suppliant and empty-handed beggar to the throne of grace. No effort of man. No Five Spiritual Laws. No Roman Road. No Christian video or television evangelist. No explaining the cross as a legal transaction, which took place because we broke the law and Jesus paid our fine. Nothing but the power of God can save a dead man who is "without strength" and "without God in the world" (Ephesians 2:12).

To believe on Jesus Christ with all our hearts appears to be one of the simplest acts imaginable, and to receive Him as our personal Lord and Savoir seems to present no great difficulty. Yet, in reality, before any soul actually submits to the Savior, there has to be the working of God's mighty power within that individual (beforehand - prior to) for them to realize their need of salvation. In other words, a miracle of grace must be wrought in any fallen natural-man before he can be saved. Before a fallen and depraved creature will voluntarily and unreservedly surrender to the just claims of Christ, before he will forsake his cherished sins and abandon his beloved idols, before his proud heart is lead to cast off all his righteousness as filthy rags, before he is willing to be saved by grace alone, before he is ready to whole-heartedly receive Christ as his Prophet, Priest, and King, God must draw him by His mighty power. Nothing short of the exercise of omnipotence is sufficient. Nothing but the Holy Spirit of God can make a dead man aware of his inoperative, lifeless spiritual position. The mighty power of the Holy Spirit of God must first bring life to a dead man before he can be saved - "So that your faith and hope might rest in God" (1 Peter 1:3-9, 13,20,21).

The fall brought fearful havoc in the whole of man's nature and condition. Every descendant of Adam was "shaped in iniquity" and is born into the world the slave of sin. No efforts of our own or any attempts by our fellowmen can, to the slightest degree, deliver us from our fearful bondage. Therefore it is apparent that a supernatural power must intervene if the sinner is ever to be emancipated from his captivity - none but the hand of God can smite his fetters loose and bring us out of prison. If the spiritual darkness of man's understanding, the perversity of his will, the disorderliness of his affections and passions were better understood, it would be more evident that no mere reformation could suffice, that nothing short of personal regeneration - the communication to him of a new nature and life - could be of any avail. The sinner must have an effectual call before he can be saved.

What do I mean by an effectual call? Broadly speaking there is a two-fold calling of God - the call from God: an external one and an internal one. The former is made to all who hear the gospel: "Unto you, O men, I call; and My voice is to the sons of men" (Proverbs 8:4). "Many are called, but few are chosen" (Matthew 20:16). That external call through the scriptures is addressed to human responsibility and meets with universal rejection. "I have called, and you refused; I have stretched out My hand, and no man regarded" (Proverbs 1:24). "Come, for all things are now ready; and they all with one consent began to make excuse" (Luke 14:18). This is an external call to all of humanity.

But God gives another call to His elect: a quickening call, an inward call, an invincible call, what the theologians term His "effectual call." "Whom He did predestinate, them He also called: and whom He called, them He also justified" (Romans 8:30). This is a calling from death to life, out of darkness into God's "marvelous light" (Peter 2:9). As the closing verses of 1 Corinthians 1 tells us, not many receive this call; it is one of mercy and discriminating grace to His elect alone.

Ephesians 1:18 speaks of this effectual call, and terms it, "His calling" because God is the author of it. The regenerate are "the called according His (eternal) purpose" (Romans 8:28), because God is the Caller. But "not many wise men after the flesh, not many mighty, not many noble are called" with His internal "calling." Only His chosen elect will ever experience this effectual call of God to the saving of their souls.

As the Father ordained peace, as the incarnate Son made peace, so the Holy Spirit brings us into the same. He communicated faith to the heart of His elect whereby we savingly believe in Christ. Then, "being justified by faith, we have peace with God" (Romans 5:1) objectively. We are brought into His favor. But more, we enjoy peace subjectively. The intolerable burden of guilt is removed from the conscience and we "find rest for unto souls." Then we know the meaning of that word "The peace of God, which passes all understanding, shall keep your hearts and minds through Christ Jesus" (Philippians 4:7). By His Spirit, through Christ Jesus, the Father has now actually bestowed peace upon

His believing child; and, in proportion as his mind is stayed on Him, by trusting in Him, the child of God will be kept in perfect peace (Isaiah 26:3).

Blessed is this biblical Gospel of our loving God and Father.

22 July 2010

The Doctrines of Grace
A Nine Part Series

"Salvation is of the Lord."(Jonah 2:9)

These articles were written for those who bow to the authority of God's Holy Writ. They are but a small piece of God's theological pie, yet, they are an extremely important slice, which most accurately reflects the teaching of the scriptures concerning the nature of God's sovereignty in the Redemption of His saints.

I hope you enjoy all eight articles.

My love in Christ,

Dr. Jay

ps. I had originally intended on writing only eight articles for this series. However, in light of the inordinate use by the Church of Arminius' and Calvin's teachings, rather than the Apostle Paul's on this important subject, I wrote a ninth, and final article."

The Doctrines of Grace
Part One

God is sovereign and He does what He pleases. An aphorism, which is one of my favorites. A blunt maxim, which articulates clearly what and who God is: independent, autonomous, self-governing, self-determining; nonaligned, free to do as He pleases. God is Sovereign. He rules by the counsel of His own will and no other.

God has foreordained everything that has come to pass; decreeing what is and what is to come; governing the world and everything and everyone in it according to His rule and authority; God has established the world and the heavens according to His divine purpose and not according to some aimless whim; God is never changing; God's purpose in all things are according to how He will have them. "According to the plan of the One, working all things according to the counsel of His own will" (Ephesians 1:11). God is sovereign and He does what He pleases - most assuredly in the Salvation of men.

FAITH - *the articles* -

God, in His sovereignness, has given us a Book which is complete and divine in its order. God loves order. "God so loved order . . ." (John 3:16). That's the Greek word here, *kosmos* - order. The world was in disorder so He sent His Son to bring Order.

God sent His Son in the likeness of our sinful flesh who, was "touched with the feelings of our infirmities, but was in all points tempted like as we are, yet without sin" to save us. God is good. He saw the prerequisite and filled it Himself. God became one of us to save us. He became sin for us; sacrificed Himself for us; was raised from the dead for us; and now sits at the right hand of the Father making intercession for us - "Salvation is of the Lord" (Jonah 2:9).

Somehow in this day and age, we've laid down Truth and picked up experience. So that we are now interpreting the Truth of God with the consistency of our experience, rather than interpreting our experience to make it consistent with the Truth of God. And the reason is simple: Our enemies have stopped fighting us; they've joined us and infiltrated us with a gospel of their own invention. Which, in most cases, has absolutely nothing to do with the Bible, but it does nicely illustrate Shakespeare's point that the "devil can cite Scripture for his purpose."

Today's Church is being baptized with a scam-artist gospel: A gospel that denies mankind's depraved and fallen, separated from God, totally dead in trespasses and sins nature. A gospel that seeks to elevate man in the eyes of his Creator, while using Christian terminology to generalize and marginalize the work of Jesus Christ on the cross. A gospel of man's good-works over the Work of God. A gospel that encourages sinners to accept Jesus in much the same way they Confirm a Facebook friend request. A gospel which has nothing to do with the Gospel of God.

So what is the Gospel of God? "Salvation is of the Lord." Our Salvation is the Work of God alone. "Lord, You will ordain peace for us: for You also have wrought (*shaped*) all our works in us" (Isaiah 26:12). This speaks of the Divine work of the grace of God "wrought" by God alone, in the heart of His People. And this text is not alone: "It pleased God, who separated me from my mother's womb, and called me by His grace, to reveal His Son in me" (Galatians 1:15,16). These passages speak of the inward workings of God's grace in His saints; from Justification, to Salvation, through Glorification. Our Salvation has been "wrought" by God . . . alone. "Not of works lest any man should boast" (Ephesians 2:9). "Salvation is of the Lord."

Divine grace works "through Righteousness," never at the expense of it. God does not make light of sin. God does not condone our transgressions. The Lord is "the Lord that heals" (*Jehovah-rophi*), but He is also "the Lord, our righteousness" (*Jehovah-tsidkneu*). One does not work without the other. God is "the God of all grace" and the God of, "be ye holy, for I am holy;" we are saved by Grace and we walk by Faith. One is the saving work of God, the other is the governmental action God requires of His people. Jesus is Lord and with His Lordship comes guiding principles of conduct.

My desire is not to squander typeface by describing in great detail the responsibility of the Saint. My task here is to shed light on God's sovereign Doctrines of Grace in Justification, Salvation, and Glorification that He "furnished" ("before the foundation of the world") for His Saints. But, before we venture into that treatise, may I (*Spartan*-ly) purport a few words concerning the unalterable responsibility of the child of God - thus, adding my two cents to the pot.

A saint is free to fail, but a saint is not free to be irresponsible. Even though "He has not dealt with us after our sins, nor rewarded us according to our iniquities" (Psalm 103:10), there are Responsibilities in behavior we Believers are obligated to demonstrate in whatever circumstance we may find ourselves in - we are to manifest, in our living, what our Father is like. We're free to fail, but we're not free to be irresponsible. As children of God we are obligated to occupy the place of Responsibility within the world our Father has placed us. In other words: Let's *not* "sin so grace can abound."

Our "Salvation is of the Lord." Alone. But why? So all the glory might be His. He is the "author and finisher," of our faith. If we have any part in it, it will not be effectual or secure. Whatever we touch we spoil. But "I know that whatsoever God does, it shall be for ever: nothing can be put to it, nor any thing taken from it: and God does it, that men should fear before Him" (Ecclesiastes. 3:14).

"Salvation is of the Lord."

30 December 2010

The Doctrines of Grace
Part Two

Three men whose Doctrine and Theology has had the greater influence upon the lives of Christians today are Jacobus Arminius, John Calvin, and the Apostle Paul. Sad to say, Arminius' and Calvin's influences are far in advance of Paul's.

Jacob Arminius was born in Amsterdam, Holland, four years before the death of John Calvin. He became a champion of Calvinistic Dutch Reformed theology. Ultimately chosen to write a defense against attacks upon Calvinism, Arminius came to the conclusion that he could not support many of Calvin's doctrines and abandoned them entirely. In rejecting Calvinism, and in the attempt to construct his own scheme of beliefs, Arminius made the Fatal Mistake of mixing 5th century Pelagian Dogma with the Scriptures.

Pelagius, the English monk who sought to reform the Roman Catholic Church, became a life-long theological antagonist of Augustine. Pelagius insisted that man did not inherit Adam's sinfulness, but was only affected by Adam's example. He believed that man's will was Free to choose for, or against, God. Hence, via Arminius, we have our present-day Arminianism or Christian Humanism, i.e., man is master of his own fate - with God's help - if he chooses.

Using Pelagianism instead of the Scriptures, Arminius based man's Salvation upon the will of Fallen man. Arminianism is an anti-sovereignty, anti-security, anti-grace, pro-works religion. Arminians believe that God, through Redemption, bestows a "Common Grace" upon all men, thereby making it possible for the individual to exercise his Free Will either for, or, against God's sovereignty.

In Arminianism, man is not Totally Depraved - man's will remains Free to decide his own destiny. It is man's Will to believe, and God's grace to assist. Biblical "foreknowledge" in Arminianism, means that God "foreknows" those who will receive the Savior, and upon that basis He may cast a vote for them. Those who Choose to reject the Savior, God opts-out. The final decision is made by Man, and God then acts upon that decision. Thus, in Arminianism man is Sovereign.

The ultimate factor in Arminian salvation is the sinner's choice of God, and not God's choice of the sinner. Those elected by God are chosen only in the sense that He "foresaw their faith and good works" - both of which arise from themselves and are not "wrought" of God. The human will is exalted to the place of Sovereignty and, according to this system, man becomes his own Savior. Grace never actually saves the sinner, but only enables him to save himself . . . if he wills.

Because the Arminian begins with his own Free Will, his end is the same as his beginning - he can come in and go out as he chooses. The little Security and Assurance of salvation the Arminian has, is founded upon whatever momentary merits and emotional experiences he can muster-up along the way. His Christian existence is experience-based, which is beset by fears, uncertainties, backslidings, and failure.

Doctrinally established Unconditional Eternal Security of the Believer, grounded upon faith in the finished work of the Lord Jesus Christ is utterly rejected by the Arminian. Their misleading error in the field of Salvation is that it persists in attempting to build the Christian's standing upon man's feeble and faltering daily life, rather than on the sufficient and Immutable Merit of the Lord Jesus Christ. The Arminian's Salvation becomes little more than a system of human conduct; for, "though the idea of regeneration is incorporated, it is, in the Arminian idea of it, of no abiding value, being supported only by a supposed human merit." L. S. Chafer (*Systematic Theology*, Book 3, pp.356).

Arminianism existed for centuries as just one more Heresy in the outskirts of true Christianity. In fact, it was not championed by an organized Christian Church until the year 1784, at which time it was incorporated into the system of Doctrine of the Methodist Church in England by John Benjamin Wesley.

Today's Christendom has been overrun by Arminianism - being spread by the Pentecostal and Holiness movements, the out-of-control Charismatic movement, and the influence of denominations such as the Assemblies of God, Church of God, Church of God in Christ, Church of Christ, Disciples of Christ, Nazarene, Mennonite, Christian & Missionary Alliances, and many others.

The basic teachings of Arminianism is this: Human depravity has not rendered man incapable of exercising his will to trust Jesus for salvation. God's grace is Resistible in the final sense so that man can ultimately thwart God's purpose to Save him. God's election is Conditioned upon His divine "Foresight of Faith" in certain men whom God, then, designates as His elect. Jesus' atonement was exactly the same for everyone with no discrimination whatever, rendering all men

Savable, but actually Guaranteeing the Salvation of none. Salvation is possible for believers, but ultimate victory rests with their Continuance in the faith, so that ultimate Apostasy and Hell may be possible for the Elect. Dominated by the Free Will of man, Arminianism is characterized by fleshly lawlessness. The Arminian's center and object is himself - not God.

Arminianism is to be avoided at all cost!

"Now I beseech you, brethren, mark them who cause divisions and offenses contrary to the doctrine which ye have learned; and avoid them" (Rom. 16:17).

Next week: John Calvin, the theologian of the Reformers.

6 January 2011

The Doctrines of Grace
Part Three

The practical application of the teaching of Scripture is so needed today. What value is Biblical knowledge or understanding, if they exert no vital influence upon our conduct? God has given His Word not only for our information, but as a Principle to walk by, and every chapter in it contains important rules for us to appropriate and put into practice. The Doctrines of Grace which is before us supplies a timely case in point.

It is absolutely essential for every Born-Again Believer to learn the scriptural difference between their relationship to the Flesh and to the Spirit. Only from the Pauline epistles will the Holy Spirit minister these Christian truths. Then, when established and hid with Christ in God, the Believer can be ministered to by the remainder of the Word without being drawn from their position in Christ, Who is their Life.

Most everyone has a knowledge of God, yet, our knowledge may be based on what we have been told by men, rather than what we know from the Spirit of God, which dwells within us. Denominations were sired by men. The Church was birthed by the Holy Spirit on the day of Pentecost; kept by the promises of God, through His Spirit, until the day of redemption - our resurrection - as the bride of Christ.

Today we have many untaught, Unregenerate men (and unscriptural women) occupying the pulpits of our Christian Churches, and, "another gospel" (Galatians 1:6) is being widely circulated. Multitudes of preachers, who have neither "tasted that the Lord is gracious," nor have "the fear of the Lord" in them, have, because of various Natural motives and considerations, invaded the sacred Calling of the ministry, and out of the abundance of their corrupt hearts they are speaking. Being blind themselves, they are leading the blind into the ditch. They have no love for the Great Shepherd or His flock. They are themselves "of the world" and therefore "the world hears them" (1 John 4:5) - preaching what is acceptable to man's Fallen human nature, and, as like attracts like, they gather around themselves a company of admirers who flatter and support them. They bring in just enough of God's Truth to deceive the unwary and give the appearance of orthodoxy to their message, but not sufficient of the Truth, especially the searching portions

FAITH - *the articles* -

thereof, to render their hearers uncomfortable by destroying their False peace. They will name the name of Christ, but will not preach Him. They will mention the Gospel, but will not expound it.

Men in this day and age have stopped preaching what the early church called, *kerygma* - a Greek word in origin, meaning the proclamation of the significance of the death, burial, and resurrection of Jesus Christ: Christ died for the sins of His elect; He was raised from the dead on the third day; He now sits at the right hand of the Father, who is on the throne of Heaven; believers believe Him . . . and are saved. That's what the early church believed and taught: *kerygma*. (Peter in Acts 2, Paul in 1 Corinthians 15.)

Kerygma is the basic unity of the Gospels. No matter to what extent the Gospel writers differ in their linguistic emphasis, they all proclaim *kerygma*. Mark's portrayal of Jesus as the suffering Messiah differs from Matthew's picture of the Lord as the fulfillment of Jewish hopes. Luke's depiction of Jesus as champion of the poor, outcast, and sinners, varies slightly from the first two, and John's account gives us an image altogether different from either of the first three, in that he speaks to our Salvation as having already been obtained. Yet - *kerygmatically* - all of the Gospels are the same: the Elect, the Believers, have been redeemed through the death, burial, and resurrection of Jesus Christ! That simple fact is lost in Arminianism, but it is preached faithfully in Calvinism.

John Calvin, the theologian of the Reformers and patriarch of the Calvinists' dictum, was born at Noyon, Picardy, on 10 July 1509. Calvin is second only to Arminius in the extent of his Doctrinal influence upon the Church today. Sometime between April 1532 and November 1533, he renounced the Roman Church and adopted the Protestant faith. Then in 1536, he wrote his epoch-making treatise, *The Institutes of the Christian Religion*.

Calvin recognized the Scriptures as the ultimate authority; religious, personal, social and political. His tenets are Bible-based; the authority of the Bible replacing the power of the Papacy, the State, or man.

Calvin's, "What is the chief end of man? Man's chief end is to glorify God, and to enjoy Him forever," is the beginning of the Westminster Shorter Catechism. The statement was formulated long after Calvin's death, and is the manifesto of Scottish and English Puritanism. I added it here because it reflects the spirit of John Calvin so well.

Calvin worked along two lines, which were to dominate his whole life: the establishment of purity of Doctrine and purity of Living. The core of Calvin's teaching is seen in the five Doctrinal points known as the T.U.L.I.P. - **T**otal depravity, **U**nconditional election, **L**imited atonement, **I**rresistible grace and **P**erseverance of the saints. The core of the Arminian teaching is seen in the D.A.I.S.Y. - "He loves me. He loves me not . . . et cetera, et cetera."

Calvin believed that any infraction of the Word of God is sin - "all have sinned and fall short" - and that there is SIN into which all men (human beings) are born into from their father, the first man, Adam, and are, by nature, at enmity with God from that birth. Which is why man needed a Savior.

Which is where we will begin next week: *the Total Depravity of man.*

13 January 2011

The Doctrines of Grace
Part Four

One of the saddest verses in all of scriptures is, Ephesians 2:12: ". . . . having no hope, and without God in the world," is followed by one of the most joyful. "But now in Christ Jesus you who were once far off are made near by the blood of Christ."

Every man, woman, and child, save the Lord Jesus Himself, is born in Total Depravity, "having no hope and without God in the world." We are born corrupt and fallen; dead in trespasses and sins; justly deserving of the wrath and punishment of a Righteous and Holy God.

It is not my place to say who is the Lord's and who isn't - "Known unto the Lord are those that are His." But in this day of inclusiveness, my desire is to know truth. The Total Depravity of man is one of the most basic Bible truths, and one which is very misunderstood. So before I set out to explain what Total Depravity is, let me first explain what it is not.

Total Depravity is not absolute depravity. The adjective, *total*, tends to presume that man is as corrupt and as evil as he can possibly be. But that's not the purpose of the adjective. The adjective doesn't establish the intensity of our Depravity, but rather it specifies its extent. Neither does it imply that we couldn't sin to any greater degree than we already do. If you could plumb the depths of Evil in the human heart, you would find it a bottomless pit. There is no end to the evil man can and will do.

Total Depravity is not the absolute absence of Relative Good. Even in man's fallen condition there are works which men call Good: bravery and sacrifice during wartime; paladins, who discover cures for catastrophic diseases, devote their life to feed the world's hungry, etc. These works can, and are called Good in a relative sense, but not necessarily Good in a God sense.

Imagine, if you would, a run-of-the-mill neighborhood. One day a well dressed older gentleman moves into this quiet, family-oriented locale, sets up house and begins to blend in with his new surroundings. After a couple of months the neighborhood embraces the old guy. He seems virtuous and respectable. He's extremely helpful to all his new neighbors. He's nice to the neighborhood kids. He keeps a clean, well mowed lawn. He's a really sweet, likable guy. So, everyone in the neighborhood speaks well of the old fellow. He's well liked.

Late one summer evening, fifty commando type guys bust down the older gentleman's front door. Guns cocked ready to fire. Blue lights flash on every corner of the neighborhood. Screeching bull-horns blast out commands. The neighbors see the older gentleman coming out of his house, head down, handcuffed, escorted by a group of well-armed Federal authorities. The old man is gingerly seated in a unmarked car and they drive away.

The neighbors are mystified. They all agree that no one had ever seen him do anything wrong. "That old man wouldn't hurt a fly."

Later on that week the neighborhood folk see the old man's face, full-framed, on the National News. They hear the newscaster describe the old man's arrest and how, as an SS guard in one of Hitler's death camps, he was responsible for the deaths of thousands of Jewish and Christian men, women and children. The neighborhood is stunned. But why?

They're stunned because of the old man's Relative Goodness. But his relative goodness in the neighborhood won't carry a lot of weight in the Israeli justice system.   The Jewish courts won't take into consideration the old man's nice clean yard and how sweet he was to the children in the neighborhood. When the old man is judged, he will be judged against the backdrop of his heinous crimes committed against humanity during World War II, not the Relative Good he did in that quite suburban neighborhood.

The same is true in God's justice system. The Relative Good we do in this life, when put against the back-drop of our sin and rebellion against a Holy and Righteous God, won't carry a lot of weight in the justice system of Heaven's Court. There is nothing Good enough in us that can satisfy God's justice. There is nothing we can do, which will remove the stain of sin we were born into this world with. Our Relative Goodness may bring a moment of praise from our neighbors, but it will not satisfy a Holy and Righteous God. We are all born in Total Depravity, "having no hope and without God in the world" - which is why we need another's Righteousness. We need a Savior.

Total Depravity is only and always being at Enmity with God. We, in our natural state, are in the state of being actively opposed and hostile to God, and to all that He is. The entire race of Adam is fallen, and in our natural state we are dead in our trespasses and sins. Every part of our nature is corrupted, twisted and deformed because of Adam's original sin - that is the *total* aspect of Total Depravity. We, as sinful mankind, of the race of Adam, are justly deserving of the wrath, punishment and judgment of the One, Righteous, Holy God. If not for the righteousness of Another, we'd all be condemned to eternal fire! But Christ has come!

The Righteousness of God is all that God demands. That righteousness is found in Christ Jesus alone, who fully met every requirement in our stead.

Next week we'll look at, Unconditional Election.

20 January 2011

The Doctrines of Grace
Part Five

Salvation can be viewed from many angles and scrutinized under various aspects, but from whatever side we look, we must remember that "Salvation is of the Lord" (Jonah 2:9). Salvation was planned by the Father for His elect before the foundation of the world; purchased for them by the Holy life and Vicarious death of His incarnate Son; applied to and fashioned in them by His Holy Spirit. "Salvation is of the Lord."

Salvation is far more than an edict for sinners to receive Christ as Savior. Salvation is God's own Sovereignty and all-powerful work of Grace toward and in those who are entirely destitute of merit; those who are so depraved in themselves that they will not, nor cannot, take the first step to be saved. Salvation is God saving His people. "Salvation is of the Lord." And this is the point of truth where so many preachers fail in their understanding. While they affirm that Christ is the only Savior for sinners, they also teach that He saves only by the sinner's consent. While they allow the fact that conviction of sin is the Holy Spirit's work, they insist that the decisive factor in Salvation is man's own Free Will. But, "salvation is of the Lord," so nothing of the creature can enter into it at any point. God is pleased only with that which He has produced by Himself. "By grace are you saved through faith, and that not of yourselves; it is the gift of God" (Ephesians 2:8).

The Word of God does demand our responsibility and accountable; yet it is also true that none of us have ever met that demand. We are all miserable failures. It is this truth, which constitutes the deep need for God to work in us, and to do for us what we are unable to do for ourselves. We are "without strength and without God in the world" (Romans 5:6). Apart from the Lord, we "can do nothing" (John 15:5). Our Salvation must be from, and by, God alone. Our "Salvation is of the Lord."

The Gospel issues a call and a command to all who hear it, but we all disregard that call and disobey that command. And this is where we commit our greatest sin and manifest our vile enmity against God and His Christ: when a Savior, suited to our needs, is presented to us, we "despise and reject" Him (Isaiah 53:3). This is where we show what irredeemable rebels we really are, and demonstrate that we are deserving only of eternal torments. But it is at this point that God manifests His sovereign and wondrous Grace to His Elect. He not only planned and provided salvation, but he actually bestows it upon those whom He unconditionally Elects.

God, in His most Holy Grace, and entirely without any merit on His Elect's part, chose and elected, out of the mass of fallen humanity, some from every tongue, tribe, people and nation to be called the Sons of God. He chose to save those few, not with the view of anything good or worthy that He foresaw within those creatures. For there was nothing good, nor worthy, to be seen in them. But by His grace, for His own Glory, for His own Pleasure, and for His own Purpose, which He determined within Himself, did He choose to save whom He would save. This is God's unconditional Choice. This is Unconditional Election.

We have seen by the Total Depravity of man, that there is no condition that we, being dead in our sins, could meet, or conditions that we would meet, if we could meet, that would bring us to God, because we (as fallen creatures) stand in rebellion and enmity towards God. Thus, our Election is Unconditional and is not respected of any faith, of any repentance, of any holiness or of any good work, or of any perseverance on our part. All of these, faith, repentance, good works, holiness etc. are the fruit and effects of God's Electing grace; not the condition or the cause of that grace.

The doctrine of Unconditional Election, basically states that: we did not choose to accept or reject God (which sounds ridiculous), God chose us; we had nothing to do with the Spirit drawing us to the Father; we had nothing to do with our names being written down before the foundations of the world; we had nothing to do with any of the process of God saving us (no matter what the preachers or the numerous evangelical tracts say) and we have nothing to do with keeping or letting go of our salvation. It's "Election!" God has a majority vote of One.

Election is not a half-hearted attempt on the part of God. Election does not mean that God is anxiously awaiting the final ballet boxes to see who gets in to His heaven, and who doesn't. Election does not mean that God has no idea how many Mansions to build. Election means that God has foreordained that the Elect will be Saved. The Elect are not those whom God hopes will be saved. The elect are those whom God will Save. And He will save them to the Uttermost! "Elect according to the foreknowledge of God" (1 Peter 1:2).

God first gives life to His Elect sinner (John 6:63). Then, repentance (Acts 11:18; 2 Timothy 2:25). Then, faith (Ephesians 2:8). Then, spiritual understanding (1 John 5:20). Then, perseverance (1 Peter 1:5). Then, fruit (Hosea 14:8; Galatians 5:22). "Lord, You will ordain peace for us: for You also have fashioned all our works in us" (Isaiah 26:12).

In Romans 9, the Lord declares, "Jacob have I loved, but Esau have I hated." You may ask, "How could God have hated Esau?" My answer, "How could God have loved Jacob?" Thanks be to God for His Unconditional Election. "Salvation is of the Lord."

Next week we'll look into another Grace, which causes much more disturbance than necessary: *Limited Atonement*.

27 January 2011

The Doctrines of Grace
Part Six

    There's a popular notion in the Church today, that "God loves everybody." The marketability of that notion aroused my suspicion. God's love for all His creatures is the odds-on favorite tenet of Universalists, Unitarians, Christian Scientists, most Evangelicals, et cetera, and is held in highest regard on numerous Gospel Tracks. According to this warm-hearted Credence, no matter how much of a black-hearted, amoral reprobate you are - in open defiance of Heaven, with no concern whatsoever for your soul's Eternal interests, still less for God's glory, His Death, Resurrection and Glorification - it doesn't matter . . . "God loves you." So widely is this maxim proclaimed, and so comforting is it to the heart at enmity with God that Truth has little hope of countermanding it's delusion. Furthermore, the Paternalistic Mantra, "God loves you," is a modern-day construct. If you search the writings of the early church Fathers, the Reformers, the Puritans, you'll search in vain for any such concept. It was D. L. Moody, a cherished 19th century saint, who did more than anyone else to popularize this concept .

    Another of today's recycled tag-lines is, "God loves the sinner, though He hates his sin" - as evidenced by most Mass-Media Evangelists. But that's a meaningless distinction. It's a figure of speech, an oxymoron as in: *faith unfaithful kept him falsely true.*

    What is there in a sinner, but sin? Their "whole head is sick" and their "whole heart faint," and that "from the sole of the foot even unto the head there is no soundness" in them (Isaiah 1:5,6).

    Does God really love someone who is despising and rejecting His beloved Son? "God is Holy," as well as "Love," and therefore His love is a Holy love. To tell the Christ-Rejector that "God loves him" does nothing more than Cauterize his conscience and give him a false sense of security in his sins. "God is love." True. But love to whom? To proclaim, "God is love!" to the enemies of God is to take the "children's bread and cast it to the dogs." With the exception of John 3:16, not once in the four Gospels do we read of the Lord Jesus telling sinners that God loves them. There, our Lord apprised Nicodemus, a man who believed that God's mercies were confined to the Jews, that God's love in giving His Son had a larger object in view and that love flowed beyond

Palestine, reaching out to "regions beyond." In other words, God had a purpose of grace towards Gentiles, as well as Jews. "God so loved the world" signifies God's love is international in its scope. John 3:16 does not mean that God loves every individual, as evidenced by John 3:17: "that the world through Him might be saved" - all (*individuals within*) the "world" will not be saved. In the book of Acts, which records the Missionary work and the "Good News" preaching of the apostles, God's love is never referred to. But when we come to the Epistles, which are addressed to His saints, we have a full presentation of this glorious truth: "God is love" - love for His own (1 John). That's where the doctrine of Limited Atonement comes into play.

The doctrine of Limited Atonement is a bone of contention within the church. Yet, it is the focus of what the Father was doing in Christ Jesus on the cross. The purpose of the Father in the work of the cross, is the heart of Limited Atonement.

As I expound upon this doctrine of Limited Atonement, or more exactly, Particular Redemption, many of you may react harshly. The number one complaint is: "It's not fair." Some of us don't like the idea of the word "Limited" in relation to God's atonement. But, "when you look at this doctrine in the light of God's Word, you see the Sovereignty of God manifested, instead of man-made conditions exerted upon the fact of God redeeming whom He will." Diana Leigh Allen.

The people of God come from different backgrounds. God has been ever so faithful to bring us out of a multitude of experiences and environments to place us into His church body. But, if we were to encapsulate the essence of the last half of the 20th century and the beginning of the 21st, as we have dealt with conservative evangelical Christianity, the substance of what we, the church, have been teaching by and large for the past 50 or 60 years, is this: God loves everyone. But there's a problem, we're all sinners. God solved that problem when He sent His Son Jesus to die on the cross for all men. All you have to do is admit that you're a sinner and accept Jesus as your Savior. That's the bulk of the Gospel message preached in today's church and it's extremely offensive. Let me explain.

The crux of my offence is that the work of Christ on the cross has been diluted and glossed over. The church in this day and age has not, for the greater part, had the attitudes of the Bereans. We hear this gospel preached: "God loves everyone. Christ died for everyone," and we believe every word without question. If you search the scriptures, you will find that the "God loves everyone, just accept Jesus" gospel is not the testimony of the word of God.

The work of Christ on the cross is the focal point of God's work of redemption. It is the great hinge of history. The cross is the most important event in the history of the world; the death of Jesus Christ upon the cross.

When the truth of the word of God concerning the teaching of the cross of Christ is illustrated, most Arminians and a lot of evangelicals, seek to depict God as "fair" by their standards. But the Bible teaches that God is Objective by His own standards, not Subjectively fair by the standards of man. God is objective, not subjective. A marked difference.

The first question we must ask and the main one which must be answered is: For whom did Christ die? We will address that next week.

3 February 2011

The Doctrines of Grace
Part Seven

For whom did Christ die?

The collective response is: "God loved the world. Christ died for the sins of the world. God is not willing for any to perish. But there are those for whom Christ died to redeem, who simply chose not to be saved." In other words, Christ died, not only for those who'll go to heaven, but also for those who'll wind up in Hell. His atoning blood was wasted on those whom He could not save because they simply wouldn't let Him.

The Bible's position is very different: "And you shall have a Son, and you shall call His name Jesus, for He will save His people from their sins" (Matthew 1:21). Christ's saving Atonement is Limited to "His people" and that's what raises the hair on the neck of the masses.

The proper noun, Jesus, (from the Hebrew, Joshua, meaning: Jehovah is salvation) itself, implies a limited area (Jonah 2:9). "I am the good shepherd; and I know My sheep, and am known by My own . . . I lay down My life for the sheep" (John 10:14-15). Not for the goats, pigs or dogs, but for "the sheep." "Husbands, love your wives, just as Christ also loved the church and gave Himself for her" (Ephesians 5:25) - Christ gave His life for His Church - His Elect. That's for whom Christ died. That's Limited Atonement.

In the light of Election, Redemption and Calling, both the Arminian and the Calvinist agree that the Father elects, the Son redeems and the Holy Spirit calls. Both use similar terminology, yet the Arminian advocates an entirely different proposition.

In Arminianism, election is Conditional on man's response to the Spirit's call. But an election that's Conditional on something man does, decides, believes, or performs, is not election. That's simply God seconding a motion man has first put into existence. We don't get to Heaven by a show of hands. *Conditional* election is, at best, a paradox: it is not an election at all, because it occurs *after* the fact.

In Arminianism, Christ died to redeem all men to God through Christ Jesus. But the Spirit of God calls with such resistible grace, that man, of his own Free Will, can and very often does, refuse the call of the Spirit of God to be redeemed. Some will accept, some will not. Christ is successful in making atonement for all, but the Holy Spirit is successful only in those, who exercise their Free Will to choose Christ and be saved.

If a Calvinist says, "The Grace of God is Irresistible!" The Arminian rebuttal is, "No, the grace of God is resistible! You can stiff-arm God on the playing field of life, and go your own way. God implores you because He doesn't want anyone to perish, and He'll be really upset if you wind up going to hell. But it's up to you. You have to exercise your own Free Will, if you want to stay in His grace and get into His heaven."

The problem arises from the noun, Choice. God is sovereign. So logically, the Limited choice in election, predestination, foreknowledge or foreordination originates in Him alone - logically, not chronologically. We do not choose God and then He is obligated to accept us. Election is wholly by the foreknowledge, foreordination and grace of God, apart from any human merit or decision. "You have not chosen Me, but I have chosen you, and ordained you, that you should go and bring forth fruit, and that your fruit should remain" (John 15:16). But, we would rather *earn* grace than *receive* it. We feel the need to earn the right to God's goodness, even though He gives His goodness freely. We have an appetite for what speaks to our own ability. We want to feel as if we have obtained Salvation by something of our own merit.

But any Grace which can be resisted to the point of eternal damnation is not Grace at all. God's Grace is not earned - it is received.

> *"According as He has chosen us in Him before the foundation of the world, that we should be holy and without blame before Him in love having predestinated us unto the adoption of sons by Jesus Christ to Himself, according to the good pleasure of His will, to the praise of the glory of His grace, through which He has made us accepted in the Beloved" (Ephesians 1:4-6).*

If Christ's Atonement is unlimited - i.e. Christ died for everyone, for all men - then you can't believe in an eternal hell. If you once admit that there will be those who wind up in the Lake of Fire, and still hold to the Freedom of the Will of man to choose God or reject Him, then there is something lacking in your Atonement. How could Christ have fully atoned for all sin in hopes of redeeming all men to God, and yet, have failed in that Atonement to the point that some men will wind up in hell. That's an Atonement limited in it's power to "seek and to save, that which is lost."

"I am the good Shepherd. The good Shepherd gives His life for the sheep . . I know My sheep, and am known by My own . . . I lay down My life for the sheep . . . there was a division again among the Jews because of these sayings . . . and said to Him, 'How long do You keep us in doubt? If You are the Christ, tell us plainly.' Jesus answered them, 'I told you, and you do not believe.'"

Why didn't they believe? "Because you are not of My sheep . . . My sheep hear My voice, and I know them, and they follow Me. And I give eternal life, and they shall never perish; neither shall anyone snatch them out of My hand. My Father, who has given them to Me is greater than all, and no one is able to snatch them out of My Father's hand. I and the Father are one" (John 10:11,14,15,19-30).

Where are His sheep? In the hand of the Father and the hand the Son. That's an Eternally Secure place. Those who are not His sheep, "do not believe." He didn't say they choose not to believe, they simply, "do not believe." They're not His sheep! He laid down His life for His sheep. And that's Limited Atonement. Limited in scope, not in power.

Next we'll look further into, God's Irresistible Grace.

10 February 2011

The Doctrines of Grace
Part Eight

There are men who acknowledge the sovereign rule of God over material activity, who, with their next breath, will object to God's sovereignty in spiritual matters. But their quarrel is with God, not me - I am not seeking to convince them. God is sovereign and He does what He pleases.

When God places His sovereign call and grace upon a fallen and corrupted sinner, God will not be disappointed. God will effectively give life to that sinner and draw that sinner to Himself with Irresistible Grace. And will Preserve that saint to Himself, forever.

But we need to be clear on the nature of the Gospel itself. The Gospel is God's good news concerning Christ, not concerning sinners: "Paul . . . separated unto the Gospel of God . . . concerning His Son, Jesus Christ our Lord." (Romans 1:1-3). The Gospel is God's "witness" to the perfection of His Son.

The Gospel is not an "offer" to be tossed around by Evangelical Peddlers. The Gospel is no mere invitation, but a proclamation concerning Christ; true, whether men believe it or not. The Gospel is brief: "By grace you are saved through faith; and not of yourselves, it is a gift of God - not of works that any man might boast" (Ephesians 2:8,9). God simply announces the terms upon which men may be saved and, indiscriminately, all are commanded to fulfill them. The righteousness of God is all that God demands and approves. That righteousness is ultimately found in Christ Jesus, Himself, who fully met every requirement of the law in our stead. Christ Jesus is "made unto us . . . righteousness."

We have an opinion that "new birth" is forgiveness of sin. But it's not! We are "born again" because we have been forgiven, not in order to be forgiven. God, through the blood of Jesus Christ, His Son, has washed us from our sins, and as a result of that washing, that forgiveness, He gave to us the gift of the person of the Holy Spirit - whereby we are "regenerated," or as Peter says; whereby we are "born again." "Not of corruptible seed but of incorruptible by the word of God." "Not through the vain conversation received by tradition from your fathers." A "vain activity," Peter says, because it is by faith in

Christ Jesus - in His completed work on the cross, whereby we have already experienced forgiveness of sin - and as a result of our faith, we experience the "new birth."

God's Salvation is given through Irresistible Grace. By His sovereign operations upon and within, He "compels" His elect to come to Christ. And none can resist! "For who has resisted His will? . . . What if God, willing to show His wrath and to make His power known, endured with much longsuffering the vessels of wrath fitted to destruction . . . that He might make known the riches of His glory on the vessels of mercy, which He had before prepared to glory, even us, whom He has called, not of the Jews only, but of the Gentiles" (Romans 9: 19-24). God's grace is Irresistible.

Our Redemption is God's gift, which can never be lost. We are Eternally Secure. Those in whom the Father has placed His eternal love, those, for whom the Lord Jesus Christ died upon the cross to Redeem, those who the Holy Spirit draws with Irresistible Grace will finally, unconditionally, without a doubt, most assuredly wind up in heaven. Those of whom the Father has chosen, "before the foundation of the world," those who have been brought into "a new and living hope," are without the slightest chance of ever going to Hell. Our salvation is Preserved in God, "kept by the power of the Spirit until the day of redemption."

One of the most powerful Biblical arguments for Perseverance, or Eternal Security of the saint, is found in the words, "eternal life" or "everlasting life."

> *"For God so loved the world that He gave His only begotten Son, that whosoever believes in Him should not perish, but have Everlasting Life" (John 3:16).*

> *"He who believes in the Son has Everlasting Life; and he who does not believe the Son shall not see life, but the wrath of God abides on him" (John 3:36 AV).*

> *"Most assuredly, I say to you, he who hears My word and believes in Him who sent Me, has Everlasting Life, and shall not come into judgment, but has passed from death into life" (John 5:24 AV).*

> *"These things I have written to you who believe in the name of the Son of God, that you may know that Eternal Life, and that you may continue to believe in the name of the Son of God" (1 John 5:13 AV).*

If you will notice, the tense of all the verbs indicate present, current possession of "Eternal Life." Not that we might receive it in the future, we have it now, in the present. It is current possession. We, the believing ones, have "Eternal Life" now!

These Doctrines of Grace - Total depravity, Unconditional election, Limited atonement, Irresistible grace and Perseverance of the saints - are written for those who bow to the authority of God's Holy Writ. They are but a small piece of God's theological pie, yet, they are an extremely important slice, which most accurately reflects the teaching of the scriptures concerning the nature of God's sovereignty in the Redemption of His saints. It was on account of offenses that Christ died (2 Corinthians 5:21; 1 Peter 2:24). He was raised and exalted at the right hand of God because of the fact that His saints are justified by His blood (Romans 5:9,16). His resurrection is proof our sins are forever gone (Romans 4:25).

> *"Now to Him who is able to keep you from stumbling and to make you stand in the presence of His glory blameless with great joy"* (Jude 24).

Be glory forever, Amen.

17 February 2011

The Doctrines of Grace
Part Nine

In the weeks past we have looked at two men whose Doctrines have had the greatest influence upon the Church today - Jacobus Arminius and John Calvin. We now come to the one who, sad to say, is the least influential, the Apostle Paul.

Due to its humanistic base, Arminianism is suited to the carnal Church-man. It succeeds because it appeals to the natural mind of man. It is a subjective Religion, swayed by human emotions, rather than the Word of God. From start to finish Arminianism is man-centered, instead of God-centered.

Calvinism, though essentially God-centered, because of its objective, legalistic base, can be, and often times is, compatible with the carnal nature of the Church-man as well. As a rule, Calvinism's emphases on the external law tends to hamper internal growth and thereby cast aside certain Spiritual effects, vigor and influences.

Paul's near-exclusive teaching of the death-dealing Cross in the life of the believer, and the glorified Lord Jesus Christ as the believer's life, is in total opposition to the carnal, Adam-dominated Church-man. According to Paul, we are dead to the law, to the world, and to the principle of indwelling sin as centered in the old Adamic man.

Paul's focal points are the believer's crucifixion with Christ, and His risen life in the believer. "For we who live are always delivered unto death for Jesus' sake, that the life also of Jesus might be made manifest in our mortal flesh" (2 Corinthians 4: 11). The death of the Cross and the life of Christ are ministered to the believer by the indwelling Holy Spirit - not the law of Moses, the rule of the cleric, but rather the life of the Lord. "For the law of the Spirit of life in Christ Jesus has made me (us) free from the law of sin and death" (Romans 8:2).

Paul is the Revealer of the "pillar and ground of the truth," which is the Church of Lord Jesus Christ. Without the writings of the apostle Paul, we would have no understanding with respect to the Church. We wouldn't understand the Church as the "bride of Christ," or that Christ is head over His body, the Church. Everything we know and understand about the New Covenant people of God, we know from the pen of the Apostle Paul. God set Paul uniquely aside to give him that

Revelation.

Take Romans to Philemon out of the Bible and you are stripped of all New Covenant Church doctrine. Take all of Paul's Epistles out of the Bible, and you're left wanting of anything concerning the Church as the "Body of Christ," for no other Apostle even brings it up. You cannot find the "mystery of faith" (1 Timothy 3:9); the "mystery" of the union of Christ and the Church (Romans 12:5, 1 Corinthians 12:12, Ephesians 1:22, 23); the "mysteries of God" (1 Corinthians 4:1); the "mystery" of the restoration and salvation of Israel (Romans 11:25); the "mystery" of the resurrection and bodily transformation of the saints of God - "Behold, I show you a mystery; We shall not all sleep" (1 Corinthians 15:51; cf. 1 Thessalonians 4:17); or the "mystery" of the present hardening of Israel (Romans 11) in any other New Testament writer's pen. Paul alone reveals the "mysteries" of the Church and her relationship to the Risen Christ in his doctrines of Justification, Redemption, Sanctification, Glorification, Propitiation, et cetera. Paul is the great, divinely-chosen Revealer of the "Gospel" for this age.

Paul alone, reveals in great detail that all of humanity is so ruined by sin that they will not, indeed, cannot bring forth genuine repentance or saving faith apart from God's regenerating power. Nor can they in any way improve their spiritual condition or prepare themselves to receive the grace of God without the help of God. Beginning in the first three chapters of Romans, Paul reveals that, "There is non righteous, no not one . . . for all have sinned, and come short of the glory of God" (Romans 3:10,23). And that, before He created the world, God in His mercy freely chose certain individuals to receive Eternal salvation (Romans 8,9,10). His choice was not based upon anything He foresaw in mankind, such as faith, good works, repentance, belief, or their willingness to cooperate with Him. On the contrary, God saw that mankind was dead in trespasses and sins, and totally unwilling to seek Him. So the cause and means of salvation is entirely in God, and not in the individual.

The Christ-centered believer knows the Father in His sovereignty, and understands His divine purpose for him: predestined to be conformed to the image of His Son (Romans 8:29). His life is based upon the Father's pure grace and His perfect will. He is thankful that he is a "vessel of mercy," and that it is God who works in him both to will and to do of His good pleasure (Romans 9:23; Philippians 2:13). He acknowledges that the Father is the sole source of his election, and not his own will (Ephesians 1:4,5). He sees that God the Father sovereignly chose and then called him to salvation, that God the Holy Spirit prepared and drew him in such a manner that he responded to this calling and received God the Son willingly and responsibly (Ephesians 1:13). He rests eternally secure in the risen Lord Jesus Christ on the foundation of His finished work on the Cross and His faithful presence on his behalf at the right hand of God the Father (Colossians 3:3).

The failure or refusal to discern the Pauline Gospel as a Separate and New Revelation and not a "development from Judaism," accounts for two-thirds of the confusion in many people's minds today as regards to just what the Gospel is. Paul's Gospel will suffer no admixture with Works on the one hand or Religious Pretensions and Performances on the other. It is as simple and clear as sunlight is from the Heavens.

24 February 2011

FAITH *- the articles -*

One Baptism
A Five Part Series

*"There is one body, and one spirit, even as you are called
in one hope of your calling; one Lord, one faith, one Baptism,
one God and Father of all, who is above all and in you all"
(Ephesians 4:4-6).*

One Baptism
Part One

There is "one Baptism."

Some of us have a problem with that phrase, "one Baptism." Why? Because there are many Baptisms found in the scripture. Baptism shows up in different fashions, locations and under differing circumstances throughout the scripture. There's a multitude: The Baptism of Moses. The Lord's Baptism. The Spirit's Baptism. The Father's Baptism. Water Baptism. The Baptism of the Spirit. The Baptism of John . . . et cetera.

Baptism as a noun is used to identify the religious ceremony of sprinkling or immersing a Believer in water (symbolizing purification or regeneration), or, as the rite-of-affiliation with a Christian Church. Baptism, as a verb, is performed on young and old alike - it all depends on the denominational persuasion.

The Greek word, **Baptisma**: indicates immersion, submersion and emergence (from the word *bapto*: to dip) and is used of John's Baptism and the judgments our Lord submitted to on the Cross (Luke 12:50).

Baptismos: indicates a ceremonial washing (Mark 7:4,8).

Baptiste: denotes a Baptist (used only of John)

Baptizo: (a verb) is used as in washing oneself (Luke 11:38); and, for identification with the Lord (Acts 19:5).

So, our English catchword (Baptism) can refer to identification, immersion, washing, dipping and so forth. Scripturally, *Baptizo* is the action which establishes the believer with the Lord. Just as Love is an action verb, so is Baptism.

FAITH - *the articles* -

Throughout the Scripture the people of God experienced Baptisms. Plural. Baptisms are always used to identify the people of God with the Lord, and are, without fail, accompanied by experiences. In the course of these experiences, the people of God are identified with, Baptized, unto the Lord. At the same time they are Baptized, they are Sanctified from what they were before Baptism, and Sanctified from the World into the Lord - separated from the World and identified with the Lord through Baptisms.

God, by bringing His people together in Covenant with Himself, brings about these Baptisms to establish His people under a new authority. His authority. Not just to establish His people under His new authority Spiritually, but to position them under His authority Spirit, Soul and Body. "I pray God your whole spirit and soul and body be preserved blameless unto the coming of our Lord Jesus Christ" (1 Thessalonians 5:23). Every covenant of God is accompanied by a physical sign. The rainbow, circumcision and Baptisms are Physical signs of a Spiritual covenant or experience.

When Miss Diana sees me, she sees my physical body. Yet, my body is only part of me. When the time comes that I lay aside my body and "go into the presence of the Lord," my body will turn to dust. But on "that day" God will come down upon my dust and bring my dust together as a seed into the fruit, which will be brought forth as a glorious body "like unto the body of His glory" (Philippians 3:21). I am one person in three parts. I am spirit, soul and body. Yet, one.

This is true for all believers. God has "sanctified us holy." God is "sanctifying us holy." And, in "that day," He will "sanctify us holy" - spirit, soul and body - baptizing us into His glorious kingdom.

Baptism was never a problem for me. It wasn't for the apostle Paul:

"Therefore, leaving the principles of the doctrine of Christ, let us go on into perfection, not laying again the foundation of repentance from dead works, and of faith towards God, of the doctrine of Baptisms, and of laying on of hands, and of resurrection of the dead, and of eternal judgment" (Hebrews 6:1,2).

Here Paul lists the first principles of our faith. And Baptism is plural: "Baptisms." The word could be translated "washings." Whichever translation you prefer, the word is plural. When I first realized "Baptisms" was plural, I said to myself, "In the New Covenant economy, 'there is one Baptism.'" So I rationalized, "Then the only Baptism, which is valid before God for eternity, is the Baptism of the Spirit." This is the way my mind works. And I wasn't wrong. But, I wasn't right either.

Just as there are three identities within each of us (spirit, soul and body), there are also three Baptisms. The Baptism of the spirit, of the soul and of the body - "of the Father, of the Son, of the Holy Spirit." And God regards these three Baptisms as "one" - which accomplishes our perfect sanctification before the Lord. Three, yet "one Baptism."

I met a man the other day at a coffee shop. While we waited for our caffeine fix, we struck up a conversation. It wasn't very long until we both realized our kinship. There was something about him that witnessed to my spirit, and there was something about me that witnessed to his spirit - "one spirit," "one body." During our exchange I used a scripture to describe the waitress bringing our coffee, "Yea, how beautiful are the feet of them that carry the Gospel of good things."

"Amen," he replied.

Glory, the man was a believer too!

It's always interesting to see how we show up in "one spirit." I never asked the man's denomination, and he never asked mine. If either of us had asked, our fellowship may have been broken immediately. We just talked, enjoying the fact that we were both Baptized into "one body" in the Lord. I didn't need to know his Church tag and he didn't need to know mine. He could have been a Decaff to my Espresso - which could have blown our whole fellowship. We didn't talk doctrine. We just talked as "one body, one spirit, one baptism" in the Lord.

More on this next week.

7 April 2011

One Baptism
Part Two

*"I therefore, the prisoner of the Lord, beseech you
that you walk worthy of the vocation to which you are called,
with all lowliness and meekness, with long-suffering,
forbearing one another in love, endeavoring to
keep the unity of the spirit in the bond of peace"
(Ephesians 4:1-3).*

All of God's economy is a Unity. And all Unity is begotten by the Holy Spirit. There is no Unity apart from the Holy Spirit. We tent to think in terms of singularity in regards to this life, but that distinction is not accurate according to Scripture. In God's economy everything is a Unity - a whole, made up of varying parts. This is true in all of God's creation. It is true in the nature of God and in God's nature. In God nothing stands alone. One man does not work alone for the Lord; we all work together, as "one body." We do not need to pray for Unity because Unity already exists. We many not see it or walk in it, but Unity is there nevertheless. A simple tree testifies to God's system of Unity.

A tree is trunk, leaves and sap. We see the trunk and the leaves, but not the sap. Yet it's there. The sap is the one essential to the life of the tree. The sap is the tree's God given Life-Giver.

If the tree looses it's leaves or a few branches or part of its trunk, it's still alive. But if the tree looses it's sap . . . it's dead. What then is the believer's sap? The Holy Spirit. The Holy Spirit is not seen, but He is the One essential element to the life of God's people. He is our Life-Giver. Moreover, He's the Life-Giving source to all that is seen. Everything in God is a Unity, and as the tree is trunk, leaves and sap, we are spirit, soul and body. As the sap gives Unity to the tree, so the Holy Spirit gives Unity to the "body" - singularly and collectively. All Unity is begotten by God, the Holy Spirit.

"There is one body" - the body of Christ. "There is one spirit." In some of your Bibles *"spirit"* may be capitalized, but it shouldn't be. The noun does not have an article before it, neither is it prefixed by the word *hagios* - holy. Therefore the "one spirit" here is the "one spirit" which unites all believers into the "one body" - the "body of Christ." "There is one spirit," and that "one spirit" like that "one body" is made up of many members which are bound together as "one body" (the Church) united by the Holy Spirit in Unity.

When our spirit is redeemed, by the promise of the Father (the incoming of the Holy Spirit which begot us as a new man in Christ), we become "one spirit" with everyone within the "body of Christ." We are Baptized into the Body of Christ.

So the first Baptism all believers experience is the Baptism of the Spirit into the body of Christ by the Father. ". . . the Comforter, who is the Holy Spirit, whom the Father will send in My name" (John 14:24-26). Which is what the apostles were waiting for in the last chapter of Luke's gospel. The promise of the Father. The promise of the Holy Spirit (Luke 24:49).

In Acts 2 the Father sent the Holy Spirit, as soon as Jesus was seated at the Father's right hand and glorified in the Heavenlies, and Baptized those first believers and all who would come after by Christ Jesus. They were, as we are, immediately Baptized by the Spirit, upon belief in the Son (Galatians 3:25,26).

The Father Baptizes the believer, by the Spirit into the body of Christ - which sanctifies the believer's spirit -not the soul or the body, but the spirit within the believer. We are Born Again.

Thus, "if any man be in Christ, he is a new creation . . ." We usually stop there. but, Paul continues, "all things are of God" (2 Corinthians 5:17, 18). Is everything in your life of God? You may be thinking soul. You may be thinking spirit. You may be thinking body. You may be thinking, "How can everything in me be of God?" Simply, because God is in the believer. And because God is in the believer, the believer is sanctified throughout, Holy. And "we know all things." That's what John said, "you have an unction from the Holy One, that teaches you all things, and you have no need that anyone should teach you, for you know all things." Where do "we know all things?" In our spirit. Our soul doesn't know yet, but our spirit knows it all. The whole idea of our growth in grace and in the knowledge of the Lord and Savior Jesus Christ is getting what's in our spirit into our soul. Our problem is that we have heart, or spirit knowledge and little head, or soul knowledge. God wants to get what's in our heart into our head, because our soul governs our body. The spirit doesn't govern our body. The spirit governs our soul. The soul governs our body. We are souls: "God breathed into the man the breath of life and he became a living soul." I am a soul. I have a spirit. I live in a body. That's me. That's you. That's all of us.

Upon our belief, the Holy Spirit dwells in us and we become the holiest of all God's creatures. The Spirit of God dwells in the spirit of the believer and sanctifies that spirit and the believer's spirit becomes the Holiest of all before God, by the Father's Baptism of the Spirit into the body of Christ. But both, our soul and our body, need to be baptized, too.

Which we'll address next week.

14 April 2011

One Baptism
Part Three

The believer is Baptized first, with the Baptism of the Father (upon our belief, the Holy Spirit dwells in us and we become the holiest of all God's creatures - we are Born Again) and then of the Son, and then of the Holy Spirit. Baptism of the spirit, the soul, and the body of the believer. Three, yet "one" Baptism.

Our soul is what makes us function, think, and what governs our activity. Our soul requires something more than residence. Our soul requires precedence. This requires God coming, by the work of the Spirit, to bring His precedence over the believer so that the believer might reign in righteousness by one man, Christ Jesus.

"But when he (John) saw many of the Pharisees and Sadducees come to his Baptism, he said unto them, O generation of vipers, who has warned you to flee from the wrath to come? Bring forth, therefore, fruits befitting repentance . . . every tree which brings not forth good fruit is hewn down, and cast into the fire"' (Matthew 3:7-10).

John was Baptizing in water to manifest "Repentance." But what does God want? "Fruit" (John 15:8,16; Romans 7:4): the "fruit" of righteousness. John's Levitical Baptism, which is not valid for the church today, was a Baptism "unto repentance," not "Fruit."

John (Luke 1) was a Levitical priest through his father Zacharias, under the Old Covenant, in the line of Aaron, who Baptized in water "unto repentance." We are not Baptized with the Baptism of John. Neither are we Baptized with the Baptism which John Baptized the Lord.

John Baptized Jesus for an explicit purpose at an explicit time for a mandated duty only Jesus could attain (Matthew 3:15). We could not attain that purpose . . . even if we wanted too.

"I, indeed Baptize you with water unto repentance, but He who comes after me is mightier than I, whose shoes I am not worthy to bear; He shall Baptize you with the Holy Spirit, and with fire" (Matthew 3:7-11). This is not the Baptism which the Father brings. This is the Baptism which Jesus, the Son brings.

"Jesus," John said, "is going to Baptize with the Holy Spirit and with fire." What does fire suggest? "Power" (Acts 1:8). The Lord Jesus' Baptism brings "power" to the believer. The Father brings us into position in the family of God when the Holy Spirit comes to dwell within the believer, bringing us into a position before the Father, by that indwelling. We are "born again." The Baptism, which the Holy Spirit is going to render, will bring the believer "power" because Jesus is going to impart to the believer another Baptism. This Baptism will sanctify the believer's soul.

The Father Baptizes first. Then, the Son, sends forth the Holy Spirit to Baptize the believer with the Spirit. The effected in the Father's Baptism is in the spirit of the believer. The effected in the Son's Baptism is in the soul of the believer.

There is an interesting distinction between Acts 1:8 and Acts 1:5. Acts 1:5 speaks to us concerning the Baptism of the Holy Spirit. "For John truly Baptized with water; but you shall be Baptized with the Holy Spirit not many days from now." John Baptized with water before, Jesus lifted the cup saying, "This is the cup of the New Covenant." Acts 1:8 speaks to us concerning the Holy Spirit coming upon us. "But you shall receive power, after the Holy Spirit is come upon you; and you shall be witnesses . . . unto the uttermost part of the earth." This is the Son's Baptism. And with this Baptism, the believer receives "power."

When the apostle Paul met a group of believers at Ephesus (Acts 19:2) he asked them, "Have you received the Holy Spirit since you believed?" Belief is how we receive the Holy Spirit. "Except a man have the Spirit of Christ he is none of His." So when we believe, the Holy Spirit comes within us, making His residence within us. We are "born again," which is the Father's Baptism. But each time Paul laid hands on any believer in the book of Acts, "the Holy Spirit came upon them." These believers didn't receive Christ. They received the Holy Spirit. "The Holy Spirit came upon them." The Holy Spirit comes upon anyone who has believed. If I want to share the Lord with someone, I don't say, "You need to receive the Holy Spirit." No! I tell them they need to receive Jesus Christ. "Neither is there salvation in any other; for there is no other name, under heaven given among men, whereby we must be saved" (Acts 4:12). But if a person has already believed, the Holy Spirit is already indwelling him, he then needs to be Empowered. So I say, "You need to receive the Holy Spirit!" Receive the Power of the Spirit, which is the Son's Baptism (Matthew 3:11).

So the second Baptism, within our "one Baptism," is the Baptism from the Lord Jesus. The Son. Which Baptizes the believer into the "power" of the Holy Spirit. Which sanctifies the believer's soul. Which causes the believer to think differently. To act differently. To see things differently. All believers who have experienced this Baptism begin to think differently. Which is why I had a hard time calling this Baptism the Baptism of the Holy Spirit. Because there is only one Baptism of the Holy Spirit. But as I read, I began to realize that there is a little more to this subject than I expected. I realized that we can have more than one Baptism and still have "one Baptism."

Next week we'll look more into Baptism: Paedo (infant) or Credo (believer)? Saved or Safe? Sprinkle or Dip? And the division among the brethren.

21 April 2011

One Baptism
Part Four

There are three identities within each of us (spirit, soul and body), so there are three Baptisms: of the spirit, of the soul and of the body: "Of the Father, of the Son, and of the Holy Spirit." Yet, there is but "one Baptism" (Ephesians 4:4-6).

First, the Father Baptizes our spirit (Acts 2; Galatians 3) and we are "born again." The Son then Baptizes our soul (Matthew 3; Acts 1) and we receive "power." The next, and final step, in our "one Baptism," is the Spirit's Baptism of our body (1 Peter 3) where we are made "safe" from the World. Three, yet, "one Baptism."

This order - spirit, soul and body Baptisms - fell upon the house of Cornelius in Acts 10, when the Gentiles were introduced into the body of Christ. First, they believed, then they were filled, and finally, they were Baptized in water. A remarkable order. Their spirit, soul and body were Baptized. "In the name of the Father, and of the Son and of the Holy Spirit."

So what does the Spirit's water Baptism do?

In 1 Peter 3:18-22, we read, "For Christ also has once suffered for sins, the just for the unjust, that He might bring us to God . . . also He went and preached unto the spirits in prison . . . when once the long-suffering of God waited in the days of Noah . . . in which few, that is, eight souls, were saved by water; the like figure unto which even Baptism does also now save us."

Peter's "save" here is the word *diasozo*, to "bring safely through." Water Baptism is not a Baptism which Redeems, or Saves us from the wrath of God, "For God has not appointed us to wrath but to obtain salvation by our Lord Jesus Christ" (1 Thessalonians 5:9-11). But rather, this is a Baptism for our body - for Safety, not Justification. The apostle Paul didn't preach water Redemption, "Christ," he said, "sent me not to Baptize but to preach the gospel" (1 Corinthians 1:13-17). Paul preached a gospel of salvation by Faith, not Water. Baptism in water makes our Body safe (*diasozo*), in and from the world. That's why we're water Baptized. To "bring (the believer) safely through" this world - which is why Peter used Noah as an example. Noah's flesh was made safe through water. In like manner, our Body is made Safe through water

Baptism: "Which even Baptism does also now save us."

This "safety" Baptism first presented itself when the children of Israel crossed the Red Sea. First, their spirit was saved by the blood of the Lamb. Then their souls were saved on the shore of the Red Sea. And finally, the water Saved them in and from the world (Exodus 12 - 14).

Water in the scriptures is a figure of the Holy Spirit. Who then, in this case, is Baptizing in water? The Spirit. This is the Spirit's Baptism. Not the Baptism of the Spirit, but the Spirit's Baptism. The same Spirit Peter said, by which "Jesus preached unto the spirits in prison "Paradise" (Luke 23:43). This same Spirit is the authority given, when any believer Baptizes another believer in water. It is the same Holy Spirit, who is the authority for the sanctifying (safe-*ing*) of the physical Body of the believer. If that Authority is not present in the act of water Baptizing, you can dunk a guy in and out all you want, and all you'll get is a dripping wet guy, who's no more saved or safe than when he was dry - because the water Baptism was not done under the authority of the Holy Spirit. The Baptism was not the Spirit's Baptism. That Baptism may have put the guy's or baby's name on a Church roll, but it will not Baptize them safe. But, if a believer is Baptized in water by another believer under the authority of the Holy Spirit, then that Baptism will make Safe the body of that water-Baptized believer - as a body "unto the Lord."

Now the questions are asked: "Sprinkled, Dipped or Dunked?" "Infant or Believer?" Well, here's what the scripture says . . .

Baptism (linguistically) is a figurative synonym that translates itself back into itself. Baptism means Baptism. So there is no irrefutable method of water Baptism. I know the Immerse choir is singing now, but you'll find no sure Biblical-Guideline for dipping, sprinkling, or whatever other method of water Baptism the Church should use. It's not there. Did Phillip dunk the Ethiopian? Don't know. It doesn't say. Odds are, he did. But I really doubt that Cornelius' household was submerged . . . unless they had an indoor pool. Yet, in both cases they were made safe through the water.

So when should we Baptize?

One school practices Paedobaptism, (Latin *Paido*, for "child"), others practice Credobaptism, (Latin *Credo*, for "I believe"). In Credobaptism, a person is Water Baptized on the basis of their profession of faith in Christ Jesus. Whereas, water Baptism in the Paedobaptism tradition is practiced on infants (believer or not) and identifies the infant as a member of the Covenant Community (implied in Matthew 19:14 & Acts 16:33). There are true believers on both sides of this issue.

I'm a Calvinist who believes in the Gifts of the Spirit and Credobaptism. Why? Because I can't (like Calvin couldn't) prove, by Scripture, paedobaptism. Calvin doesn't defend paedobaptism by the Biblical narrative, but by "deduc[ing] its nature and meaning". . . "from the promises given in Baptism" (*Institutes of the Christian Religion*, IV: xvi).

Water Baptismal regeneration is not Scriptural; we are "saved by Faith," not Water (Acts 18:8; Galatians 3:26-29; Mark 16:16). New Covenant believers are there by Election, not Water. But all, after they have believed, will desire to be water Baptized.

Next week, the conclusion.

28 April 2011

One Baptism
Part Five

There are "Baptisms"(Hebrews 6:2), which find their testimony in Matthew's gospel: "of the Father, of the Son, and of the Holy Spirit" (Matthew 28:19). Three, yet, "one baptism" (Ephesians 4:5).

The uniqueness of Matthew's gospel, other than the fact that he is writing in particular to Israel, is his concern with the Righteousness of God. His message is the Kingdom of Heaven. His theme is the Lord Jesus. His conclusion - a portion which is not in another gospel - concerns itself with the Authority and Righteousness of God.

"Then the eleven disciples went away into Galilee, into a mountain where Jesus had appointed them. And when they saw Him, they worshiped Him; but some doubted." A strange narrative indeed, when you consider that these guys had been three years with the Lord, witnessed His death, His Resurrection, and yet, "some doubted." Strange. But doubt is the blight of man.

"And Jesus came and spoke unto them, saying, 'All authority is given unto Me in heaven and in earth.'" If your Bible uses the word "power", which is the Greek word, *dunamis*, the translation is not correct. The word here is, *exousia*, "Authority." There is a vast difference between "power" and "authority." If you have authority, you can demonstrate power. If you don't have authority, you'll never have power. But authority can be demonstrated without using power. I was shown proof of this when, in a rush for an early morning radio interview in Jackson, Tennessee, I was pulled-over by Authority.

Authority walked up to my car window, and, in a very polite tone, said, "May I see your driver's license?" Now this cordial intonation gave me ample opportunity to answer with either respect or animosity. I chose the former - because I realized that the state of Tennessee stood behind this Authority. Which meant the state of Tennessee was standing in the window of my car - actually, because of Authority's physical proportions, it really looked like the whole state of Tennessee was standing in my car's window. Be that as it may, if I had said, "I think you need to prove your right to ask for my driver's license." Authority could have then exercised the Power hanging at its side. But, being the well-informed citizen I am, I immediately acted in accordance with

Authority's request and handed over my driver's license. I submitted to Authority so Power didn't need to be verified.

I see a lot of people in Church today waving around a lot of power, trying to prove they have authority, when they don't. The apostle Paul didn't need to do that. The seven sons of Sceva tried it, when they went into the house of a demon-possessed man bellowing, "we adjure you in the name of Jesus, who Paul preaches, Come out of him!" The demon said, "Jesus I know. Paul I know." But who are you guys? Where's your Authority? They tried to use power without authority. So the demon jumped on them, ripped off their clothes and tossed them into the street bleeding (Acts 19:14-16).

"All authority is given unto" the Lord, and He distributes His authority unto His Church, by the power of the Holy Spirit. And we go out, "Teaching them . . . Baptizing them in the name of the Father, and of the Son, and of the Holy Spirit." (Matthew 28:16-20).

Matthew lists three Baptisms here:

The Baptism of the Father: - our spirit is redeemed by the incoming of the Holy Spirit, which begot us as new men in Christ (Acts 2; Galatians 3), Baptized, "born again" into the Body of Christ.

The Baptism of the Son: - "Jesus," John said, "is going to Baptize with the Holy Spirit and with fire" (Matthew 3; Acts 1:8). We receive "power" from the Lord Baptizing us with the Spirit (Acts 1).

The Baptism of the Spirit: - our body is made "safe" through the water. Baptized by the same Spirit, Peter said by which "Jesus preached unto the spirits in prison . . . when once the long-suffering of God waited in the days of Noah . . . eight souls, were saved (*diasozo*, to "bring safely through") by water . . . Baptism does also now Safes us" (1 Peter 3).

Three Baptisms, yet, "one Baptism." This is the complete sanctifying work of God teaching us "to observe all things whatsoever I have commanded you" (Matthew 28: 20). Thus, we are Baptized into Position from the Father; Power from the Son; and Safety from the Spirit.

We are Baptized in "one Baptism," yet three: Baptism of the spirit, of the soul and of the body - "of the Father, and of the Son, and of the Holy Spirit." And God regards these three Baptisms as "one Baptism." Without the totality of these Baptisms the work isn't complete. You can make it to heaven without the Water, because you believe (Mark 16:16; Romans 3:22), but You'll find life pretty hard-going while here on earth. You are not complete without the three Baptisms at work as "one."

Deuteronomy announces, "Behold O Israel, the Lord our God is one Lord." Is He? Yes, He is. He is Father, Son and Spirit. He is One. Yet, He is three in the One. Some ancient manuscripts read, "Behold O Israel, the Lord our God is a unity." The Father, Son and Spirit work as One. We, the Church, are a single unit in the Lord, yet, we are many members of that single unit (Romans 12:4), individually Baptized "of the Father, of the Son, and of the Spirit."

"There is one body, and one spirit, even as you are called in one hope of your calling; One Lord, one faith, one baptism, one God and Father of all, who is above all and in you all" (Ephesians 4:4-6).

There is "one baptism."

5 May 2011

FAITH - *the articles* -

Revival in The Land

The book of Hosea (whose name means "Salvation") was written to the northern kingdom of Israel, who was on the brink of disaster. Outwardly, the nation was enjoying a time of prosperity and growth, but inwardly, moral corruption and spiritual adultery permeated the lives of the people of God. The prophet Hosea was instructed by God to marry an unfaithful woman, and he found within his own life a vivid illustration of the unfaithfulness of God's people and the faithfulness of God. Hosea repeatedly echoes his threefold message: God abhors the sins of His people; judgment is certain; but God's love stands firm.

Hosea pleaded for the people of God to turn back to God. He cried for revival in the land. But his cries fell on deaf ears. Why?

The reason is simple, the people of God then, as now have the term "revival" misrepresented - misconstrued in our thinking. We think of revival as a time marked by the people of God jumping up and down, quivers going up and down our spines, all manner of gifts of the Spirit being manifested and people dropping like flies, the saints of God moved by the Spirit of God and an alter full of sinners weeping for forgiveness of their sins. But that's not revival. That's something else entirely.

Revival begins, as always, proceeded by conviction of sin - conviction of sin in the people of God. Understanding as Hosea understood, "judgment begins at the house of God" (1 Peter 4:17). Not by singing in the Spirit. Not by a preacher working the people of God into a frenzy. Not by anything the flesh would glory in. But rather, the one sure sign that God is moving in real revival among His people is conviction of sin in His people. Not "tongues of fire." Revival is always proceeded by the people of God down on their faces weeping before God. Because - for many of them, this is the first time in their lives - they see the degradation, the wretchedness of their own sin, their own flesh, and they are humiliated in the presence of a Holy God.

Every great revival which has ever struck this world - whether it is the Welsh revival, the Shantung revival (in eastern China), the Herrnhut (the Moravian Church) revival, the Great Awakening or whatever revival, which has ever moved across this world, notably in England and the United States, has always been in combination with the humiliation of the flesh and the conviction of sin in the children of God - conviction of sin as they stand in the presence of a Holy God. I am deeply concerned that the chief problem with the saints of God in this day (and our country as a whole) is that the people of God have never been convicted of sin. We have been convicted just enough to realize that we do not want to go to hell - we want revival, but we do not want to stop enjoying all our stuff.

We can pray (corporately and individually) seeking God's deliverance from governmental subjugation, peace for our brothers, warmth from the cold, etc., but if we, as the Church, are never moved by the Holy Spirit with the conviction of our sin first (repentance) we'll accomplish nothing. The Lord may answer our request, but send leanness into our soul (Psalms 106:15). A sad state of affairs indeed.

The Lord made it clear that, "Everyone shall be salted with fire, and every sacrifice shall be salted with salt." Every one. Every sacrifice.

Fire, like salt, has a two-fold effect. Both can bring life or death. A fire can provide a romantic glow on a frosty night or a blister on the finger kissed by it. Fire, just as salt, brings life or death; it depends on whether you have propagated the nature of the fire.

A great example of this is found in the book of Daniel. Three faithful Hebrews were thrown into the fiery furnace of Babylon for refusing to bow down to a Babylonian decree. They refused to follow an unholy dictum, even under pain of death. The furnace was heated "seven times more than it was usually heated." The Hebrews were "cast into the mist of the burning fiery furnace" - clothes and all. But the flames of Babylon had no effect. Why? Why didn't the flames consume the three Hebrews? Because they had previously shared in a greater fire. They had propagated the nature of the fire of God. They had been salted with the fire of God long before they entered the blaze of the Babylonian furnace. They had earlier tasted of the nature of God. And the nature of God's fire - as it comes to the believer - will either bless or blast. Depending on the walk of the believer.

We can pray for revival all we want, but if we haven't been "salted" by the "fire" of the Holy Spirit of God with the conviction of our sin . . . watch out.

We are living, just as in the days of Hosea, in a time of one-sided love and faithfulness that represents the relationship between the people of God and the Lord Himself. As Gomer was married to Hosea, so we are betrothed to the Lord Jesus. As Gomer's relationship to Hosea gradually disintegrated, so we as the Bride of Christ "have left our first love" - as Gomer ran after other men, we the Church have run after other gods: position in the world, our government, etc. Our spiritual idolatry is illustrated by Gomer's physical adultery.

Hosea's message reflects the terrible fascination of Israel with Baal worship. Baal means "husband" or "lord." We, the Church, for so long have looked to our government to provide, to defend, to act as our "husband" and "lord," to be the other lover to whom we have unfaithfully turned to.

Just as confusion and decline characterized the last years of the Northern Kingdom, so it is with the people of God today. And just as the people of God, Israel, we are refusing to heed Hosea's warning of imminent judgment.

Yes, we need revival in the land, but first we need, as the Church of the living God, to repent of our spiritual adultery, our unfaithfulness, our sins! Then and only then will the Lord of Glory bring the much needed revival to our land.

Much love in Christ,
Dr. Jay

FAITH - the articles -

Sin & Redemption

In my pantheon of heroes, the best of men are God's warriors, who are alive with moral outrage and who enter the arena to wrestle with the mystery of evil in its many disguises. Fierce men, rich in considered judgment, who still have thunder & lightening in them; not dispassionate spectators, or cynics. Men who call sin, sin. Men who confirm the way of redemption through the One and only means provided: "Believe on the Lord Jesus and be saved!"

My heroes believe the Living message of Sin & Redemption.

What is sin?

Sin is unlikeness to God. We are born excluded from God; contrasting in character, nature & temper. We were created in the image and the likeness of God, but that image is defaced and unrecognizable.

Sin is distance from God. We are born excluded from intimate fellowship with God. We do not know God, do not love God, do not serve God. We are in a condition of which it is impossible for us to rise out of our sinful state, save by the way of redemption - according to the purpose and power of God, alone.

Sin is wrong done to God. This is God's supreme message concerning sin. The sinfulness of sin is always emphasized in its aspect of relation between mankind and God. While it is difficult for our finite minds to comprehend the fact that wrong can be done to God, it is nevertheless true that wrong done to our "neighbor" is ultimately wrong done to God. Thus, all sin is wrong done to God. If we hold that sin consists only of wrong done to our "neighbor," it will inevitably weaken our sense of sin, and its degree will be decided by the character of the "neighbor" wronged. The only way in which the heinousness of sin against our "neighbor" can be kept alive is by the recognition of the fact that our "neighbor" belongs to God. If, upon every "neighbor" we see the imprint of God, as revealed in Genesis; and if, therefore, we consider that to hurt our "neighbor" is to harm God, the sinfulness of sin against our "neighbor" will be recognized. On the other hand, if we lose sight of this, any "neighbor" will be seen as a separate unit; and distinctions will be made as between sin against one, and sin against another. To recognize that all sin is wrong done to God, is to possess the sense of sin's awfulness, which produces repentance for the Wrong done, and the motive for the doing of Right. The Lord stated this in a nut shell in His summery of the Law and the Prophets, "You shall love the Lord your God with all your heart, and with all your soul, and with all your mind. And . . . you shall love your neighbor as yourself" (Luke 10:27). Simple.

All sin is Wrong done to God. David recognized the true meaning of sin in his, " Against You, You only have I sinned" (Psalm 51:4). It was that fundamental conviction of the true meaning of sin, which created David's consciousness of the Wrong that he had done to Bathsheba and Uriah was ultimately, a Wrong done to God. Take away the truth that when we sin, we sin against God, and we'll grow careless about any Wrong done to our "neighbors" Bathsheba and Uriah.

What is redemption?

Redemption is founded upon righteousness. There can be no redemption of mankind to God, unless it is based on Right; and the activity of God's tenderness is always that of the severity of righteousness.

Redemption is only possible by blood. The writer of the letter to the Hebrews gathered up the whole message of God's redemptive economy in the words, "Apart from shedding of blood there is no remission" (Hebrews 9:22). The shedding of blood is Life given-up. We can only be saved by life given-up through suffering, not just by blood, but by blood-shedding. That ancient symbolism is awful and appalling to the modern eye, but our horror ought rather to be that of the Sin, which made such symbolism necessary - revealing sin's real meaning to God. There are those who speak of the doctrine of Redemption by the shedding of blood as being objectionable and vulgar. And they're right. The shedding of blood is objectionable; it's awful, heinous, barbarous & cruel. But it is the ultimate expression of the activity of our Sin, and the whole meaning of the appalling truth that Sin, in the universe, touches the very life of God with insult, blows and wounding. Sin is wrong done to God.

Like me, most of my thunder & lightening heroes realize that some parts of the Old Testament is frightful reading - tragic stories of blood and fire. But that message needs to be heard again. Mankind needs to take into account that Sin smites God in the face, and wounds Him in the heart. That our redemption is the outcome of His tender compassion, in which He receives our wounding and pardons us by virtue of that infinite and unfathomable mystery of which the shedding of blood is the only equivalent symbolism.

Redemption is our means to holiness. God's final message is that our redemption does not excuse any of us from holiness, but that it is the method by which we are made holy. To trust in Jesus for our redemption, and yet continue in sin, is to commit the most heinous sin of all (Romans 6:1,2).

The Bible speaks of the awfulness of Sin in the light of the holiness of God, of the abundant Redemption springing from the love of God, and of the possibility of holiness of life, created by communion with God, "who gives us victory through our Lord Jesus Christ" (1 Corinthians 15:57).

29 September 2011

FAITH *- the articles -*

People Without the Law

*"Death reigned from Adam to Moses,
even over those who had not sinned
after the similitude of Adam's transgression."*
(Romans 5:14)

I want to explore the judgment of sin "when there is no law." How are they judged?

The simple answer: "when there is no law," they are judged on the basis of the fact that they were born of the first man Adam. Just like us. But let's expand upon our inquiry.

Before the law, God dealt with the nations in a time sphere on the basis of their behavior - which is why He brought the flood upon all the world of the ungodly. But man's eternal position was never predicated on what he did. That is why Paul said, "For until the law sin was in the world; but sin is not imputed when there is no law. Nevertheless, death reigned from Adam to Moses, even over those who had not sinned after the similitude of Adam's transgression" (Romans 5:13-14).

What was the similitude of Adam's transgression? God said, Adam don't "eat of that tree." So Adam, "ate of that tree." The woman didn't hear God say, Don't "eat of that tree." Eve got the message from Adam, but "ate of the tree" anyway. So they were both thrown out of the garden because of their disobedience.

After Adam and Eve left the garden, God didn't say anything to anyone about how to live - but they did have "the knowledge of good and evil." There were no stipulations sat down as to how man was to behave, until after the flood. But "death reigned from Adam until Moses, even over those who had not sinned after the similitude of Adam's transgression." In spite of this fact, God did not deal with men on the basis of their personal sins on an eternal basis, He, nonetheless, did deal with them on a natural basis. Thus, He brought in the flood.

Between the time of the fall of Adam and the flood of Noah, the basis of God's judgment upon man was the revelation that a redeemer will come: a redeemer will come from, "The seed of the woman" (Genesis 3:14-15). This was the promise embraced: the pledge, that a

Redeemer would appear on the scene in that Day - *One* who would bring redemption to mankind. The men who believed that record and offered offerings to God in accordance with that revelation: Abel, who *"brought the firstlings of his flock and the fat thereof. And the Lord had respect unto Abel and to his offering"* (Genesis 4:3-5; Hebrews 11:4.); Enoch, who *"was not found because God had translated him"* and . . . *"he had this testimony, that 'he pleased God'"* (Genesis 5:22-24; Hebrews 11:5); Noah, who was, *"moved with godly fear, prepared an ark for the saving of his household, by which he condemned the world and became heir of righteousness which is according to faith"* (Genesis 6:14-22; Hebrews 11:7); etc. , all stood in righteousness before God. And as a result of their standing (Ephesians 6:12-17), they maintained a sensitivity in the sphere of their inner man, their conscience. Conscience, being the rule of God written on the heart of every man, the "knowledge of good and evil," as the apostle Paul states. But the men who did not operate in that record, moved farther and farther away in sensitivity to the Lord, who created them. "Every imagination of the thoughts of his heart was only evil" (Genesis 6:5) - so when the Lord, the Spirit of God, spoke, they could not hear.

The word *conscience* is a contraction of two Greek words, which means *to know together*. The idea is the Spirit has an utterance and the soul has an attitude. When the Spirit speaks, if the soul of a man can not embrace the words with an attitude of sensitivity to the Spirit, what the man has is a grieved conscience. An individual can grieve their conscience long enough, and to the point where there is no sensitivity to the speaking of, or better, the hearing of the Spirit of God to that man, therefore the man cannot hear what the Spirit is saying. The Spirit's words cannot then push through the seared conscience.

Before the flood, the men of the earth grieved their conscience, defiled their conscience, and finally seared their conscience - so the Lord brought the Flood. Only Noah had a conscience that wasn't seared; he believed - "Noah found grace in the eyes of the Lord" (Genesis 6:8).

Today we have approximately six billion people living on the earth. Fifty years or so ago, we had only two or three billion. The earth's population grows exponentially as time goes on, becoming more and more rapid. The population of the world reached one billion in 1804, two billion in 1927, three billion in 1960, four billion in 1974, five billion in 1987, and six billion in 1999. It is projected to reach seven billion by late 2011, and around eight billion by 2025. By 2045-2050, the world's population is currently projected to reach around nine billion, with alternative scenarios ranging from 7.4 billion to 10.6 billion. The earth's population, in the space of two hundred and forty six years (246), has grow from one billion in 1804, to a projected seven or so billion by 2011. This fact made me wonder what the population of the earth was at the time of Flood.

It is theorized (by secular science) that during the 4th millennium B.C. the earth's population was approximately seven to fourteen million people, "when men began to multiply on the face of the earth" (Genesis 6:1). If we take their secular numeric guesswork, we can guesstimate that there was most likely a few million people living on the earth in the years before the flood - approximately the time of Methuselah's birth (Noah's grandfather). But how many people were living on the earth at the time of Methuselah's death? Methuselah lived almost a century, "nine hundred sixty and nine years" (969) and died the year of the Flood. I am not an expert in or student of mathematics, but after "nine hundred sixty and nine years" the population must have been enormous! Yet, out of the myriads of fallen humanity, only one man, Noah, had not grieved his conscience. This seems strange unless you consider that the Lord could not find "ten" righteous in the city of Sodom and Gomorrah (Genesis 18, 19).

Noah lived in a world where "all men have sinned and come short of the glory of God," but Noah believed. Noah could hear the Spirit of God because of that belief. The Lord quickened Noah's spirit and he believed - God saves sinners. The man who is sensitive to the Lord can maintain that relationship, i.e., spirit and soul, before the Lord. As he remains in that sensitive state, he can walk in righteousness, in obedience before the Lord, as far as that obedience is revealed. But since "sin is not imputed when there is no law"; and man, at that time had no Law - no Law had been given between the fall and the Exodus - God was not dealing with man during that time on the basis of individual actions, but on the basis of his nature given him from his father Adam. Even at that time, those who believed were saved. They had the Word from God, "the seed of the woman;" and they believed God. So God saved them in the Ark.

There are risks to living by faith in the Lord, but the rewards far outweigh any risk. The key to success is to always keep Christ Jesus ("the seed of the woman" - our Ark) as the object of our faith. He has never, nor will He ever fail.

12 August 2010

FAITH *- the articles -*

Two Doors

How did the Hebrew people enter into the Tabernacle of Moses in the wilderness? They entered through the gate of the Tabernacle - through the front door. And why did they want to enter through that gate? They wanted to enter through that gate because they believed there was something inside the Tabernacle - on the other side of it's front gate - which they needed and which could not be possessed, unless they entered through that gate.

Jesus, parenthetically, is that Gate.

Jesus is revealed in the Gospel of John as a two-fold door (gate). First, He is seen as "The Sheep Door," whereby we find access; and second, as "The Door," whereby we find fellowship. We can go in and out through Him and find pasture.

The Gospel of John, as the record begins and indicates, is a setting forth of the Tabernacle of God with men. The testimony of Jesus - God being made man - is the reason John was written. "The Word became flesh" and literally, *tabernacled*, or pitched His tent, among us - in us.

From John 1 through John 21, we have a declaration of the Tabernacle of God, which is with men. The entire gospel of John can be divided into the three divisions, which are found in the Tabernacle of Moses - from the sacrifice, to the place of communion, to the place of fellowship. But, it is "the doors," which are located in John 10, that we are concerned with at this point.

"Verily, verily, I say unto you, he that enters not by the door into the sheepfold, but climbs up some other way, the same is a thief and a robber. But he that enters in by the door is the shepherd of the sheep. To Him the porter opens, and the sheep hear His voice; and He calls His own sheep by name, and leads them out" (John 10:1-3).

There are three doors in John 10. Jesus is two of them. He is not the other. The first door is the door through which Jesus entered. "The sheepfold."

It has been suggested that the one entering through the first door is referring to the believing sinner seeking salvation, to the believer who has entered into the kingdom by the proper door - which is not what this passage is saying; that's not what's involved here.

FAITH - *the articles* -

Jesus said that everyone whoever came before HIM was a thief and a robber. That's what the text goes on to say, does it not? Everyone that ever came before HIM was a thief and a robber (Acts 5:33). All of the others, who came on the scene before the Lord Jesus, had climbed-up some other way. The Pharisees were climbing-up some other way. They were coming up over the wall. They were not coming through the "door of the sheepfold" - through the lineage of David.

The door of the sheepfold is the Levitical law through which the Messiah had to enter. The One born of a virgin had to fulfill every just requirement of that Law. Jesus came fulfilling the Law. He came through the "door of the sheepfold." He came through the passage, the door, if you will allow, of His earthly mother, Mary (Matthew 1:1-17; Luke 3:23-38). He came to fulfill the sacrificial necessity before God. Jesus came *through* the first door, the sheepfold, and He *is* the second and the third door. He is not the "door of the sheepfold." He is the "Door of the sheep" and "the door." "Then said Jesus unto them again, Verily, verily, I say unto you, I am the door of the sheep. All that ever came before Me are thieves and robbers; but the sheep did not hear them. I am the door; by Me if any man enter in, he shall be saved, and shall go in and out, and find pasture" (John 10:7-9).

So we have three doors: A door into the sheepfold - through which Jesus entered. A door for the sheep - which He supplied. And a door - which we, the redeemed, (believing sinners) enter and find fellowship.

This is represented in the Tabernacle of Moses: One door for entrance, which brought Israel to the sacrificial altar. Another door, which brought Israel into the Holy Place. And a third door, which brought Israel into the Holiest of all, which was the place of fellowship, communion, and prayer.

There is a conjoint unity in the Gospel of John with the Tabernacle of Moses: the altar of incense in the Tabernacle of Moses is a parallel to the high priestly prayer of the Lord Jesus; and both are said to "come up before the Father as sweet incense into His nostrils."

So Jesus is, "The Sheep Door," whereby we find access and "The Door," whereby we find fellowship. Jesus is the Two Doors. And we can "go in and out through Him and find pasture."

One more thing before we leave this subject, I think it interesting that through the Law of the Old Testament scripture, the Golden Altar was always seen outside the veil - the veil which separated the Holy Place from the Holiest of Holiest - the dwelling place of God. But when the apostle Paul deals with the positioning of the furniture in the Tabernacle of Moses, all of a sudden the Golden Altar is on the inside of the veil (Hebrews 9:1-4). Interesting.

Maybe we'll look at that next.

22 September 2011

FAITH *- the articles -*

The Vine & The Branches

Within the Tabernacle of Moses there was a Lampstand (Exodus 25), crafted of pure beaten gold: seven golden lamps, burning pure beaten olive oil - six golden branches and one golden shaft, (Exodus 27:20).

That golden Lampstand was a picture of the Church of the Lord Jesus Christ: "And in the midst of the Lampstand, One like the Son of man . . . the seven churches are the seven Lampstands" (Revelation 1:13-20). And the golden branches and the oil burning lamps, growing out of the Lamp's stand, is a picture of the New Covenant Believers. The Vine & The Branches (John 15).

In the Exodus description of the Lampstand, the branches grew out of the Lampstand. So, if the branches are growing out of the Lampstand, what then is the Lamp's stand? Moses describes the Lamp's stand as the "shaft." The "shaft" was the Lampstand's stand. The "shaft" held the Lampstand's branches and lamps. What then is a stand? Isn't a stand, something stands on? And if the "shaft" is the stand, then something must stand on the stand. So it stands to reason that Jesus is the Stand on which the Exodus "Lampstands" and "the seven Lampstands" of Revelation, both stand and grow out of.

What does the Church stand on? What, for that matter, does all the world and the universe stand on? Jesus of course! "For by Him were all things created, that are in heaven, and that are in the earth, visible and invisible, whether they be thrones, or dominions, or principalities, or powers. All things were created by Him, and for Him; And He is before all things, and by Him all things consist" (Colossians 1:15-17, KJV). Jesus Christ is the Eternal-Glue, the Heavenly "shaft," which holds the whole of all matter, seen or unseen, together!

So, in fact and in parallel with the Book of Revelation, Jesus is the Lamp's stand. And out of Him is growing the Lamp's branches - His redeemed people. One perfect unit: Vine & Branches (John 17:11,21,22). On top of each of His branches is a lamp (light) "the light of the world", which Jesus was first called, and now He calls His Church. Under each of the Exodus lamps was a set of knobs, bowls, and buds [flowers]. Each of the branches had three sets of these knobs, bowls, and buds - three sets of three on each branch - (a wonderful picture of the nine gift ministries, given by the Holy Spirit, in 1 Corinthians 12), until you reach the "shaft," the center of the Lampstand, which had four sets of knobs, bowls, and buds (this of course, is a brilliant picture of the four perfecting ministries in Ephesians 4).

The three sets of three, knobs, bowls, and buds found on each branch of the Lampstand, is also a picture of the nine graces of the fruit of the Spirit found in Galatians 5:22,23. The fruit of the Spirit can be divided into three sets of three. Love, joy, peace. Long-suffering, gentleness, goodness. Faith, meekness, temperance. The pomegranates, calamus and spikenard, from The Song of Solomon (4:12-14).

The first set of three are nourishing agents (the *pomegranates*), which parallels love, joy and peace. The second set is our healing agents (*calamus*), the long-suffering, gentleness and goodness, which heals in the body of Christ. The last pictures faith, meekness and temperance (*spikenard*), a perfume, which has a sweet smell to all who are blessed by its fruit. We are a garden of the Lord growing the Lord's fruit.

The whole of the Exodus Lampstand and "the seven Lampstands" in Revelation, both speak of the Lord Jesus, His light, His gifting, and His church (Exodus 25:30 ff) as one.

The Shaft is the Lamp's stand; the Lord Jesus, "the light of the world;" and the Holy Spirit, the burning oil of the lamp. We are the branches growing out of Him giving light to the world (John 15). The Vine & The Branches are one!.

The Lord is not just the Stem of the Vine. He said that He is, "the Vine!" The Root, Stem, Branches, all of it! He said, "I'm the whole thing!" His people are small segments growing out of Him. We are the branches, bearing "fruit," growing out of the Vine, filled with the Holy Spirit (the oil, the fruit), giving His light, His fragrance to the entire world. The Vine & The Branches are one!

And how do we grow? We grow out of Him with His "fruit" that blossoms, from our "knobs, bowls, and buds" into light. He is the Shaft, the Stand, the Vine. We are His golden branches growing out of Him. That place of Life, His life, produces His branches. And in turn, we, His branches, produce His fruit. The Holy Spirit providing the burning fire.

> *"I have chosen you, and ordained you, that you should go and bring forth fruit, and that your [nourishing, healing, sweet smelling] fruit should remain" (John 15:16).*

And the glory that the Father gave into His Son, He has given unto us "that we may be one" with Him as He is with the Father (John 17:21).

The Vine & The Branches are one!.

9 June 2011

FAITH - the articles -

Spirit & Fire

Luke, "the beloved physician" and companion of Paul, in commenting on Israel's expectations concerning John the Baptist writes, "John answered saying unto them all, I indeed Baptize you with water; but One mightier than I comes, the latchet of whose shoes I am not worthy to unloose: He shall Baptize you with the Holy Spirit and with fire" (Luke 3:15,16).

John was prophesying of the One who was coming after him, who was mightier than he, and who would "Baptize" them, individually, with the "Holy Spirit and fire."

In John 1:33, we see John the Baptist again speaking of his testimony concerning Jesus, "And I knew Him not: but He that sent me to Baptize with water, the same said unto me, Upon whom you shall see the Spirit descending, and remaining on Him, the same is He who Baptizes with the Holy Spirit."

John here is testifying of Jesus, declaring that He really did not know that Jesus was the One, until he saw the Spirit of God descending and remaining upon Him. For the One, who sent him to Baptize, told him that the One, upon whom he saw the Spirit descend and remain, was the One that would "Baptize with the Holy Spirit."

After His resurrection, we see Jesus assembled together with His disciples, when He commanded them not to depart from Jerusalem, but to wait for the promise of the Father, of which, He said, "You have heard of me. For John truly Baptized with water; but you shall be Baptized with the Holy Spirit not many days hence" (Acts 1:4,5 KJV).

So what do we learn from these verses? First of all, there is an experience that is properly called the "Baptism with the Holy Spirit." John said, "There is One coming after me, (who is) mightier than I am. He will Baptize you with the Holy Spirit and fire." And later, John affirms that Jesus is that One.

Secondly, these verses bear witness that the "Baptism with the Holy Spirit" is separate and distinct from Regeneration (being "born again" - 1 Peter 1:23). It is one thing to be "born of the Spirit" (which is not a reformation of mankind's carnal nature, but rather, a creative act of the Holy Spirit making a "new creation" in Christ) and yet another thing to be "Baptized with the Holy Spirit."

In John 20:22, we read that Jesus "breathed on them (His disciples) and He said unto them, 'Receive the Holy Spirit.'" It was at this point the disciples received that indwelling presence of the Holy Spirit.

I know that there are those who will object to this indwelling presence of the Holy Spirit, by remarking that the action Jesus took - by "breathing on" His disciples, saying "Receive the Holy Spirit" - was only symbolic. But they're wrong in their objection. They are totally without scriptural warrant in making that assumptive interpretation. There is nothing in the Scripture that would indicate His disciples did not receive the Holy Spirit when Jesus "breathed on them" and told them to "Receive the Holy Spirit." In fact, it's hard for me to imagine that Jesus could "breathe on" anyone and say, "Receive the Holy Spirit," and that person not "Receive the Holy Spirit."

Be that as it may, from the time that Jesus "breathed on them," the Holy Spirit indwelt His disciples. However, in Acts 1:4, Jesus told those same Spirit indwelt disciples that they should not depart from Jerusalem, but wait for the promise of the Father saying, "John indeed Baptized with water unto repentance, but you will be Baptized with the Holy Spirit in a few days."

So, according to Jesus, regeneration, water Baptism and "Baptism with the Holy Spirit" are not one and the selfsame experiences.

In the Greek language, there are three prepositions that signify our relationship with the Holy Spirit: *para*, *en* and *epi*. He is *with* you (*para*). He shall be *in* you (*en*). And you will receive power when He comes *upon* you (*epi*).

Everyone, who has been "born again" (1 Peter 1), has experienced both the *para* and *en*: He is *with* you, and, He shall be *in* you. Every believer had the Holy Spirit *with* them to convict them and to bring them to Jesus Christ. "According as He has chosen us in Him before the foundation of the world" (Ephesians 1:4). And the moment they, individually, believed, the Holy Spirit came, and He began to *indwell* them. But, in Acts 1, Jesus told those believing, Holy Spirit *indwelled* disciples, to wait in Jerusalem (not to depart, but to wait there for the promise of the Father). Then He said, "For you shall receive power, when the Holy Spirit comes upon you." And here He uses the third Greek preposition, which is *epi*. The Holy Spirit comes *upon* or *over* the believer. I personally prefer when He *overflows* the believer. But the preposition, is *epi*.

So, it is one thing to have the Holy Spirit *with* you - *para* - which brought you, individually to Christ. It is another thing to have the Holy Spirit *in* you - *en* - to be individually, as a single believer, indwelt with the Holy Spirit. But it is even more to have the Holy Spirit, individually, *upon* you, or *over* you - *epi* - with which you, individually, "receive power," when He Baptizes "you with the Holy Spirit and with fire."

26 May 2011

FAITH - *the articles* -

The Lord's Supper

Recently, while ministering in different churches, assemblies, and fellowships, we began noticing many of the people were sick, dying and some had even died. Dr. Jay began asking the Lord why was this going on. The article proceeding this one addresses the Lord's answer. But before reading "Broken For You," here is an excerpt from an earlier article addressing the initial question:

Why should we have the Lord's Supper?

The simple answer: Jesus said to, "Do this unto My remembrance" (Luke 22:19). Also, to honor the person and work of Christ: "My body which is given for you . . . the new covenant in My blood" (Luke 22:20); to "proclaim the Lord's death until He comes" (1 Corinthians 11:26); to fellowship in Christ: "sharing the body of Christ" and "sharing in the blood of Christ" as "one body" (1 Corinthians 10:16-17).

The Lord's Supper pictures the new and living way of the New Covenant.

> *"Therefore, brethren, since we have confidence to enter the holy place by the blood of Jesus, by a new and living way which He inaugurated for us through the veil, that is, His flesh, and since we have a Great High Priest over the house of God, let us draw near with a sincere heart in full assurance of faith, having our hearts sprinkled clean from an evil conscience and our bodies washed with pure water. Let us hold fast the confession of our hope without wavering, for He who promised is faithful; and let us consider how to stimulate one another to love and good deeds, not forsaking our own assembling together, as is the habit of some, but encouraging one another; and all the more as you see the day drawing near" (Hebrews 10:19-25).*

There's a severe warning in Hebrews 10:29 about dishonoring "the Son of God," "the blood of the covenant," and insulting "the Spirit of grace" by drifting away from obedience to Christ. The person and work of Christ should be central when God's people gather. The Lord's Supper, along with the other activities of Acts 2:42, is meant to keep us focused on Jesus - not as individuals privately consuming a token liturgical snack, but as God's collective household "encouraging one another" within a context of a Family Feast.

When should we share-in the Lord's Supper?

Paul teaches, "when you come together as a church . . . when you meet together . . . when you come together to eat" (1 Corinthians 11:18, 20, 33).

Luke writes how Jesus broke bread, "On the first day of the week, when we were gathered together to break bread" (Acts 20:7), and then adds, "They were continually devoting themselves to the apostles' teaching and to fellowship, to the breaking of bread and to prayer" (Acts 2:42). These are significant, Christ-centered, Christ-magnifying activities given by Jesus Himself as our model after He was enthroned, after the Spirit of promise, who would "take the things of Christ, teaching us" all we need to know for making disciples and building Christ's church, was poured out (John 14:26; 15:26-27; 16:13-15; cf. Matthew 16:18).

Taken from "Since You've Asked"
8 September 2011

Broken For You

"Whosoever shall eat this bread, and drink this cup of the Lord, unworthily, shall be guilty of the body and the blood of the Lord"
(1 Corinthians 11:27).

As a young-man, I attended a Church whose interpretation of this verse was, "You have to be worthy to partake of the body and blood of Jesus Christ, and if you're taking it unworthily, you're drinking damnation to your own soul." So, many times, I let the cup & bread pass me by. I was really concerned about my unworthiness. But, I was wrong. My worthiness was not, and is not, predicated upon my goodness, my works or my efforts. It is totally established on the grace of God and my believing in Christ Jesus. Today, I partake freely, resting in His grace.

What Paul is referring to here, is the manner in which the Corinthian Church was eating & drinking. It was disgraceful. During their weekly Agape Meal (we'd call it a Potluck), they'd gorge themselves, get drunk, and then join-in Holy Communion. So Paul rebuked them, "Whosoever shall eat the bread, and drink the cup of the Lord, in an unworthily fashion [or an unworthy way], shall be guilty of the body and blood of the Lord. So let a man examine himself, and so let him eat of that bread, and drink of that cup. For he that eats and drinks unworthily, eats and drinks damnation to himself, not discerning the Lord's body. For this cause many are weak and sickly among you, and some have even died" (1 Corinthians 11:27-30).

They were not discerning the Lord's body, ergo, many were "weak, sick & dead."

As the Communal Wine is symbolic of the Lord's shed blood (irrefutably), the broken Bread symbolizes what? Jesus' "body broken for you." But when was the Lord's body broken?

The Gospels tell us, because it was the preparation for the Sabbath, the Jews came to Pilate and asked permission to break the legs of the prisoners so they wouldn't be hanging on the Sabbath. Pilate said, "Break 'em." So they broke the legs of the two thieves, but when they came to Jesus, He was already dead - they didn't break His legs, fulfilling scripture, "Not a bone of Him shall be broken." But, just to be sure He was dead, one of the soldiers took his spear and thrust it into Jesus' side. When he pulled it out, there came out "blood and water."

Under the Law, a Passover lamb could not be offered for a sacrifice with broken bones (Exodus 12:46; Numbers 9:12). Thus, for Jesus, the perfect "The Lamb of God," to be sacrificed for the sin of the world, He could not have broken bones. But, if Jesus' bones were not broken, what did He mean by, "This is my body broken for you?" How and when was His body broken?

The answer comes from, "And Pilate took Him and scourged Him."

Scourging was the Romans method of interrogating - that's how they got confessions. The detainee would be tied to a post, bent-over, and stretched. A soldier, armed with a whip - embedded with bits of glass and lead - would lash the detainee's back until he confessed. If he confessed quickly, the lashing would be a little softer and a little softer as the whipping continued. If he didn't, the lashing would be harder & harder, until the individual's back was ripped to shreds. The Roman government solved a lot of unsolved crimes by this method of interrogation.

In Acts 21, Paul was rescued from a mob of irate Jews by the Roman captain, Lysias. As Paul, and his guards made their way up the steps of Antonio's Fortress, Paul asked, "Can I speak to these guys?"

Lysias said, "You speak Greek?"

Paul said, "Of course."

Lysias, a little confused, said, "Aren't you that Egyptian?"

Paul said, "No!" and started speaking to the crowd in Hebrew, which the captain couldn't understand. As Paul spoke, the Jewish mob became hysterical, throwing dirt in the air, screaming, and ripping their clothes. So Lysias said, "Get him inside." Adding, "Scourge him to find out what he said." Interrogate this guy. So Paul says, "Is it lawful to scourge a Roman citizen, who has not been condemned?"

Lysias, a little freaked, asked, "Are you a Roman citizen?"

"You bet I am," said Paul.

"I bought my citizenship," Lysias confesses. "How much did you pay?"

Unruffled, Paul answers, "I was free born."

Paul's scourging was nipped in the bud . . . No Roman citizen could be scourged (interrogated) without charges filled against them.

Jesus, according to Isaiah was, "As a lamb before her shearers is dumb, so He opened not His mouth" (Isaiah 53:7). So, when Pilate scourged the sinless "Lamb of God," to get a confession, He had no crime to confess, no sin, so He "opened not His mouth". . . This was no accident. This was prophesied in the book of Isaiah: "He was wounded for our transgressions, He was bruised for our iniquity. The chastisement of our peace is upon Him, and with His stripes we are healed" (Isaiah 53:5). This was what Jesus mean by, "This is my body broken for you" - no doubt, to the point of ground beef.

Thus, the Corinthians, or anyone eating the Bread, the broken body of the Lord, not discerning the Lord's body, does not, nor, can not receive that beneficial spiritual & physical healing nutrient provided for in that broken Bread . . . And for this reason, many Christians are "weak, sick and some have died."

This is why Paul told us to examine ourselves when we eat the Bread. Take a look at yourself.

"For if we would judge ourselves, we would not be judged [chastened, disciplined] of God" (1 Corinthians 11:31).

And why does God discipline us? "That we would not be condemned with the world" (1 Corinthians 11:32).

2 February 2012

FAITH *- the articles -*

God's Love Perfected

If fear grips our heart, it's because God's love is not perfected in us. We're not totally assured that God loves us.

So we create speculative notions: "I'm not really sure that this situation is gonna work out for good, it may destroy me." "This may be the end of my road." "This may be all she wrote." "I don't see any way out." And why do we do this? Because God's love is not perfected in us.

If God's love were perfected in us, if we really knew God loved us, so totally loved us, that whatever may happen to us can only happen because God allows it to happen, we wouldn't be concerned with any situation we find ourselves in. If we're truly confident that God loves us supremely, then we'd never worry about what happens to us.

Oh, the confidence that comes when we know that God loves us. When His love is perfected in us, we can accept what comes without fear. Because, "there is no fear in love, perfect love casts out all fear. He that fears experiences this torment. And he that fears is not yet made perfect in love. We love him, because he first loved us" (1 John 4:18-19).

Beware of teaching that would make us the initiator and God the respondent. This is a very popular teaching within many churches today:

"We should initiate, so God can respond." "We need to fast, so God can respond to our fasting." "We need to praise the Lord, so the Lord can respond to our praises and bless us." "We need to give to God so God can respond and give back to us." And in so doing, we make man the initiator and God the respondent. But in reality, God is the initiator and we're the respondents. We respond to Him, because He first responded to us.

We praise the Lord, not to bring a blessing upon our life. No! We praise Him because the blessings of God are so abundant and bountiful on our life already, that we can't handle it. "I love You, Lord. I praise You and thank You, oh Lord." And, with that response, we're responding to the grace of God that we've experienced.

God has initiated His love and His grace towards us, and we love Him because He first loved us. We're responding to His love. But, we must know God to respond to Him. We must know the love of God. We must know the grace of God. We must know the goodness of God. We must know God's love, grace and goodness in Christ, and then, when we know, we respond. God is the initiator and we're the respondents.

God loved us first, and we respond to that love. "We love Him because He first loved us." But it's hard to respond to something we're not aware of.

One lovely phrase we're prone to say is, "I love God", which sounds beautiful. We all should be saying that. We all should be able to say that. And I'm not putting down saying that. But, "if a man says, I love God and hates his brother, he is a liar; for he that loves not his brother whom he has seen, how can he love God whom he has not seen?" (1 John 4:20).

We can't say "I love God," and hate any of our brothers. That's an inconsistency. That's a lie. Because, "this commandment we have from him, that he who loves God loves his brother also" (1 John 4:21).

Jesus was questioned by a lawyer as to what was the greatest commandment. And Jesus said, "Thou shall love the Lord thy God with all your heart, with all your soul, with all your mind, and with all your strength. And the second is like unto the first: you shall love your neighbor as thyself, and on these two are all the law and commandments" (Matthew 22:37-40). Jesus immediately tied together the love for our neighbor with our love for God.

When the rich young ruler came to Jesus and knelt at his feet and said, "Good Master, what good thing must I do to inherit age-abiding life?" And Jesus said, "Why do you call Me good? There is only one good, and that is, God. But keep the commandments."

But, "Which ones?"

Jesus said, "You shall love the Lord your God. You shall not steal. You shall not commit adultery . . . and so forth."

So the young man said, "Lord, all these I've kept from my youth up, what do I lack?"

Well, Jesus said, "If you're going to be perfect, then go sell all that you have and distribute it to the poor and follow me. Then you'll have great treasures in heaven . . . And he went away sorrowful because he had great riches." (Mark 10; Luke 18).

If that young man had said, "Lord, I have kept all these commandments from my youth up. I haven't stolen. I haven't committed adultery, and I haven't lied against my neighbor, and so forth. I've kept all those from my youth. But tell me, what is the real commandment?" Jesus would have said, "Love your neighbor as yourself."

This is where most of us find ourselves. We're very wealthy. We have more than we can eat, more than we can wear, more than we need. And our neighbors are in rags and starving, but we're not willing to help them. What would Jesus say to that? "You guys don't love your neighbor as yourself." So we respond, "Oh, but Lord, I love God and I keep all the commandments." But when it comes down to a practical example, no, we're not keeping the commandment. In truth, it isn't what we say, it's our deeds that express the reality of our experience, of our salvation, of our assurance of God's love, of God's love perfected.

21 July 2011

Love One for Another

I love words. The shape and shade and size and noise of words as they hum, strum, jig and gallop along, compelled me to become a writer. That's what springs from me naturally.

Spiritual love, in contrast, must proceed from my spiritual nature and must be attracted by the sight of the divine image I see in other saints. "Every one who loves Him who begot also loves him who is begotten of Him" (1 John 5:1). I love others because of the love given me from Another. That's what my spiritual nature must be. But no one can love God in another unless he has God's love in his own soul. Love begets love.

Many of us hold an entirely wrong idea as to the nature and fruits of love. Most of us misconstrue natural ability and temperament for love. A hardy handshake, a warm smile, a well chosen word works in the natural, but not in the Spirit. Many of us love particular Christians because we find them to be sweet-tempered or generous-hearted, but that is merely natural, and not spiritual love. If we would love the saints spiritually, we must disregard what they are temperamentally by nature, and observe them as the objects of God's love, loving them for what we see of Him in them. Only then will we be able to rise above individual peculiarities and personal infirmities, and value them with a true spiritual affection.

Now don't misinterpret what I'm saying. I do not mean that we should ignore our brothers' offenses or condone their sins (Leviticus 19:17). On the other hand, what we most often regard as "snubs" or "scorn" from someone, may be due to our own pride - not the abrasive-tempered brother, whose personality rubs us the wrong way. We may feel hurt because we do not receive the notice, we consider our due. At times, it's not good for the people of God to know too much of each other (Proverbs 25:17). Familiarly may breed contempt. You may love my writing (which I hope you do) but if you had the chance to know me, you may spot so many personality imperfections, that you'd run at the very sight of me.

Neither the reality, nor the depth of Christian love should be measured by honeyed words or endearing expressions. Actions speak louder than words. Gushy people are proverbially superficial and fickle. Those common folk who are less demonstrative are usually more stable. Still waters run deep. Spiritual love always aims at the good of its object. It is exercised in edifying conversation, in seeking to strengthen and confirm faith, in exalting God's Word, and promoting piety, holiness and godliness. The more another magnifies Christ, the more he should be endeared to us. I do not mean mere skin-deep, silver-tongued talk about Christ, but that overflowing of the heart towards Him which compels the beloved's mouth to speak of Him. We should love the saints for the truth's sake, for being unashamed to affirm their faith in such a day as this. Those who reflect most of the image of Christ and carry about with them most of His fragrance should be the ones we love the most.

Love for the brethren is ever in proportion to our love for the Lord Himself, which explains why the former is at such a low ebb. The sectarian bigotry and the personal bitterness growing all around us is easy to explain. Love to God has decreased in vigor, power, and extent. "You shall love the Lord your God with all you heart, soul and strength" comes before "you shall your neighbor as yourself." But the love of material things and the cares of this world have chilled the souls of many of us towards God. Our affections must be set steadfastly upon the Head of the Church, before they will warm its members. When the Lord is given His rightful place in our hearts, His redeemed, our brothers and sisters in Christ, will also be given theirs. Then our love will not be confined to that narrow ecclesiastical circle in which our lot is cast; we will embrace the entire household of faith. Then we shall have "love for all the saints" (Ephesians 1:15), and that will be evidenced by "supplication for all the saints" (Ephesians 6:18) - those in the four corners of the earth whom we have not seen. "Salute every saint in Christ Jesus" (Philippians 4:21 KJV) - poor as well as rich, weak as well as strong.

"By this all will know that you are My disciples, if you have love one for another" (John 13:35).

28 October 2010

Wrong Response to His Cross

The nature of Christ's salvation is woefully misrepresented by the present-day evangelist - announcing a Savior from hell, rather than a Savior from sin. And that is why so many are fatally deceived, for there are multitudes who wish to escape the "Lake of Fire", who have no desire to be delivered from their carnality and worldliness.

There are a number of people whose response to the Lord is influenced, not from recognizing a personal need for Him, but because they rather dislike the circumstance they find themselves in and want God to change it. Multitudes of people call on the Lord, not because they are willing to have any loss in this life to gain Christ, but they call on Him because they are loosing in this life. They don't like the condition they find themselves in, so they call on the Lord to change their circumstance. They don't like loosing their wife, house, car, health, freedom, etc., and they want God to change that. They want God to make them healthy, wealthy and wise. If they must accept Jesus in the process, then they'll accept Jesus - over and over. In these cases, very often it requires such a convicting work by the Spirit of God – a complete devastation of their circumstances to bring them to the point of wanting only the Lord - even if they never get anything from this life - that only pure devastation – a complete loss in this life, is the only verdict which will bring them to the Savior.

We commit a great error in the way we preach in many cases, in that we preach about the good things that are available to the individual who will come to the Lord. We preach, "He will straighten out your family, your job, your credit, etc." All of which may be true in many cases. But, a lot of people only come to the Lord to have their family, work, etc., straightened out - they don't come because they want redemption. Therefore, they come again the next Sunday, and the next. They come over and over, because they are not getting their problems addressed. Jesus offers redemption. But they are not receiving redemption. They're not coming for redemption. They are coming for another reason.

The convicting work of the Spirit of God is the first imperative to anyone's response to the Lord. Yet, many people come to the Lord for

FAITH - *the articles* -

the wrong reason. They are not coming saying, "Though He slay me, yet will I trust Him" (Job 13:15). Theirs is a response to His provision, not to His redemption. I wonder how many professed believers would serve the Lord if He removed everything from them and left them nothing but Himself? That's one of the reasons Job is in the Bible - to make us understand that a man who believes God, is a man who recognizes that nothing else is important. He needs nothing else, he only needs the Lord. God did not redeem us to improve our environment, He redeemed us because He loved us even while we were lost, undone sinners. The man (or woman) who comes to the Lord because he realizes he is an undone lost sinner in need of the Savior, will receive redemption. If your first need is not redemption, your needs will never be met.

"Two men went up into the temple to pray; the one a Pharisee, and the other a tax collector. The Pharisee stood and prayed thus with himself, 'God, I thank You that I am not as other men are, extortioners, unjust, adulterers, or even as this tax collector. I fast twice in the week; I give tithes of all that I possess.' And the tax collector, standing afar off, would not lift up so much as his eyes unto heaven, but smote upon his breast, saying, 'God be merciful to me a sinner.' I tell you this man went down to his house justified rather than the other; for everyone that exalts himself shall be abased; and he that humbles himself shall be exalted" (Matthew 18:9-14). The word used by the tax collector, "merciful," is the Greek word *hilaskomai*. The word is used in connection with the mercy seat (Exodus 25:17-21; Hebrews 9:5). The tax collector was not thinking of mercy alone, but of the blood-sprinkled mercy seat in the temple. There is no forgiveness apart from sacrifice. There is no salvation apart from the blood of Jesus.

We, like the tax collector, must recognize that our first need is redemption, and our need will be met.

Have You Really Come To Christ?

All the excellencies, both Divine and human, are found in the Lord Jesus, yet fallen mankind sees in Him no beauty. No desire. No need. They may be instructed in "the doctrine of Christ," they may believe all that the Bible affirms of Him, they may speak His name, profess to be resting on His finished work, sing His praises, yet their hearts may be far from Him. The things of this world have the first place in their affections. The gratifying of self is their dominant concern. Their life is not surrendered to Him. He is too Holy to suit their love of sin; His claims too exacting to suit their selfish hearts; His terms of discipleship too severe to suit their fleshly ways. They will not yield to His Lordship. Until God performs a miracle of grace upon their hearts, they cannot, nor will not, Come to Christ.

"Come unto Me, all you that labor and are heavy laden, and I will give you rest" (Matthew 11:28) contains a gracious invitation, made by the compassionate Savior to a particular class of sinners. Notice, the "all" is qualified by the words, which immediately follow. This declaration is clearly defined to those who "labor" and are "heavy laden." It does not apply to the vast majority of light-headed, pleasure-seeking fellows, who have no regard for God's glory and no concern for their eternal welfare. No, the word for such creatures is: "Rejoice . . . and walk in the ways of your heart, and in the sight of your eyes; but know you, that for all these things God will bring you to judgment" (Ecclesiastes 11:9). But to those who have "labored," who are "heavy laden" with their utter inability to meet His requirements, who long to be delivered from the power of sin, Christ says, "Come unto Me, and I will give you rest."

"No man can come to Me, except the Father which has sent Me draw him" (John 6:44), tells us that Coming to Christ is not an easy matter, as many imagine. The incarnate Son of God declares that such an act is utterly impossible to a fallen and depraved creature, unless His Divine power is brought to bear upon that creature. Coming to Christ is far different from coming forward and taking an evangelist's hand, signing a Decision card, joining a Church, or any of the "many inventions" of man (Ecclesiastes 7:29). Before any one can, or will, Come to Christ their heart must be supernaturally changed, their stubborn will must be supernaturally broken.

"All that the Father gives Me shall come to Me, and him that comes to Me I will in no wise cast out" (John 6:37) is unpalatable to the carnal mind, yet it is precious to the child of God. It is the blessed truth of unconditional election, the discriminating grace of God. It speaks of a favored people whom the Father gives to His Son. It declares that every one of that blessed company shall Come to Christ. The effects of their sinful birth in Adam, the power of indwelling sin, the efforts of Satan, the deceptive delusions of blind preachers, will not be able to hinder them. When God's appointed hour comes, each of His elect is delivered from the power of darkness and translated into the kingdom of His dear Son. No matter how unworthy and vile we are, no matter how long the catalogue of our sins, He will by no means despise or fail to welcome us, and under no circumstance will He ever cast us off.

"If any man come to Me, and hate not his father, and mother, and wife, and children, and brethren, and sisters, yea, and his own life also, he cannot be My disciple. And whosoever does not bear his cross, and come after Me, cannot be My disciple" (Luke 14:26,27) makes known the terms on which Christ is willing to receive sinners. His uncompromising claims of His holiness are set out. He must be crowned Lord of all, or He will not be Lord at all. All that pertains to "the flesh" - a loved one or self - has to be hated. And with that, we must "bear" the badge of Christian discipleship, our "cross," our self-denial, with self-sacrifice ruling our heart.

"To whom coming, as unto a living Stone, disallowed indeed of men, but chosen of God, and precious" (1 Peter 2:4) tells us to continue as we began. We are to Come to Christ not once, but frequently, daily. He is the only One who can minister to our needs, and to Him we must constantly turn for the supply. In our emptiness, we must draw from His "fullness" (John 1:16). In our weakness, we must turn to him for strength. In our ignorance we must turn to Him for wisdom. In our sin, we must seek His cleansing. All we need for time and eternity is stored up in Him: refreshment when we are weary (Isaiah 40:31), healing when we are sick (Exodus 15:26), comfort when we are sad (1 Peter 5:7), deliverance when we are tempted (Hebrews 2:18).

"Wherefore He is able also to save them to the uttermost that come to God by Him, seeing He ever lives to make intercession for them" (Hebrews 7:25) assures us of the eternal security of those who do Come.

Christ saves "to the uttermost," forever. He is not of one mind today and another tomorrow. No, He is "the same yesterday, and today, and for ever" (Hebrews 13:8). None whose name is indelibly stamped on the heart of our great High Priest can ever perish.

"This Jesus whom I preach to you is the Christ" (Acts 17:3). Have you really come to Him?

28 July 2011

FAITH - *the articles* -

Not After The Flesh

"If any man be in Christ he is a new creation;
old things have passed away; behold,
all things have become new"
(2 Corinthians 5:17).

The Mosaic Law, which was holy, just and good, could not make us righteous before God. Why? Because of the weakness in our flesh. But, "God sending his own Son in the likeness of sinful flesh, and for sin, condemned sin in the flesh" (Romans 8:3).

What we could not do for ourselves, God did for us through sending His Son in the flesh. "That the righteousness of the law might be fulfilled in us, who walk not after the flesh, but after the Spirit " (Romans 8:4).

Righteousness is not fulfilled by us, but it is fulfilled in us by Christ Jesus.

Mankind is composed of three parts, an inferior trinity: body, mind, and spirit. Our mind is synonymous with our soul, our consciousness. Our consciousness is responsive to whatever controls us. So, if we are controlled by our body appetites, if we are living predominately after the flesh, then we have the mind of the flesh. We are mindful of fleshly things, physical needs. This is the state of all mankind apart from Christ Jesus. They are body conscious. The person apart from Christ Jesus, speaks about things that relate to their body. They speak about new recipes, exotic new desserts, drinks, sex - things that relate to their bodily appetites - because that's where their mind is. Their flesh is in control. What they're thinking about constantly is their body-needs, their body-drives.

"They that are after the flesh are constantly mindful of the things of the flesh, but they that are after the Spirit, then, are mindful of the things of the Spirit." The mind, the carnal mind, "is death" (Romans 8:5,6).

But when we are "born again" by the Spirit of God, the Spirit, then, is in control of our life. Our desires, our conversations change dramatically when we are in Christ. We become concerned with spiritual things. We begin speaking about God, our relationship with

God, the work of God within our hearts, and how we can please and serve Him. Our conversations are addressed to spiritual things.

Someone who lives dominated by their bodily appetites is living like an animal, because animals are body-controlled beings. They have a consciousness that is constantly absorbed with their body's needs, which is why Humanists today are so certain that they are related to the animal kingdom. They'll look at a baboon and say, "All he thinks about is his bodily needs. His only concern is feeding himself, of procreation, and he looks a little bit like me. I guess I am related to that baboon." And they feel a close affinity, because the baboon is living just like they live. But, someone, whose spirit has come alive and who is living after the Spirit of God, realizes that they're not related to the animal kingdom, they're related to God.

So Paul declares, "To be carnally minded is death" (Romans 8:6).

That is, spiritual death, which biblically, is the separation of mankind's consciousness from God. But mankind classifies death differently. When the EEG reads flat for twenty-four hours, there's no brain activity, and our consciousness is gone, we're declared dead. But the Bible says that if our consciousness is separated from God, that is, we don't have a real consciousness of God, that's when we're Really dead. So our mind, our consciousness is dead, because it is separated from God and absorbed with the things of its own needs.

"The mind of the Spirit is life and peace" (Romans 8:6). "But the carnal mind [or the mind of the flesh] is enmity against God" (Romans 8:7).

Our flesh is opposed to God, because God has declared the spirit superior to the material. So those who have the mind of the flesh find themselves at enmity with God. "For the mind of the flesh is not subject to the law of God, and neither indeed can it be. So then they that are in the flesh cannot please God" (Romans 8:7-8).

That's an interesting statement, because so often we ask God to accept the works of our flesh. But God will no more accept the works of our flesh than He would Cain's, who was rejected by God.

In Revelation 4, God is upon His throne, surrounded by the twenty-four elders, cherubim, and angelic beings, all worshipping the eternal God, the Creator, saying, "Holy, holy, holy, Lord God Almighty, who is, who was, and who is to come." Declaring, "You are worthy, O Lord, to receive glory and honor, for You have created all things, and for Your pleasure they are and were created." Fascinating. Like it or not,

God created us for His own good pleasure. That's the basic purpose for our existence. We have twisted that and feel that we should live for our own pleasure, but the Bible tells us that if a person is living for their own pleasure, they are "dead" while physically alive. Why? Because they're not answering to the very basic cause of their existence.

Thus, if we are living in the flesh, constantly thinking and speaking about our body-needs, our life is doomed to emptiness and frustration, because we are not answering to God for the very basic purpose of our existence.

"Therefore, brethren, we are debtors, not to the flesh, to live after the flesh. For if you live after the flesh, you are going to die: but if you through the Spirit do mortify the deeds of the body, then you shall live. For as many as are led by the Spirit of God, they are the sons of God" (Romans 8:12-14).

"He that has an ear, let him hear . . ." (Revelation 3:22).

14 July 2011

FAITH - *the articles* -

The Meaning of Sincerity

The apostle Paul prayed in Philippians 1:8-10 that the saints' love would abound more and more, "in knowledge and in all judgment" that we "may be sincere and without offense till the day of Christ." The Greek word, (*eilikrines*, sincere), used here, occurs only once more, as an adjective, in the New Testament, where Peter states: "I stir up your *pure* (sincere) minds by way of remembrance" (2 Peter 3:1). Paul again uses this same Greek word as a noun in 1 Corinthians 5:8 and 2 Corinthians 1:12 and 2:17, where in each case it is rendered, "sincerity."

What then is "sincerity?" What does it mean to "be sincere?" "Sincerity" is the opposite of counterfeit and dishonesty. It is the opposite of pretense - of pretending to be someone else in order to deceive others. To be "sincere" is to be free from pretense or deceit. To be "sincere" is to be genuine. To be sincere is to be in reality what you are in appearance: to be frank, true, unfeigned. "Sincerity" is one of the characteristics which distinguishes the true Christian from the empty professor. The latter, though they may have much knowledge in their heads and words in their mouths, have no standard of integrity in their hearts and give little thought about the uprightness of their daily walk.

"Sincerity" properly means, "that which is judged in the sunshine, that which is clear and manifest." "For our rejoicing is this: the testimony of our conscience that we conducted ourselves in the world in simplicity and *godly sincerity*, not with fleshly wisdom but by the grace of God, and more abundantly toward you." It is "godly sincerity" as here in 2 Corinthians 1:12. "Godly sincerity" is in reality, "the sincerity of God" - the "sincerity" of which the Lord is not only the Giver and Author, but also the Witness, which may be brought to Him and held up before Him for His scrutiny. This idea is expressed clearly in John 3:21: "He that does truth comes to the light, that his deeds may be manifest, that they are wrought in God." "Judged in the sunshine . . . clear and manifest."

Our English word *sincere* is derived from the Latin *sine cera*, which means "without wax," and the origin of that Latin expression approximates very closely the etymology of the Greek word, *eilikrines*. In both expressions we have the impression of appraisal by light. The ancient Romans cherished a very delicate and valuable porcelain, which was extremely fragile, and only with much trouble could it be fired without being cracked. Dishonest dealers were in the habit of filling in the cracks of flawed porcelain with white wax, but when their wares were held up to the light, the wax was evident, being darker in color than the porcelain. Thus, the honest dealers started marking their porcelain with *sine cera*, "without wax." Their porcelain would pass the test of being held up to the sunlight. Thus, "he that does truth comes to the light."

So as we can see, this spiritual "sincerity" is the opposite, not only of false pretence, but also of unholy mixture. As the apostle said of himself and his companions, "We are not as many, which corrupt the word of God: but as sincerity, but as of God, in the sight of God speak we in Christ" (2 Corinthians 2:17). The words, "which corrupt," literally means "which huckster." A huckster is a mercenary person eager to make a profit out of anything. Hucksters "corrupt," deceitfully mingling false and worthless articles among the genuine.

Sincerity is opposite of mixture: the opposite of truth & error, of godliness & worldliness, of loveliness & sin. A sincere person has not assumed Christianity as a mask, but their motives are pure; their conduct is free from double-dealing and cunning; their words express the real sentiments of their heart. They are ones who can bear to have the light turned upon them, the spring of their actions scrutinized by God, Himself. They are of one piece through and through, and not as the hypocrite who vainly attempts to serve two masters and make the best of two worlds. They are not afraid to be tested by the Word of God, for they are without guile or shame and are straightforward and honest in all their dealings. As we have seen in 2 Corinthians 1:12, "sincerity" is joined with "simplicity," which is expressed in: "The lamp of the body is the eye. If therefore your eye is healthy (single) your whole body will be full of light" (Matthew 6:22). The one with a "single" eye refuses to mix fleshly craftiness with spiritually: they aim *solely* at pleasing and glorifying God. Thus, a sincere heart is a true heart (Hebrews 10:22), a heart genuinely holy, true to God, faithful in all things. A sincere heart is a pure heart (2 Timothy 2:22), *sine cera*, without wax.

2 September 2010

". . . to the obedience of Christ"

Many of us take great delight in thinking. Our thoughts become our life. We thrive on our ideas. To tell us not to think, is like asking us to give up our very life. But, if our minds are continually turning, the Spirit of God cannot reach, cannot enlighten our spirit. Our minds cannot accept God's Light, because His Light requires objectivity, not subjectivity, which demands no dependency on our mind. Anyone who is subjective, who is influenced by personal feelings, tastes, or opinions, cannot see God's Light. "God has given them the spirit of slumber" (Romans 11:8).

If our thoughts are our life, how can we perceive God's Light? It's impossible because we are too subjective. For our mind to become a useful organ, it must be dealt with by God. It needs to be shattered. Broken. Our outward man must be broken. If our thoughts remain the center of our being, then we are totally unusable when God's light shines. As a result, the Word is blocked. There's no fruit. Because God's Word, His speaking, His Light is blocked by our subjective thoughts. God's Word must pass through man. Yes, man is God's channel. But God's channel must not be blocked. Just as natural water needs an unblocked channel to flow freely, God's needs an unblocked channel for His "living water" to freely flow.

Wasting of thought is not insignificant. How many of us waste our thoughts? How many of us waste our thoughts on trivial matters? This waste of thought blocks God's Light. Now don't get me wrong, I'm not saying that thought is useless. O' contraire, revelation is completed through man's thoughts. Everything God gives is useful, good. Our minds are created by God; they're not useless. It is only when our thoughts become the center of our life, issuing forth in, and from our own ideas and feelings, that they becomes useless, unprofitable. Our mind, should be God's servant.

Paul admonished us to, take "every thought captive to the obedience of Christ" (2 Corinthians 10:5). In that capturing, God doesn't abrogate our mind. He wants to take it "captive to the obedience of Christ." The issue then, is whether our mind is under our control, or God's. Are we led by the Spirit or by self (Romans 8:1)? If we are self-assured of our own wisdom and mental ability, God is not our mind's Master. Our thoughts have been taken captive to the obedience of self, not Christ. So God must begin to break us. But don't misunderstand this work. This breaking does not destroy our mind itself or its function. This breaking merely breaks down its life source, its false center. God still uses our mind. There is a vast difference between the mind as Life and the mind as self. God doesn't want our mind, our thoughts to be the life source which controls us. He wants our mind, our thoughts to be "captive to the obedience of Christ," to be His servant. The mind, the fleshly subjective thoughts that act as our life source, must be broken. Our mind, our thoughts, acting as God's servant is His objective.

How then are we set free from our subjective, fleshly self-thoughts? By "the law of the Spirit of life in Christ Jesus" (Romans 8:2). By walking according to the Spirit. "That the righteousness of the law might be fulfilled in us, who walk not after the flesh, but after the Spirit" (Romans 8:4). If we walk according to the Spirit, "the law of the Spirit of life in Christ Jesus" will be manifested in us. But, if we walk according to, or "after the flesh," the law of sin and death will be manifested in us. "For as many that are after the flesh do mind the things of the flesh; but they that are after the Spirit the things of the Spirit" (Romans 8:5). Whoever walks after the Spirit overcomes the law of sin and death.

Who then are the ones who walk according to the Spirit? They are the ones who set their mind on the spirit. "For to be carnally minded is death, but to be spiritually minded is life and peace" (Romans 8: 6). Those whose minds are set on the Spirit walk according to the Spirit, and those who walk according to the Spirit have the law of the Spirit of life in them, and they overcome the law of sin and of death.

What then does it mean to set the mind on the Spirit? Simply, to set our mind on, to think on, the things of the Spirit. If we spend our time thinking about wild and strange things, we becomes scattered and confused and thus, we are surely of "the flesh." But if we are brought by the Lord to the point that we can think on things of the Spirit, we become spiritual, understanding spiritual things. How can we whose mind and thoughts are occupied with human affairs, live by the law of the Spirit? It's impossible! No one can live by the Holy Spirit, whose mind is set on the flesh!

Our mind and our thoughts should not be the center of our being. They should be servants, who listen carefully to their Master's voice. Otherwise, we fall into that which we think naturally, fleshly, subjectivity. But, if our outward man is broken, our self is no longer the center, self is no longer our focus. We no longer act according to our thoughts. We wait for God's voice, like obedient servants. Then, when God's light flashes within us, our spirit catches that light, and our mind, our understanding apprehends its meaning. We have been brought "... to the obedience of Christ."

15 September 2011

FAITH - the articles -

Three American Holidays
A Handful of Articles

The following articles were originally as single works. However, we have included them here as a series, loosely termed, for the reader's benefit.

It is more than likely obvious at this point, Dr. Jay doesn't suffer the traditions of men gladly, but he does love the elect, and he does love Truth. So, as a result of the increasing societal widespread panic caused during the general observation of holidays popularized by greeting card vendors, Dr. Jay responded in the only way he knows - by exhorting the saints through the Word of God to live free - "being in the world, but not of it.

The Thanksgiving Story

There's too much squawking these days about the Decline of Thanksgiving. Macy's Parade ratings are down, the fan-base is shrinking, and even the Democratic Party says radical changes are needed to keep the Show alive.

But none of this is true. It is a landslide of gibberish, dutifully parroted by News Media Talking-Heads.

So who cares? Somebody has to fill all those holes in the 24-hour news cycle. We live in fast Times. Big news that once took nine weeks to cross the Atlantic now travels everywhere in the world at the speed of light, and gossip travels even faster.

Any geek with a cheap computer can log-on and spread terrifying rumors about Anthrax bombs exploding in Birmingham or, state as fact, that half the population of the 1620 Pilgrims would have been killed by the brown fog of Ague Fever that blew in on a vagrant wind from Mongolia, if the Indians hadn't stepped in to save them . . . And no American History class would doubt for an instant that these things might not be true. That is the wonderful perversity of News Gossip in the 21st Century. Nothing's impossible to believe . . . except maybe the truth.

FAITH - *the articles* -

So what's the Truth about Thanksgiving?

On March 24, 1603, James 1, the only son of Mary Queen of Scots, became King of England. Not long after, the Church of England, by rule of their New King, began persecuting anyone and everyone who didn't recognize The Crown's absolute civil and spiritual authority. Anyone who challenged the King's ecclesiastical authority and anyone who believed strongly in everyone's Individual Freedom to worship God as they choose, were hunted down, imprisoned, and off-times executed for their beliefs. So a group of God-fearing Pilgrims decided to make tracks to Holland and established their own unshackled Christian community.

After a decade or so, forty of those Pilgrim resolved to make the touch-and-go trip to the New World, where they could hopefully, without loss of life-and-limb, live and worship God as they pleased. So on August 1, 1620, forty Pilgrims, led by William Bradford, set sail on the goodly ship Mayflower. During the pilgrimage, Bradford wrote-up a Compact, that would establish just & equal laws for all members of the New-World Colony, irrespective of their religious beliefs. Smart thinker, Bradford.

Where did Brother William get these revolutionary ideas penned in his Mayflower Compact? The Christian Bible of course . . . And he never doubted it would work.

When the Pilgrims landed in New England, they found: "A cold, barren, desolate wilderness," which Bradford wrote in his journal. No friends, food, or shelter. And that was just beginning. During the first winter, half the Pilgrims (including Bradford's wife) died of starvation, sickness & exposure. When Spring finally came, the New-World Natives taught the Pilgrims how to plant, fish, hunt & et cetera.

For a year or so, the Pilgrims lived in a world that seemed like some contrived fantasy - their reality bore little resemblance to what they had imagined. This, of course, is where most modern American History ends. Thanksgiving is spelled-out in many Textbooks as a holiday for which the Pilgrims thanked their Indian friends for saving their lives, rather than as a devout expression of gratitude grounded in the tradition of their Faith in God.

So what's omitted?

First off, the original contract the Pilgrims had with the guys who paid for their Mayflower trip called for everything the community produced to go into a common storehouse, and each member of the community was entitled to one common share of whatever was produced. This was the original "Share the Wealth" ploy.

All the land they cleared, the houses they built, the produce they grew, belonged to the community. Everything was distributed equally. Nobody owned personal property. No individualism. The Colony was kith-n-kin to a Hippie Commune. And it was a dismal failure. Environmental, feel-good structures never work. But they learned a valuable lesson: the most creative and industrious people have no incentive to work any harder than anyone else, unless they can utilize personal motivation & gain. The able men complained that they were working for other men's families without reward . . . Why should you work for other people when you can't work for yourself? What's the point?

William Bradford made a bold move. He began assigning plots of land to each family to work, manage & hopefully reap profit. He turned loose the power of the Free Marketplace. He let lose Free Enterprise by the principle of private property. Every family was permitted to market their own crops and products . . . And they prospered. "This had very good success," wrote Bradford, "for it made all hands industrious, so as much more corn was planted than otherwise would have been." Long before Karl Marx was a sparkle in his father's eye, the Pilgrims had given socialism a trial-run, and figured out, it don't work! So they scraped it permanently.

What Bradford wrote in his journal about their social experiment is true American History: "The experience that we had in this common course and condition, tried sundry years . . . that by taking away property, and bringing community into a common wealth, would make them happy and flourishing - as if they were wiser than God."

In due course Trading Posts were set up and home-grown commodities were exchanged with their Neighbors. As the success of the Plymouth settlement reached Europe, more trailblazing English Protestants began arriving, kicking-off what's known as the "Great Puritan Migration."

So the real story of Thanksgiving is the Pilgrims giving thanks to God for His mercy, faithfulness, & guidance. The Pilgrims and the New-World Natives did have a Thanksgiving dinner - maybe it was turkey. But one thing's for sure, it was not the New-World Natives who saved the day. It was the Lord, and the Pilgrims' faith in Him, who never fails.

23 November 2011

FAITH *- the articles -*

Christ was born on . . . ?

Christmas is a dangerous vice, but millions of people are hooked on it's yearly Bacchanalia of "peace on earth, good will towards men." It's always a good time of the year for the Rich. It is a time for Profit-making and gross displays of Wealth, for giving huge Rubies and Diamonds to each other, and for seeing themselves on the covers of their own Magazines. . . although for most of us, it's a Ritual Observance we suffer through, while we max-out our Credit, visit estranged Family Members and maintain a Happy Face ,'till it's over. And the reason is simple: the traditional "Christmas spirit" runs completely against the grain of Human Nature, a nature which has nothing to do with silly Christian weaknesses like Generosity, Kindness, Brotherly Love, or Gift-Giving.

Now don't get me wrong. I love a good Carnival, Eggnog, Fruitcake, and I'm no Teetotaler. I love a kiss from Miss Diana under a leathery-leaved Parasitic Plant. But, just like Christmas, none of those personal-treats have anything to do with the Church. Christmas, as celebrated in the Western Church, is just one of the many carry-overs of neo-paganism that survived the Reformation - nothing more - a highly varied mixture of ancient and modern elements, in which nature worship, influenced by modern environmentalism (see *The Message Bible*), plays a major role. Other influences include Shamanism, magical and occult traditions, and Radical Feminist critiques of Christianity. *"The Hanging of the Greens/Crismon Worship Services,"* started in 1957 by a woman in an Apostate church and practiced in many main-lined Churches today, is a great example of this mixed bag of Holiday Tricks.

And it all began so innocently: *Via Media*, the link-up of Paganism and Christianity which took place under Constantine the Great (the Emperor and first Pope of Rome) in the early 300's A.D.

Constantine wanted a wedded Kingdom. He wanted Unity: Unity within his Empire and the Church - but how does one do that? How does one blend the *bona fide* with a *knockoff*? No one in their right mind counterfeits three dollar bills. That's stupid. You counterfeit something that looks like the real article. So Constantine set about creating a mixed-Marriage of Church and State. An imitation of the Real. The Pagans, unlike the Christians who worshiped one God, worshiped a plethora of objects symbolizing all sorts of gods. So how does one fuse that? Simple. You bind the two with truth, lies and half-truths. You flood a valley with Truth so you can float a row-boat full of Lies. The Pagans honored Icons. So Constantine brought in the homage of Christian Saints, Images, Crosses, Fishes, Marble Statues, etc., which *appease*d the Pagans, but *compromised* the Church. This religious Potpourri drew it's first breath in the form of so-called Christian rites, rituals and customs. Statues of Isis and Horus were renamed Mary and Jesus. The Festival of Saturn (winter solstice) was replaced by a Christ-Mass. Incense, Candles, Evergreens, Holly, Processions, Vestments, all of which had been in Pagan Cults, were cleansed in ordained Rituals of the Church. Everything the Pagans worshiped, plus more, was incorporated into the Church and proclaimed Christian.

And it's easy to see how this all happened. Christians, by and large, are a simple, no-frills, honest lot. The people of God want the world to see the Church as relevant to their lives right now - Christianity is not just about the past, but has life-giving impact in the present. Then comes questions, longings, experiences, expectations about life, and over time, instead of the Church being disturbed, surprised, caught off guard and offended by the judgment and justification that *God* brings into our lives, we begin to Domesticate the Church. We fashion Bibles that are more readable to the Modern ear - creating a Handbook of life principles to improve our earthly lives. We make the Lord of Glory a supporting actor in our personal screenplay, instead of seeing the Bible as the script with the LORD as the central character. And when that happens the Church loses Her sense of being the radical, un-Worldly, Supernatural Nation preaching the Word from Heaven that Kills and makes Alive. When evangelism dies, heresy is born.

When the Church stopped asking itself whether the Bible with its own message, questions, and answers is already more relevant on its own terms than whatever Modern relevance operation we've performed on it, many Churches lost their way. And when that happened, those Churches emerged as some weird version of a "nowhere man living in a nowhere land . . . who doesn't have a point of view, knows not where he is going to." The Bible became a fortune-cookie, inspirational-thought-for-the-day Novel, which left everyone in their original Sin, Guilt, Fear, and Death. But, to jog the world's memory of why the Church is still here, those Churches created a yearly Celebration, of dead trees, prickly red-berried Shrubs, Pagan Ornaments, and Bonus Awards, to bring "Joy to the World," while the world continues to live in the slums.

There's a big different between *hearing* the Bible and *using* the Bible for whatever we already think is important, interesting, and relevant. Our salvation cost God *everything* - the most precious treasure: His Son. From the Beloved of His eternal joy, the Father turned His face in wrath to His only begotten Son, even though He, Himself, had done nothing to deserve it. Grace *is* free, but it's not cheap. God paid the heaviest price of all.

This is not the era of driving God's enemies out of a Temporal Land and establishing a Geo-Political Theocracy somewhere. Jesus made that clear in His Sermon on the Mount, and also in His rebuke of James and John for wanting to call Fire down from Heaven on a Samaritan village that refused the Gospel. Now is the hour of Grace, of going to the highways and byways to gather guests for the Sabbath feast, to proclaim the Forgiveness of Sin and Freedom from Bondage - not just on December 25th, but every day of the year.

23 December 2010.

FAITH - the articles -

The Incredible, Eatable Easter Egg

The world is plagued by old wives' tales, queer traditions and folklore. Most are harmless, and the bulk of them are never questioned. But, being a curious sort, I have to know why people "knock on wood," or why a Sports-Jock wears the same pair of un-washed socks his entire Professional career. In like fashion, I had to know what's-up with the Church's time-honored Easter Egg. Specifically, when, where and why the Egg? Well, I've found out . . . from various folktales, urban myths, time-honored legends & Canon V of the first Nicene Council.

The use of Eggs in all sorts of Pagan festivities dates back to antiquity, when the Egyptians and Romans, among others, saw its shape as an emblem of the Universe. But our Easter Egg didn't get its start until around 325 A.D. - after Constantine crowned himself the first Roman Pope and summoned the first Church-Council. Easter, Lent, Christmas, and the like, were dated, deemed and dictated "Holy Festivals" - all set and settled by the end of Constantine's reign. As the feast of Easter developed in the early Roman Church, so did the festival's preparatory period, known as Lent. This 40 day precursory involved fasting and abstinence from certain foods, including Eggs. Canon LVI of the Council in Trullo, 692 A.D., again, urged Egg abstinence: "It seems good therefore that the whole Church of God which is in all the world should follow one rule and keep the Fast perfectly, and as they abstain from everything which is killed, so also should they from Eggs and cheese, which are the fruit and produce of those animals from which we abstain."

Biblical or not, that was the verdict.

By the time of the medieval theologian Thomas Aquinas (1225-1274), Eggs, milk, and meat were all strictly forbidden during Lent: "Eggs and milk foods are forbidden to those who Fast, for as much as they originate from animals that provide us with flesh . . . the eating of flesh meat is forbidden in every Fast, while the Lenten Fast lays a general prohibition even on Eggs and milk foods."

In pre-refrigeration days, it was difficult to preserve milk and meat for 40 days until Easter, but that was not necessarily true of Eggs. The use of Eggs, which unlike other foods do not perish quickly, was a natural way to Break the Lenten Fast on Easter Sunday. So, presenting gifts of Eggs at Easter became a long and culturally diverse Church lineage. Practicality was one factor, given that hens would be laying Eggs throughout Lent, a surplus would exist by Easter - probably at lower prices. (Notably, the Jewish Passover Seder meal includes a hard-boiled Egg symbolizing the sacrifice at, and subsequently the destruction of, the Jerusalem temple. Whether this had any influence on the development of the Easter Eggs, I really don't know.)

Okay, that's where Constantine's Easter Egg came from, but why do we dye them? Again, folktales, legends . . . yada, yada, yada.

There's an ancient story about Mary Magdalene being summoned to the Roman Emperor Tiberius. After telling him that Christ had been resurrected, the skeptical Caesar pointed to an Egg and exclaimed, "Christ has not risen, no more than that Egg is red" - after which, according to legend, the Egg in question miraculously turned blood-red.

One Eastern Orthodox myth tells the story of either Mary Magdalene or Mary, the mother of Jesus, placing a basket of Eggs under the Lord's Cross. Why she did this is not explained, but, according to lore, the blood of Christ fell on the Eggs, turning them blood-red.

According to an oral wives' tale, Simon of Cyrene (Luke 23:26) was, in fact, an Egg merchant, who was forced to leave his Egg Kiosk to help Jesus carry the Cross. Miraculously, when Simon returned, he found that all his Eggs had changed color. Yep, blood-red.

These, and other identical sagas, have traditionally been taken as the basis for why we dye Easter Eggs. Why we ask children to hunt them is a story for a later date. But, we've been dyeing Easter Eggs for centuries. "O, when will Easter come,' runs an ancient Macedonian children's rhyme, 'bringing with her red Eggs?"

As expected, Red was the favored Easter color until pastels became vogue in the mid-1970's. In the early 1980s, M&M's® became available in pastel-spring colors. Reese's® now makes peanut butter Easter Eggs, and Smucker's® produces Easter jellybeans.

In 1290, the English King Edward I collected a bunch of Eggs, had them "boiled and stained, or covered with gold leaf, and distributed to the royal household at Easter" (William Hone, William, *The Every-Day Book*). An Egg in a silver case was sent from the Vatican to King Henry VIII (1491 –1547 A.D.). The most famous modern counterpart of this is the renowned Fabergé Egg, first made in 1885 for Tsar Alexander III as an Easter present to his wife, Tsaritsa Maria. People were dyeing Easter

Eggs by one method or another in various parts of Britain, especially northern England in the 18th century, which they called "Pace-Eggs," from the Greek word *paschal* - relating to Easter or Passover. Chocolate Easter Eggs emerged in the 19th century and, because they could be mass-produced, took over the Easter market by the following century. The Church hasn't been the same since.

So, in conclusion, why the Easter Egg? Tevye the milkman in *Fiddler on the Roof* said it best: "Tradition!"

14 April 2011

Easter and the Equinox

Our Western dating system - or calendar - was first given us by a Roman Abbot named Dionysius Exiguus (500-560 A.D.) "Little Dennis," as he was called - a brilliant mathematician and astronomer, as well as a scholar in both Latin and Greek. In 525 A.D., Pope John I asked if Little Dennis would calculate the Easter date for the next year's celebration. So he calculated the true Easter date, being an astronomer, by noting the age, or phase, of the moon during a given year on a set date in the solar calendar - which was now in use, as opposed to the lunar, or moon phases, calendar. He set an arbitrary date, March 22, the day after the official spring equinox, as determined at the time of the Council of Nicaea (325 A.D.), as the next year's Easter.

Let me explain the good brother's dating technique. In 532 A.D., the moon's age (Little Dennis calculated) was 0 days old on March 22 - a new moon. So the moon will be 11 days older on March 22, the next year. Thus in 533 A.D., the moon was not 0 days old, but rather 11 days old. His calculations changed the year he began to date Easter from 525 A.D. to 532 A.D. With the wave of his pen, he changed forever our dating system.

This calculating of Little Dennis was based on a 19 year lunar cycle, within each 95 year period - a lunar cycle changed each 95 years. The problem with this cycle? The moon runs on a 30 day cycle, so the dates snowballed out of symmetry and season with each passing year. His dates were wrong only in hours; but by the time a thousand years had passed, the whole thing was really a mess.

A few hours didn't sound like a big problem to the Pope then, and most likely, doesn't sound like a big problem to us, now. But, if you multiply say, 3 hours a day times 1,000 years you get 3,000 hours. 3,000 hours divided by 24 hours in a day equals 125 days. 125 days equals one big mess of a calendar. So in 1582 AD, the new "Gregorian" calendar was introduced - to try to restore the dates to their correct time and season periods.

The "Gregorian" calendar still held to Little Dennis' original calculations for the first year - or the date of our Lord's birth - which was off by nearly 4 years. Yet, a bigger problem with this system was the impossibility of matching up the 7 day week, in which Sunday fell, with a 95 year cycle of 19 years. Seven does not divide into 95. A fellow named Victorius had previously figured out a solution to this problem: the Easter dates repeated themselves every 532 years; 532 is divisible by 19 and 7, thus the problem could be solved. But this information unfortunately never reached our dear Little Dennis.

Little Dennis' contribution to our calendar went far beyond his 95 year Easter dating cycle - he gave us our system of dating, *anno Domini* (A.D.), "the year of our Lord" - which is still in use today - with the exception of our modern day intellectuals.

Little Dennis calculated that Christ was born exactly 531 years earlier, which became his base year of A.D. 1. He did not designate a year 0 because the concept of zero had not yet been invented. Don't ask me why. Where the good Abbot got his date for Christ's birth is unknown. But A.D. is what we take for granted as the beginning of our calendar – Christ's birth, "year of our Lord," A.D.; and so it goes.

Little Dennis almost certainly got his beginning date wrong. Matthew tells us that Christ was born in the time of Herod the Great, who died in 4 B.C. - according to the historian Joesphus. Which means the Lord's birth must have been before that date. Which would place His birth in the B.C. sphere in stead of the A.D. realm where Little Dennis placed it. The inverse of *anno Domini*, B.C., - the English for "before Christ" - wasn't used until 1627 A.D., when the French astronomer Denis Petau became the first to add B.C. to dates while teaching at the College de Clermont in Paris, so how was our Little Dennis to know?

What does this mean to us today? It means that the year 2007, 2008, or so, is probably our true year 2012 in the (A.D.), " the year of our Lord" - if you do the arithmetic without a year 0, you'll come to the same conclusion.

What we in West call **2012** is in actuality . . .

2008 (give or take a year or two) reckoning from Christ's birth in c.4 B.C.

2765 according to the old Roman calendar.

2761 according to the ancient Babylonian calendar.

6248 according to the first Egyptian calendar.

5772 according to the Hebrew calendar.

1432 according to the Moslem calendar.

2546 according to the Buddhist calendar.

1390 *according to the Persian calendar.*
1728 *according to the Coptic calendar.*
220 *according to the Calendar of the French Revolution.*
5131 *in the current Maya Great Circle.*
The year of the Dragon *according to the Chinese calendar.*

I could say much more on this subject, but my hands do not have the endurance of my heart - at this point in time anyway - but this is why we celebrate Easter when we do.

FAITH - *the articles* -

The following article spurred many "thank yous" from Christians all over the world, including a Greek Orthodox woman, who wrote a five page letter to the author and shared the article with numerous Clergy and friends.

I Hate Easter!

Yes I do! I hate Easter! Not the observance, the F119east, the validity, the authenticity, the honoring of, the celebration of the Lord of Glory being raised from the dead. No! I hate the Noun! I hate the proper noun, Easter! Why? Because that Anglo English noun causes every un-schooled, half-whit-so-called-theologian to come out of the woodwork with overused banal, trite, hackneyed, stock platitudes of: "Easter" is Pagan!" "Easter means *Eastre!*" "*Eastre* is the celebration of the Pagan goddess associated with spring." Yada, yada, yada, don't care, don't care, don't care. When they learn their Greek, Hebrew and Latin, like I had to, then we'll talk. Until then . . . shut up! These so-called learned men of the Cloth, invariably misinterpret, misread and confuse, verses like, ". . . *intending after Easter to bring him forth to the people*" (Acts 12:4), insisting that "Easter" is not in the original manuscript. Phooey! Baloney! It is, and I'll prove it!

Easter, or, as I prefer, Resurrection Day, is the most important Feast in Christianity. In fact, it is the pivot of the Belief and Doctrine of the Christian faith. ". . . *if Christ be not raised, you are yet in your sins*" (1 Corinthians 15:17). But, "*God has both raised up the Lord, and will also raise us up by His own power*" (1 Corinthians 6:14). This is what we believe. This is what we Celebrate.

In the first century of Christianity, Sunday (a Germanic interpretation of the Latin, *dies solis* - "day of the sun"), replaced Saturday as the Lord's Day. The Church, in her early days, celebrated a weekly remembrance of Easter (*Pascha* - from ecclesiastical Latin, *paschalis*, from *pascha, 'feast of Passover,'* Resurrection Day, our Anglo, Easter) each Sunday, or First Day of the Week. In fact, this *Pascha* Feast was so reverenced by the early Eastern Church, they designate their First Day of the Week, *Voskreseniye* (meaning Resurrection) to weekly commemorate the Lord's victory over death. In Russia today, *Voskreseniye,* is still their First Day of the Week. Sadly, in secularized cultures like the United States, *Pascha* is not celebrated, except once a year in public worship. *Pascha* (Easter, Resurrection Day), is too religious and too Christian for people who are immersed in the things of this world to pay much attention to the world to come and their life after death, yet that is what Easter is all about . . . to those who believe.

If you read history, you'll find that Christians who the did most for the present World were those who thought most of the next. Christians have largely ceased to think of Heaven, which why we are becoming so ineffective in the World.

Our English noun, "Easter" is the Latin *Pascha*, also written "Passover," or properly, the "Feast of the Resurrection of the Lord." The Latin *Pascha*, is a transliteration of Greek, which is itself a transliteration of the Hebrew *Pesach*, meaning "Passover." So the original manuscript of the Bible does use the analogous of our English noun "Easter" from the Hebrew, to the Greek, to the Latin, to Middle English, and finally to our Anglo English. The noun "Easter" itself, is from late Middle English: from Old French, from the ecclesiastical Latin *Paschalis*, from *Pascha* "feast of Passover," via Greek and Aramaic, from Hebrew *Pesach* "Passover," on to our Anglo English, "Easter." That's a long sentence for a short thought, but I won't hang around and worry about. It's simple & true. "Easter" is in the original manuscript of the Bible - just not in English. Now, I don't mean to point a "digitus impudicus" (finger) at the Easter Feast naysayer, but the rest of the original manuscript of the Bible isn't written in English either.

So, why doesn't the Church simply refer to this Easter Feast as "Passover" or "Resurrection Day?" Well . . . because of our Germanic heritage! Not our pagan roots.

The origin of our English noun, Easter, comes from the Germanic name for the month in which the original Christian Easter Feast usually fell, and so, just as the American civic holiday of the Fourth of July has nothing to do with Julius Caesar for whom July was named, neither does Easter have anything to do with the Pagan goddess *Eostre*, the namesake of the month in which *Pascha* fell. Coincidence? Yes. Conspiracy? No. Easter (the noun) was developed from the Old English word which refers to *Eostur-monath* or Easter-month - *Eostur-monath* was simply the month of the Germanic Calendar in which the celebration of the "Feast of the Resurrection of the Lord" (Easter) was observed. Nothing more, nothing less.

The potential difficulty only exists for speakers of Germanic tongues. Most languages in the world use a cognate form of the Greek/Latin term "*Pascha*," and so are free of any Pagan connotations for the name of the Easter Feast. That is, unless someone wants to sell a Christian Easter-Conspiracy Book on TV.

"O death, where is your sting? O grave, where is your victory?"

"Veni, Vidi, Vici!" Christ Jesus came, He saw, He conquered!

(My transliteration from the Latin.)

Happy Easter.

21 April 2011

FAITH - *the articles* -

400 Years & Counting!

Today, May 5, 2011, is the 400th anniversary of the King James Bible. The cultural atmosphere, as well as the reception the King James Version (KJV) itself is getting from different quarters, is quite interesting.

Thomas Nelson, partnering with The History Channel, launched a 400-day celebration last year. *Publishers Weekly* announced: "Save the date . . . the King James translation of the Bible, first published on May 5, 1611, and widely considered to be one of the most influential shapers of English language, literature and culture."

Which brings me to an odd aspect of this story: I found it intriguing that *Publishers Weekly* gave the KJV a mention, because for years the KJV has been marginalized in so many ways by . . . Christians.

As a culture we've bought into the idea that the KJV is "hard to read." And so its venerable translation has been set aside and thrown over for a hodge-podge of harmful translations that reflect Liberal Scholarship bias . . . a byproduct of Enlightenment thinking.

When Christian Publishers realized they could dazzle customers with innovative versions of the Bible, the dam broke. Today nothing is beyond the boundaries of our Post-modern thinking. We have the *Grandmother's Bible*, the orange and blue *Teen Study Bible*, the red and blue *Teen Devotional Bible*, the *Take-It-Anywhere Bible*, the *Boys Bible*, the *Camouflage Bible*, and even the *Back-Pack Bible* for kids on the go. Metal Covers, Magazine and Comic Book formats and, . . .well, the list goes on. Sadly, most of the modern texts scarcely resemble the original manuscripts.

Miss Diana and I have multiple Bible translations, but our favorite is our matching set of the 1967 translation of the King James. This particular translation contains no footnotes telling us that the Old Testament passages related to prophecy are metaphors. There're no notes that reconcile Darwinian philosophy with the Genesis accounts. It's a Bible, that's all.

It's hard for some people to accept that our sovereign God chose a method of communication, which includes written language accessible to His people in all times and places.

The mindset, that says we need Ivory-Tower Egg-Heads to

decipher, decode, decrypt, unscramble & interpret the Bible for us is simply silly in two ways: One, The KJV is not too hard to read. Two, those preconceived opinion notes contained in modern translations do more harm than good.

Don't get me wrong, I'm not arguing that the KJV use of "hoary headed" should be forced on modern audiences. But the "gender-friendly" new translations, which changed certain Biblical pronouns like "men" to "brother and sister," etc., is nothing but awful scholarship. If a Christian (man or a woman) simply reads their Bible, with the help of the Holy Spirit, they'll grasp its meaning. But if it's read along with most Modern Intellectuals' notes, their bias - masquerading as scholarship - will more likely be absorbed.

In the *New Living Translation* study Bible published by Tyndale, the tampering by Modern Intellectuals is blatant. Their notes for Job 40 & 41, the famous "Leviathan" and "Behemoth" passages, reveal to us that these creatures are thought by "most" scholars to be a crocodile or a hippopotamus - even though Behemoth has a tail "strong as a cedar."

The KJV reads, the Behemoth "moveth his tail like a cedar."

This might seem to be a trivial distinction, but it is not.

The King James translators were not influenced by Darwinian philosophy, so they saw no need to liken these two creatures to modern animals. Modern translators cannot accept that these creatures could be akin to dinosaurs. The KJV translators just let the text do their talking, unlike the "geniuses," who operate as Bible translation editorial boards today.

Some modern scholars go further in their notes for Job 40 & 41; they treat us to the idea that some of these creatures could be leftover descriptions from ancient Near East mythology. Get it? In other words, The Bible might have been influenced by Sumerian myth, not the other way around.

Another modern tampering with Scripture is the forcing of an environmentalist, "green" agenda into the Bible - taking the discussion far beyond what the Bible intended regarding stewardship.

A great example of this is Eugene Peterson's 10-million selling *The Message Bible*, which alters Scripture in the name of environmentalism. Peterson translates John 3:17, with, Jesus "came to help, to put the world right again." The KJV reads, "that the world through Him might be saved." Big difference, eh? Peterson doesn't stop there. He also adds "green" to Romans 15:13: "Oh! May the God of green hope fill you up with joy."

The Green Bible is another example of this environmentalistic greening of the Word of God. Produced together with the Sierra Club, The Humane Society and the National Council of Churches, this Bible has an intro by Desmond Tutu and contributions from N.T. Wright and Brian McLaren. Befitting its name, *The Green Bible* is virtually obsessed with environmental concerns, encouraging "people to see God's vision for creation and help them engage in the work of healing and sustaining it."

Whereas, the Bible is not terribly concerned with this present world - this is where Worldview and Eschatology come to the fore. The Bible actually says this planet is under judgment and will one day be completely remade (Matthew 24:35; Revelation 21:1).

Back in the 90's, the *NIV Men's Devotional Bible* saw fit to include a statement by the Catholic mystic, Merton, who claimed that "sin is the refusal of spiritual life."

Sounds spiritual? Deep?

The problem is, it's nonsense. If sin were the refusal of spiritual life, we'd have billions of sinless people. Many people are spiritual. I was shocked at the time that a Christian publisher would produce something like that. I'm not anymore.

Well, I've digressed. Here's to the 400th Birthday of the King James Bible. May her "hoary headed" translators rest in peace.

5 May 2011

FAITH *- the articles -*

Right Judging

"Judge not, that you be not judged"
(Matthew 7:7)

In His Sermon on the Mount, the Lord declared, "Judge not, that you be not judged" - by no means one of the simplest prohibitions to interpret - yet, we should not to come to a hasty conclusion as to its intention.

The disciples of Christ Jesus are to conduct themselves in a manner exactly the reverse from that of the Pharisees or those who would have you keep the Law or their opinion of the Law; we unsparingly judge ourselves and refuse to invade the office of God where others are concerned.

The word "judge" in, "Judge not, that you be not judged" is one which occurs frequently in the New Testament, and is used in quite a variety of senses. "I speak to wise men; judge you what I say" (1 Corinthians 10:15). Also, "judge in yourselves: is it becoming that a woman pray unto God uncovered?" (1 Corinthians 11:13). The word "judge," in these instances simply means to carefully weigh a matter and then form an opinion.

> *"There was a certain creditor who had two debtors; the one owed five hundred denarii, and the other fifty. And when they had nothing to pay, he frankly forgave them both. Tell me, therefore, which of them will love him most?"*
>
> Simon answered and said, *"I suppose that he to whom he forgave most."*
>
> And He said unto him, *"you have rightly judged"* (Luke 7:43).

The Lord applauded Peter's "right judgment". Peter had drawn a right conclusion. So then, "Judge not, that you be not judged" does not imply that we shouldn't have an opinion (which is literally impossible), to never come to a conclusion concerning anyone or anything, nor to fully accept whatever anyone says because we are not to "judge" anyone - thus implying that we are to never "judge" anyone's words or actions no matter how dictatorial and fruitless they may be. This would be a negation of reason.

The capacity of judging, of forming an opinion, is one of the elects' most valuable faculties - the right use of judging, is one of the most important duties we have as believers. If we do not form judgments as to what is true and false, right and wrong, good and bad, false and true doctrine, true and false teachers, preachers and prophets how can we embrace the one and avoid the other? So "Judge not, that you be not judged" does not indicate that, under any circumstance, we are never to "Judge".

I was told as a child, "You shouldn't judge." "You can't judge another man." "Now Jay, stop judging." Yet, the Bible tells me to judge "right judgment." We have two attitudes here, "judge not that you be not judged," and "you have rightly judged." So what's the difference?

What if we see a brother sin? If we say he's sinning, aren't we judging? If we don't judge his sin, aren't we harming our brother, and the church? So what kind of judging are we not to judge? Jesus Himself said, "Why even of yourselves judge you what is right" (Luke 12:57); "judge righteous judgment" (John 7:24). If we don't form judgments as to what is right and true as opposed to what is false and wrong, how can we embrace the one and avoid the other? It is very necessary for us to have our "senses exercised to discern" - thoroughly judge - "both good and evil" (Hebrews 5:14), so we will not be taken in by every oily-mouth imposture we encounter.

The Lord never forbade us to act according to the dictates of common prudence. He did not prohibit us from judging men's character and actions according to their avowed principles and visible conduct. The actions of men absolutely requires us to form a judgment - with respect both to their state and their conduct. This is being responsible "sons." Unless we come to a decision of what is germane, what is good or bad in those we meet and situations we are in, we will be found rejecting the one and condoning the other. "Beware of false prophets, which come to you in sheep's clothing, but inwardly they are ravening wolves. You shall know them by their fruits" (Matthew 7:15): how can we honor this injunction, unless we carefully measure every Churchman we see and hear by the Word of God? How will we be able to know which man is truly a man of God or simply some self-appointed holy Joe or sky-pilot, unless we inspect their fruit - their life, words and converts? This is judging - right judging.

But we do not, nor can we, judge another man's heart - reckoning him a believer or not - reckoning his motives to be from a sinful heart. That's the Lord's job. In that instance "we judge not lest we be judged." Just as, "whosoever shall say to his brother, Raca (empty, an abusive epithet), shall be in danger of the council; but whosoever shall say, you fool, shall be in danger of hell fire" (Matthew 5:22). We do not call, or judge, a man a fool - "a fool in his heart" - because we really don't know whether he's a fool in his heart or not. It should be noted, the fool here is not some short-sighted fellow who comes to work wearing one brown shoe and one black. No, this fool is a fool in his heart. "A fool has said in his heart, 'There is no God'" (Psalm 14:1;53:1). Only the Lord can judge the heart of a man. We can't. We don't know the heart of any man. So we, "judge not." Right judging.

FAITH *- the articles -*

The End-Times Apostate Church
A Four Part Series

Part One

Best-Selling Snake Oil

I'm a Christian. And, along with many of my Fellows, we are seen by some as, "Rubes." The title, "Rube" is an old-time phrase, coined in the merciless culture of the Traveling Carnival gangs that roamed from town to town in the early 20th Century. Every stop on the circuit was just another chance to fleece another crowd of free-spending "Rubes" - Hicks, Yokels, Marks, Dullards who buy diamonds from Gypsies, and anyone over the age of nine who still believes in his heart that all politicians are honest and would never lie on TV.

These people are everywhere. They are Legion, soon to be a majority, and 10,000 more are being born every day. It was P.T. Barnum, the Circus-man, who explained the real secret of his commercial success by repeating his now-famous motto, "There's a sucker born every minute," and his job was to keep them amused - which he did - with a zeal that has never been equaled in the history of American show business. That is, until now.

Modern Christian Authors, Publishers and Book-Sellers have snapped-up P.T.'s Big Top; and his Blockbuster Gamut is up and running again. And these peddlers know what "Rubes" want: dignified Freaks, well-dressed Clowns, and spine-tingling wild Animals. Looking at the list of best-selling Christian books, with self-serving titles like "So Long, Insecurity" and "The Me I Want to Be," one wonders how much longer it will be before non-Christian authors are on the list. Maybe some of them are on it now. Who knows? And their publishers don't care.

For six thousand years, Satan has had full opportunity afforded him to study fallen human nature to discover our weakest points and to learn how best to make us do his bidding. The Devil knows full well how to dazzle us by the attraction of power, and how to make us cower before its terrors. He knows how to gratify our craving for knowledge and how to satisfy our taste for refinement and culture; he can delight our ear with melodious music and captivate our eye with entrancing beauty. If he could transport the Savior from the wilderness to a mountain, in a moment of time, and show Him all the kingdoms of the world and their glory, he is no novice in the art of presenting alluring objects before his victims today. There's a "Rube" born every minute.

Just two days ago I was given a book by Eugene H. Peterson, *Living the Resurrection* - this book would be comical, if it weren't so tragic to see where so-called Christian writers are sitting right now. You can read this book in a couple of hours, because it's written for Biblically Illiterate Government-Schooled third-graders: wide-eyed "Rubes," who are under the impression that "The Resurrection" is a new British Punk-Band. Peterson, like so many Christian authors today, aims for the lowest common denominator and taps into the human love of . . . self. After reading this book, I wondered if Peterson ever walks away from his *soi-disant* intellectual Ivory-Tower Magic Mirror. This guy is a buffoon, theologically.

One of Peterson's literary claims to fame is his commercially rhapsodized, *The Message Bible*. I read Greek, and, with a little help from my Rabbi buddy, I can translate Hebrew, so what are my thoughts on Peterson's "The Message"? It's a joke-book theologically, written by an enlightened Jester. It's a fallacious transliteration, which must be avoided at all cost! Simply, because it's a transcriptional abhorrent collection of hallucinations of an intellectual fool - not a Bible! *The Message Bible* has been birthed from within popular professing Christianity, which invites the reader to learn more about Jesus from a pluralistic perspective - amalgamating Christ with the world. Its goal is to establish a Jesus (along with His Church), who is acceptable to people of all faiths - or no faith. Avoid! Avoid! Avoid!

Sadly, the Christian publishing Cartels make sure that personality-soaked authors, like Peterson, get center stage. This naturally shrinks the opportunities for authors, who actually have something Biblically Truthful to say, but might not have access to Botox, Capped-Teeth or Heavy Media coaching.

Witness the 30-million-or-so best-selling *The Purpose Driven Life*, by Rick Warren: a Christian Title masquerading as a benevolence-inducing read, when in fact it is just as self-serving as, say, a Deepak Chopra tome.

I've read *The Purpose Driven Life*, and I've also seen "Its" Theologically-challenged hold on much of the evangelical world. This book is for Used-Car-Salesmen, not the Church! Harsh? No more so than the mood among Christian publishers who foster this kind of Leadership.

The most compelling authors on Christian best-seller lists are the dead ones, such as C.S. Lewis and Henrietta Mears. They wrote in a time when people weren't so Biblically Illiterate. Today, authors "write down" to an audience that largely have no Biblical knowledge, which perpetuates Biblical Illiteracy.

This Illiteracy is why Christian authors on the Bestseller Lists today can actually change Scripture to fit points they want to make in their books - actually changing the words of the Bible. They create square pegs and hammer them into any pop-psychology round-hole the Bestselling Christian Author wants to make. *The Shack* is a very good example. When this trumped-up style actually gains traction among readers . . . Surprise! "Said" author becomes a franchise, a machine for the publisher and the reading public are then treated to at least one volume of this kind of clap-trap Snake Oil each year. Christian Bookstores stock 'em, promote 'em and sell 'em - to every "Rube" they can flimflam.

Give me the Holy Bible any day of the week

4 November 2010

The End-Times Apostate Church
Part Two

Lucifer's Gospel

"I fear, lest by any means, as the serpent beguiled Eve through his craftiness, so your minds should be corrupted from the simplicity that is in Christ"
(2 Corinthians 11:3).

What is Lucifer's Gospel?

Lucifer's Gospel is a product of a Culture that claims to be shocked at its very existence: an ecclesial Community represented by the editors of *Christianity Today* and the producers at TBN, who live in a world full of Christian Celluloid and CD bandits, hustling toothpaste and hair oil. This is a Citizenry, who are no longer capable of confronting the real thing. For years they have sat with their children and watched the world go by from the glow of their TV screens . . . and now they're bringing up children, who think Paul of Tarsus is a DVD character. This is a generation that went to war for God, Mom, Apple Pie and the American Way of Life. When they came back, they retired to the giddy comfort of their TV parlors, to cultivate the subtleties of Christian history as seen by Hollywood.

To them the appearance of Lucifer's Gospel must seem like a publicity stunt. In a nation of frightened dullards, there is a sorry shortage of bona fide Christian Lionhearts; and those few who make the grade are always welcomed in any age: RC Sproul, John MacArthur, Jonathan Edwards, John Owen, Charles H. Spurgeon, Charles Hodge, A. W. Pink, John Calvin . . . they all have that extra "Something" - the Holy Spirit of God, proclaiming the true Gospel of Christ Jesus.

The Apostle Paul referred to Lucifer's Gospel in his letter to the Galatian Church, "I marvel that you are so soon removed from Him that called you into the grace of Christ unto another gospel: which is not another, but there be some that trouble you, and would pervert the Gospel of Christ" (Galatian 1:6,7). Then he continues, "But though we, or an angel from heaven preach any other gospel unto you than that which we have preached unto you, let him be accursed."

The End-Times Apostate Church / Lucifer's Gospel

In 2 Corinthians 11, Paul addressed himself to the false apostles and prophets of Lucifer's Gospel, who come into the body of Christ and preach, what Paul refers to as "another Jesus" - the word *another*, is the Greek word, *alas*; meaning: another of the same kind. (Our English word *alias* is also drawn from the same Greek word.) This is "another Jesus," who looks and acts like the Jesus we've heard about - but he's not the same Jesus at all. He doesn't have the same Reliable Qualities as the Jesus we know from our Bible - he's another Jesus of the same kind. An alias savior. A Jesus who seems compassionate, loving, and redemptive; everything the people of God know the real Jesus to be, but when we are exposed to this other Jesus, we experience Another Gospel of a different kind: a false gospel - a gospel of regulations and requirements jumbled up with grace. By accepting this message, we thereby receive Another spirit of a different kind, which carries the Church away from God-loving to people-loving. Jesus did not preach, "Embrace love and thereby redeem the world." Jesus preached, "Embrace Me and forsake the world!"

Lucifer's Gospel is not a system of revolutionary principles, or a program of anarchy. It does not promote strife and war, but rather it aims at Peace and Unity. It does not seek to set the mother against her daughter, nor the father against his son, but fosters the Fraternal spirit, whereby the human race is regarded as one great "Brotherhood." It never seeks to drag *down* the natural man, but to improve and uplift him.

Lucifer's Gospel advocates education and cultivation and appeals to "the best that is within us all". It aims to make this world such a Congenial and Comfortable habitat that Christ's absence from it will not be felt and God will not be needed. It endeavors to occupy man so much with this world that he has no time or inclination to think of the World To Come. It propagates the principles of self-sacrifice, charity and benevolence, and teaches us to live for the good of others, and to be kind to all. It appeals strongly to the *carnal* mind and is popular with the masses . . . Lucifer's Gospel nullifies the Death of Christ!

In contrast to the Gospel of Christ, Lucifer's Gospel teaches salvation by works. It inculcates justification before God on the ground of Human merits. Its Sacramental phrase is "Be good and do good" . . . it announces salvation by Character, which reverses the order of God's Word, as distinctive by, as the fruit of, salvation. Its various ramifications and organizations are manifold. The Emerging Church phenomenon, Signs and Wonders movements, Prosperity theology,

FAITH - *the articles* -

Christian Socialist Leagues, Peace through Unity Congresses are all employed (maybe unconsciously) in proclaiming Lucifer's Gospel: Salvation By Works. The pledge-card is substituted for Christ; social purity for individual regeneration, and politics and philosophy for doctrine and godliness. The Cultivation of the old man is considered "more practical" than the creation of a new man in Christ Jesus; while universal peace is looked for apart from the interposition and return of the Prince of Peace.

The apostles of Lucifer's Gospel minimize sin by declaring that sin is merely ignorance or the absence of good . . . thus making God a liar by declaring that He is too loving and too merciful to send any of His own creatures to Eternal Torment. Lucifer's Gospel preachers hold up Christ as the great Examplar and exhort their followers to "follow in His steps." Their message may sound very plausible and their actions appear very praiseworthy . . . *Lucifer* himself is transformed into an angel of light. Therefore it is no great thing if his ministers are also transformed as the ministers of righteousness, whose end shall be according to their works.

The Essence which lurks behind the preachers of Lucifer's Gospel is their concern for freedom, merit, and good works in human pride - a desire to have something to offer God that will blunt the enormity of our need for Grace.

Today hundreds of churches are without Leaders who faithfully declare the whole counsel of God and present His way of Salvation; and the majority of people in these Churches are very unlikely to learn the Truth for themselves. The Bible is not expounded in the pulpit and it is not read in the pew. The demands of this hubbub age are so numerous that the multitudes have little time and still less inclination to make preparation for their meeting with God. Hence the majority, who are too indolent to search for themselves, are left at the mercy of those whom they pay to search for them; many of which betray their trust by studying and expounding economic and social problems, rather than the Oracles of God . . .

Thousands are deceived into supposing that they have "accepted Christ as their personal Savior," who have not first received Him as their LORD. The Son of God did not come here to save people *in* their sins, but "From Their Sins" (Matthew 1:21). To be saved *from* sins, is to be Saved from ignoring and despising the authority of God; it is to abandon the course of self-will and self-pleasing; it is to "forsake our way" (Isaiah 55:7). It is to surrender to God's authority, to yield to His dominion, to give ourselves over to be ruled by Him. The one who has never taken Christ's "yoke" upon him, who is not truly and diligently seeking to please Him in all the details of his life, and yet supposes that he is "resting on the Finished Work of Christ," is deluded by the Gospel of Lucifer himself - and will pay the price in the World To Come.

11 November 2010

The End-Times Apostate Church
Part Three

Silencing The Elect

"I have a few things against you because you have there those who hold the doctrine of Balaam, . . . you also have those, who hold the doctrine of the Nicolaitans, which thing I hate"
(Revelation 2:13-15).

What is the doctrine of Balaam? "If you can't lick-um . . . join-um" (Numbers 22; 23) The way of Balaam is to sell your gift for hire. Balaam's doctrine said to Balak, "Hey, you'll never wipe out the people of God, so go and mingle in with them." So, false teachers move in with all their doctrines of immorality, and mix in with the people of God. And the Bad Apples spoil the whole bunch.

What is the doctrine of the Nicolaitans? "If we can shut 'em up, we can control 'em." If you can take from the people of God, the privilege of ministering to the Lord individually - if you can take the privilege of interpreting the scripture away from the people of God, and place that privilege into the hands of a select group of Church Officials - then the people of God become slaves of the group who know and hold the Book. That's the Nicolaitans!

The word Nicolaitans means, *people rulers,* or *converters of the people.* The word comes from the Greek, *nikao* which means, "to conquer," and *laos* which means, "people." We derive our word, *laity* from the word *laos.* As soon as we began referring to the people of God as "The Laity," this was the beginning of the separation of The Clergy from the People of God. The church became a Priest class here, and a Laity class there. And God said "I hate it!" This separation brought about spectator-sport Christianity: the preacher up front and the congregation down below . . . and God "hates it!"

All of this is a result of, and the ultimate end of what happened in the Pergamum church (Revelation 2:12-17).

Pergamum, the state church, was first established by the emperor Constantine - thus, it became first church of Rome and introduced the first Pope, or Pontifex Maximus. As time went on, all the bishops of

Rome were given imperial (and pagan) titles. The emperor and Pope (one in the same) also became known as the Vicar of Christ (Latin *vicarius* '*substitute*' of Christ) and as the Bishop of Bishops. After Constantine's death and continuing to this day, these three titles are retained by the popes of the Roman Catholic Church.

Of the seven cities mentioned in Revelation, Pergamum was indeed the most wicked, for Satan's seat or throne was established there (Revelation 2:13).

As its name implies, Pergamum (*twice married* or *mixed marriage*) was a city of mixed religions and temples. A title held by the inhabitants of Pergamum was "Chief Temple-Keepers of Asia." Behind the city was a cone shaped mountain rising 1,000 feet above sea level, which was covered with heathen temples. Towering above all the temples, and visible for miles around, was a giant altar to Zeus, the Grecian father of the gods. The city was also headquarters of the serpent god, Asklepios, and like Smyrna, Pergamum had erected a temple to the Roman emperor. The most prominent religious system of the city and most likely the one that plagued the local church for what Christ had condemned it, was the worship of Bacchus, the Greek god of revelry and licentious orgies. The annual drunken feast held in honor of Bacchus in the spring, called the Bacchanalia, included eating meat sacrificed to idols and climaxed in a sexual frenzy. (Mardi Gras has its roots in the Bacchanalia, which is religiosity followed by Ash Wednesday, fasting, abstinence, and penitence: i.e. Lent.)

Are there Pergamum churches today? Yes.

One signpost of a Pergamum church is Nicolaitanism, or the overthrow by the Clergy of the Laity. Some Protestant churches are run by a hierarchy who dictates all policy, forbidding members to vote on certain issues. The selection and placement of pastors in many denominations are handled by bishops, deacons or superintendents. The vote of church members, if indeed there is one, is simply an endorsement of a prior selection.

Nicolaitanism's doctrine is identical to that of the doctrine of Balaam: "If you can't lick 'um, join 'um" (Revelation 2:14). There are today, whole denominations who are controlled by organizational demons, who have come into the church as "angels of light." They are Balaam's acolytes and they are not interested in the Lord Jesus Christ, though they pretend to be.

Another requirement of a Pergamum church is the System of

FAITH - the articles -

Unity:- of church and State: "mixed" or "twice married" - a mixture of pagan doctrine with church doctrine. Today it's called *a consensus of faiths*, which has found a platform in many Protestant churches. The results of this "marriage" is staggering.

Not long ago, 10,000 Protestant clergymen were mailed a questionnaire, a poll to which 7,441 replied:

To the first question, "Do you believe that the scriptures are the inspired and inerrant word of God in faith, history and secular matters?"

24% of Missouri Lutheran pastors answered No;
77% of American Lutheran pastors answered No;
67% of American Baptist pastors answered No;
82% of United Presbyterian pastors answered No;
87% of United Methodist pastors answered No;
95% of Episcopalian priests answered No.

To the second question, "Do you accept Jesus' physical resurrection as fact?"

7% of Missouri Lutheran pastors answered No;
13% of American Lutheran pastors answered No;
33% of American Baptist pastors answered No;
35% of United Presbyterian pastors answered No;
51% of United Methodist pastors answered No;
30% of Episcopalian priests answered No. None of these accept Jesus' physical resurrection as fact.

Replace any of those churches with whatever denomination you choose, and you'll find a similar "mixed marriage" of Church and State, Divine and Pagan in them all. And when this "mixed marriage" has a foothold in any denomination, evangelism ceases and heresy enters the church. If your church has mixed Patriotism with Christianity or Pagan, New Age or Hipster Christianity with Church doctrine, your Church has passed the final test of being a Pergamum church. You are being ruled by Nicolaitans, who are following the doctrine of Balaam. And the Elect has been Silenced.

18 November 2010

The End-Times Apostate Church
Part Four

Rebels Without A Clue

What happens when Hip meets Holy?

Let's say you're a teen-ager looking for something to do on a Saturday night. After you've tired of cruising the McDonald's parking lot, you decide to check-out a new venue in town. You park your parents' four-door Impala and saunter into a non-descript, warehouse-like auditorium. Inside, it's filled with fledgling Hipsters sporting the latest Couture the New York garment industry can offer. There's sultry mood lighting, Fog Machines, and bass-throbbing music being shocked-waved through a sound system, which is just loud enough for the Throngs to carry-on scream-level conversations. Off to one side is a bar operated by a couple of twenty-something's serving a motley collection of libations. At the far end of the building is an over-sized bandstand crammed full of mics, drums, amps, and an assortment of electric keyboards and guitars. Above the stage are jumbo screens flashing what appears to be the latest music videos. iPhones are everywhere.

As you make your way through the trendsetting, à la mode gaggle of spectators, two nose-ringed tattooed Hipsters approach you. They make small talk. One comments about the cool surroundings. The other asks if you've heard the new Fire Brand album. Something is said about the environment and the need to control Global Warming. Eventually they ask if you'd like to exchange contact information

Now the question: Are you in a Bar or a Church? Hard to say . . . in today's Christianity.

Welcome to the world of the Rebel Church: A world where the Bible, heart-felt evangelism, and holiness are relevant only as a source of paradox or wistful nostalgia. A world where Biblical discipline and accuracy are anathema. A world where adolescent evangelicals have grown-up on Contemporary Christian Music, Adventures in Odyssey, vacation Bible School, and novel fictitious prose of the Left Behind pulp.

The widespread appeal of the Rebel Church is worth pondering. With little or no benchmark, axiom or Rules of Engagement, they are driven by emotion and governed by defiance. Their desire is to see the world saved by using the world as the means. And this is where they show what incorrigible Rebels Without a Clue they really are. As they "kick against the goads" of true evangelism, it is just at this point that God manifests His sovereign and wondrous Grace. He not only planned and provided salvation, but he actually bestows it upon those whom He has chosen - with or with out a state-of-the-art presentation. The Lord will save His Church.

Salvation may be viewed from many angles and contemplated under various aspects, but from whatever side you look, you must ever remember that "Salvation is of the Lord" (Jonah 2:9). Salvation was planned by the Father for His Elect before the foundation of the world. It was purchased for them by the Holy Life and Vicarious Death of His Incarnate Son. It is applied to and completed in them by His Holy Spirit. It is known and enjoyed through the study of the Scriptures, through the exercise of faith, and through communion with the triune Jehovah.

I fear that there are multitudes in Rebellious Hipster Christendom, who fervently imagine and sincerely believe that they are among the saved, yet who are total strangers to a work of Divine Grace in their hearts. It is one thing to have clear intellectual conceptions of God's Truth, but it is quite another matter to have a personal, Real Heart acquaintance with it. It is one thing to believe that Sin is the awful thing the Bible says it is, but it is quite another matter to have a Holy Horror and Hatred of it in the soul. It is one thing to know that God requires repentance, it is quite another matter to radically mourn and groan over our vileness. It is one thing to believe that Christ is the only Savior for sinners, it is quite another matter to really trust Him from the heart. It is one thing to believe that Christ is the Sum of all Excellency, it is quite another matter to love Him above all others. It is one thing to believe that God is the Great and Holy One, it is quite another matter to truly Reverence and Fear Him. It is one thing to believe that "Salvation is of the Lord," it is quite another matter to become an attested partaker of it through His gracious workings.

There is a "believing" in Christ by the natural man, which is not a believing unto Salvation. Just as the Buddhist believes in Buddha, so in today's Christendom there are multitudes who believe in Christ. And this "believing" is more than an intellectual one. Often times there is much feeling connected with it, because fleshly emotions may be deeply stirred. The Lord taught in the Parable of the Sower that there is a class of people who hear the Word, and with joy receive it, yet they have no root in themselves (Matthew 13:20, 21). Sadly, this is occurring daily in our New Rebel Church. Scriptures tell us that Herod heard John "gladly." Thus, the mere fact that someone basks in the pneuma of Contemporary Christian Music or gets a kick out of flamboyant gospel preaching is no proof at all that they are a regenerated soul. The Lord Jesus said to the Pharisees concerning John the Baptist, "You were willing for a season to rejoice in his light," yet the sequel of events following, proves clearly that no real work of Grace had been created in them. And all these things are recorded as solemn warnings for today's Church!

Unfortunately, to the subculture of today's Rebellious Evangelicals, all of this is laughable. As they try their best to torch away the truth of Historical Christianity, there is no escaping the echo of Mistah Kurtz's final words from *The Heart of Darkness*: "The horror! The horror! . . . Exterminate all the brutes!"

Lord, in Your wrath, remember mercy (Habakkuk 3:2).

2 December 2010

FAITH - *the articles* -

Truly Just & Truly Fair

Genesis 19 deals with the destruction of the cities of Sodom & Gomorrah. They are miniature sketches of the world in which we live. And now, just as then, the world is the magnet, and mankind the iron filings that lie within its field.

The Lord came to Abraham (Genesis 18) and informed him of the fact that because of the wickedness of those cities, it was necessary for the judgment of God to come. Abraham pleaded with the Lord for Sodom, actually saying "But what if there are fifty righteous; would You destroy the righteous with the wicked?" The basis of Abraham's argument was: the Lord of the earth should be fair, or be just. Even in judgment, God must be fair or just. God cannot be unjust in any action at any time ever.

This is an area that Satan is constantly seeking to make a case against God. How can a God of love, or would a God of love, condemn a man to eternal hell who has never heard of Jesus Christ? What about a man who lived and died never knowing, or hearing of Jesus Christ? Is he going to have to suffer forever in hell, when he never had a chance to hear? Interestingly, the Bible doesn't give us the answer directly, but it does give us an indirect answer and that is, God is Truly Just & Truly Fair.

Abraham's argument with God was, "Shall not the Lord of the earth be fair, or be just?" When God spoke of the judgment that was going to come, Abraham saw an inequity, if God would judge the righteous with the wicked. That wouldn't be fair. That's the premise and the basis of Abraham's argument with the Lord. It wouldn't be fair to judge the righteous with the wicked.

Jesus said to His disciples, "In this world you will have tribulation: but [He said] be of good cheer; I've overcome the world" (John 16:33). The Church has had tribulation since it's birth. Today we're under great persecution. In Albania, Islam is tightening their hold, persecuting the Church. Many Albanian pastors have been imprisoned in the past few weeks.

Christians have been persecuted in Communist dominated countries, such as China and Russia, for years. But Islam is perhaps the

FAITH - the articles -

greatest foe of Christianity today. In Islamic countries, it's a Capital Crime to seek to convert an Islamic person to Christianity - punishable by beheading.

The church will always experience persecution from the world. So, Peter tells us to not count it "strange concerning the fiery trial which is to try you, as though some strange thing has happened unto you" (1 Peter 4:12). In fact, if the world loves you, then you better examine your position. But, "if the world hates you," don't be alarmed, Jesus said, "It hated me. The servant is not greater than his Lord" (John 15:18,20).

The tribulation & persecution the Church has, and continues to experience, has at its source or origin, the world, the flesh and the Devil, since Pentecost. But, the Great Tribulation that's coming, or the Great Judgment of God (Revelation 7:14), whenever that comes, the Church will not be a victim of, because God will be Fair and Just in His judgment. "If there be fifty righteous", the Lord said, "I'll spare it for fifty righteous." Abraham finally talked Him down to ten. And God said He would spare Sodom for "ten righteous."

God's judgments, are always absolutely Just and absolutely Fair.

So the Lord sent His angels into Sodom, and they couldn't find ten righteous individuals in the entire city. The only truly righteous person there was Abraham's nephew, Lot. His family wasn't thoroughly righteous, but being merciful, God let his family go out with him.

Twice in the New Testament, once by Jesus and once by Peter, Sodom is used as an example of the last days. Jesus said, "As it was in the days of Lot, so shall it be at the coming of the Son of man" (Luke 17:28,30). His example points to the fact that God's judgment did not come, until the day Lot was taken out of the city. As soon as Lot was out of range, God rained fire and brimstone upon Sodom. Lot was delivered before God's judgment came.

Peter also points to the deliverance of Lot saying, "God knows how to deliver the righteous, and to reserve the ungodly for the Day of Judgment" (2 Peter 2:9). God delivered righteous Lot, who was vexed by the manner of life of those around him - like us.

Christians living in this day are under constant bombardment and pressure to accept evil, to tolerate evil, and to accept most perversions as natural. If we dare speak against homosexuality, we'll have a parade in front of the Church the next day. So we've become sort of cowered into a position of not stating our beliefs.

If a Christian student, or teacher, dares say in a university class that, "Jesus is the only way to salvation," they'll be laughed at. They'll call them, narrow and bigoted. If a Christian makes an affirmation of faith and a belief in living a moral, pure, righteous life, they're accused of living in the past. We're under pressure. And it's hard to live in a society that's so corrupt, without it rubbing off a little on us.

So taking the same argument as Abraham, "Shall not the Lord of the earth be just?" Would it be just that God would bring His great wrath and judgment upon the Church, along with the unbelieving world? No.

Even as God delivered Lot, God shall deliver His Church before His great period of Judgment that is to come upon the earth. It's a matter of God's principle in judgment. God is truly Just and truly Fair.

30 June 2011

FAITH *- the articles -*

Without Controversy

" ... great is the mystery of godliness"
(1 Timothy 3:16).

Godliness is godlikeness. Great is the mystery of being like God. These characteristics and traits are the characteristics and traits of God. God wants us to be like Him.

In 1 Timothy, Paul addresses the qualifications for Elders and Deacons in the Church. Paul had left Timothy in Ephesus to strengthen the Church. It is to Timothy that Paul is writing and instructing him in the government of the Church. "I want you to know how you ought to behave yourself in the house of God" (1 Timothy 3:14-15).

A man who is an Elder or an Overseer in the Church is, in reality, one of God's representatives. And this office carries with it the most awesome responsibility of being like God - Godlikeness. God wants His leaders to be like Him so that as people look at them, they can better understand what God is about. And that, in some cases, is all the understanding many people will ever have of God - what they observe in the life of God's leaders.

Each child of God is God's representative. But those who take the position of an Elder or an Overseer have a greater responsibility. And God doesn't take lightly how they represent Him. James warns us: "be not many teachers, knowing that we shall receive the greater judgment" (James 3:1). The Lord cautioned, "to whom much is given, much is required" (Luke 12:48). So, for those in the position of Overseeing, there is a tighter standard by which they must live. "Blameless, of good reputation" - inside and outside the Church.

It is a tragedy when an Overseer doesn't take his responsibility seriously. Because he, "falls into reproach and the snare of the devil" (1 Timothy 3:7).

Satan definitely seeks to snare ministers. To trap them. To bring reproach upon the Gospel. As Nathan said to David concerning his sin with Bathsheba, "You've caused the enemies of God to blaspheme" (2 Samuel 12:14). Satan works harder on those who have a greater influence, than those of lesser influence. The more the Lord uses someone, greater are the temptations the enemy places in their path.

Great is the mystery of being like God. God wants us, all His children, to be like Him. That's His purpose in creating us. And when He created us, He created us like Him, "in His image and after His likeness." It was the purpose of God that we'd be like Him.

Great. But what is God like?

God is love. So love must dominate our being. God is pure. God is holy. He wants us to be pure. He wants us to be holy. God is kind. God is compassionate. God is patient. He wants us to be kind, compassionate, patient. He wants His children to be like Him. Great is the mystery of being like God.

All of us shout, "Yes! I want to be like God." But how that is accomplished, is another thing, indeed.

Being like God is the greatest thing that could possibly happen to a person. So, as His obedient children, we try to be like God. But we find that whenever we try to be like God, there are other forces at work within us, hindering us from our goals.

Paul was there in Romans 7, "I consent to the law of God that it is good. But I find that there is another law at work within my members, within my body. And the good that I would, I do not: and that which I would not, I do" (Romans 7:16,19,23).

We all consent (approve) to that which is good. But how to perform it . . . we just can't find. We consent to what is right, what is good. We know what we ought to be doing. But how to perform it? That's where the problem lies. So we cry out, "O wretched man that I am! Who shall deliver me from this body of death" (Romans 7:24)?

And we are comforted in, "There is therefore, now no condemnation to them who are in Christ Jesus" (Romans 8:1). And we sigh a great sigh of relief because that great mystery has been solved. It was solved in the incarnation - "without controversy, great is this mystery of godliness." God solved the mystery of Godlikeness through the incarnation of Jesus Christ for, "God was manifest in the flesh" - a clear declaration that Jesus Christ is God. "God was manifest in the flesh." The purpose of the incarnation was to bring man to a Godlikeness: To help us, Pastors, Teachers, Elders, Deacons, and all the rest, to be like God.

"Without Controversy, great is the mystery of godliness . . . God was manifest in the flesh."

19 May 2011

Starvation Of The Lambs

"Behold, the days come, said the Lord God,
that I will send a famine in the land,
not a famine of bread, nor a thirst for water,
but of hearing the word of the Lord . . .
and they shall run to and fro to seek the word of the Lord,
and shall not find it"
(Amos 8:11).

Eight hundred years before the birth of Christ, the northern kingdom of Israel was riding high and living low. Moral standards had all but disappeared, honesty was a thing of the past and the poor were treated as social lepers. But money was flowing and trade was booming, so they didn't trouble themselves with the negatives. Strange as it may seem, in this mix of milk and honey and hunger, Temple attendance was booming. Mega synagogues, with their fine-tuned music and high pageantry, entertained the public in masses. But not with preaching, for they "commanded the prophets, saying, 'Prophesy not'" (Amos 2:12). Every one believed, because Israel was built on faith in God, that God was on their side and would see them through any and all adversity . . . no matter what they did. They were living on the endowment of their ecclesiastical past.

By this time God had abandoned all hope of winning this self-satisfied, farce of a nation. How the mighty had fallen. So God decided to launch an A-bomb in the form of a sheep-herder named Amos. Amos exploded through Israel's heartland like a blitzkrieg prophet of doom! "Thus says the Lord," Amos shouted, "for three transgressions of Israel, and for four, I will not turn away its punishment . . ." The Lord was going to judge His people! The clock had been ticking, and the time was now! The recently occurring natural disasters, drought, poor harvests, sickness, and earthquakes were all announcements of the Lord's displeasure, but no one was paying attention (Amos 4:6-11).

And this was just the beginning. Soon the whole Nation would be enslaved and deported (Amos 5:27). But the worst of all had happened, there was "a famine of hearing the word of the Lord." Israel had been promised, through God's prophets, direction, whenever they needed it. All through Israel's history God had sent His prophets to give them His word for guidance and comfort. But since His people wouldn't pay heed to the prophets He'd sent, then no more prophets would be sent! This was a picture of spiritual starvation, destitution and abandonment. Israel's hearts were hungering for a word from the Lord, but their hunger would not be satisfied. The word of the Lord was nowhere to be found. There was "a famine in the Land."

Amos is a prophet for this present day. His vision is a picture of the spiritual starvation of today's Church. The famine he saw is ours.

Spiritual starvation in the Church is the most unnatural state possible! The New Testament positions the Church as inheriting all of God's promises: life, joy, love, welfare, et cetera, *ad vitam aeternam* (for all time, for eternity) through Christ. "For He is faithful that promised" (Hebrews 10:23). The Church is guaranteed assurance and guidance from God - the Holy Spirit - for eternity. In the New Covenant we do not, nor will we have an endless succession of corporeal prophets, "clothed in camel's hair, eating locusts and wild honey" preaching to us, by the inspiration of the Spirit of God, as the Old Testament saints did; instead, the Holy Spirit, "who spoke by the prophets", has been given to reside within each individual member of the Body of Christ to interpret, authenticate and apply both Old and New Testament teachings to each Christian in every generation - "I will pray the Father, and He shall give you another Comforter, that He may abide with you forever" (John 14:6). The Church is the fulfillment of the promises of God.

So what do we see in the Church today? Do we see the promises of God manifest, or something else? Shouldn't we at least expect to see the Church today believing that the witness of the two Testaments, is the Word of God? Shouldn't the Church be clear on the central message concerning "God in Christ; Christ in you" our "hope of glory"? Shouldn't the Church see plainly how God's Message effects all men, with its demands for a life of faith, hope, love and obedience? Yes... but we're not! Clarity on these matters is so lacking in the life of today's Church, that the Church today is unhealthy, out of sorts and is in the midst of spiritual starvation.

Was starvation inevitable? I believe it was. For the past few years the Church has not been preaching the biblical Gospel. The nature of Christ's salvation and His relation to the Church has been woefully misrepresented by the present-day evangelist. The Church has laid down the Bible and picked up experience. So that we are now interpreting the Word of God with the consistency of our experience, rather than interpreting our experience to make it consistent with the word of God. And the Church is starving to death!

To the world, the Church must seem like a rank and file mass, staggering in a fog, not knowing where we are or which way we're going. Our preaching is hazy; our heads muddled; hearts fret; doubts reign; uncertainly abounds - all to the tune of Contemporary Christian Music. Why is this? We could blame modern pressures, but that's like Eve blaming the serpent. The real trouble is us. We have grieved the Holy Spirit with biblical skepticism and unbelief, and God has withheld Him. He has not removed Him, but rather He has ceased speaking through Him. We are experiencing divine judgment - the Starvation of the Lambs.

Is there a solution? Yes. And a simple one.

The Church, individually and collectively, must begin to feed on its "bread of life," the Word of God. We must begin, once more, to believe and preach, that the Bible is God's Word written. It's His Book. He wrote it. It's God breathed. It can be believed in. We can cast our life and our all upon it. We can have absolute confidence in it. In the words of the Psalmist, "It is tried in a furnace of fire, purified seven times." And the promise of God, respecting His Book is: "He will preserve it from this generation even into forever."

We must, once more, believe that God's written Word is the rule of faith and life. We must desire God's Holy Words; love them; embrace them; and be transformed and changed by them.

And finally, We, the Church must be completely dependent upon the Word of God as the means of grace. The Bible is the meat for our souls; a light for our feet; a sure and steadfast, everlasting instrument for our salvation; a comforting agent which makes us glad; it is the Words of everlasting life.

We cannot call back the Holy Spirit into the Church and revive God's work by our own actions: that quickening is the prerogative of God alone. But we can at least remove the stumbling-stones over which we have fallen. We can set ourselves to rethink the true God-breathed doctrines of revelation and inspiration of His Word in a way that will eliminate skepticism and uncertainties about their divine and eternal truth. We can again believe God, and no other. No task is more urgent

FAITH - *the articles* -

in our time - unless we 're content with starvation.

30 September 2010

Preach The Gospel

What does it mean to Preach the Gospel? Simply put, it means to state every doctrine contained in God's Word, and to give every Truth its proper status. But what we call Truth today is oftentimes merely the traditions of our denomination. I've learned that from experience.

When I went to Seminary (Southwestern, Dallas Theological, Oxford's Magdalen/Christ Church College, UK), I went to learn the Bible. But instead, I was taught the doctrines of those individual denominations. And they used the Bible as proof.

If you attend a Presbyterian School, what you'll learn is all the Calvinist verses. Go to a Baptist Seminary, and you'll be taught that tongues have ceased. In a Pentecostal College, you'll learn that tongues are mentioned all through the Bible. A Seventh Day Adventist School will teach you that the seventh day is the right day to worship. All of us who have attended Theological Schools have, most often, learned denominational traditions . . . and they've got Bible verses as proof!

Most preachers are so conditioned by denominational traditions that if they are ever to do God's will, He will have to open their heads, take out their brains, wash them in His Spiritual detergent, brush them off and put them back in Right-Side Up!

So what is Preaching the Gospel?

Well, it's not giving people a slice of philosophical pie and neglecting the Truths of His Holy Book. It's not leaving out fundamental doctrines of the Word, and preaching a denominational religion - which is no more than a Vapor, without any crystal-clear Truths.

No man can Preach the Gospel, without mentioning Christ's name; nor can he preach Christ and Him crucified, and leave out the Holy Spirit's work. If a preacher never says a word about the Holy Spirit, his hearers will reply, "We do not so much as know whether there be a Holy Spirit"(Acts 19:2 KJV).

A man cannot preach a Gospel, which lets the saints fall away after they are Called - suffering the children of God to burn in the fires of damnation, after having Believed. Such a "Gospel" (if one can call it that) is loathsome and contemptible - and is not the Gospel of the Bible.

A man cannot Preach the Gospel, unless he preaches Calvinism. I say that, not to offend, but because no man can Preach the Gospel if he does not preach Justification by faith without works; not unless he preaches the Sovereignty of God and His administering of Grace in this age; not unless he exalts the Electing, Unchangeable, Eternal, Immutable, conquering Love of God; nor can he preach the Gospel, unless he bases it upon the Particular Redemption, which Christ made for His Elect and Chosen people. Calvinism is simply a common term, which conveys the whole of Truth inherent in the Gospel.

Some men preach a fractional Gospel - only one single doctrine of it. You can't say that those men don't preach the Gospel at all, if they maintain the doctrine of Justification by Faith - "By grace are you saved through faith." Call him a Gospel preacher if you will, but not one who preaches the whole Gospel.

Some men preach from what I call a Fifth Gospel. They have Matthew, Mark, Luke and John's Gospels, but they preach from another, Fifth Gospel. This Gospel consists of every verse and passage they've underlined and highlighted and that's all they preach from. And thus the whole of the Gospel is never heard.

No man can Preach the Gospel if he leaves out, knowingly and intentionally, one single Truth of the blessed God and Savior. That may seem cutting, and may strike the conscience of preachers who make it a matter of principle to keep back certain Truths - but it is God who will Judge, not me.

Some men purposely confine themselves to four or five topics. You expect to hear, either, "Not of the will of the flesh, but of the will of God," or, "He that believes and is baptized" or "For all have sinned and come short of the glory of God." You know the moment these men step in to preach, you're sure to hear nothing but Election, Baptism or the Roman Road that day. Such men fumble if they give too great prominence to one Truth to the neglect of the others. But, the whole Bible, and nothing but the Bible, is the standard of the true Gospel.

Some preachers make an Iron-Ring of their doctrines, and if you dare to step beyond that narrow circle . . . watch out! You're likely to be labeled a heretic. God bless heretics, then! God send us more of them!

Some preachers make Theology into a kind of treadmill, consisting of five doctrines, which are endlessly rotated; they never go on to anything else.

Every Truth must be preached. And if God has written, "he that believes not is condemned already," that is as much to be preached as, "there is no condemnation to those that are in Jesus Christ." If it's written, "O Israel, you have destroyed yourself," then preach that, as well as the next clause, "in Me is your help found."

All who are entrusted with the ministry, should seek to preach all Truth. I know that may be impossible. That Holy-Mount of Truth has clouds on its summit. No mortal eye can see its pinnacle. But at least try to sketch the cloud, if you can't paint the summit. Depict the difficulty itself if you can't unravel it. Don't hide anything. If the Mount of Truth is cloudy, then say, "Clouds and darkness are around him." Don't deny it. Don't chop down the Mountain to your denominational standards, simply because you can't see its summit. Preach all the Gospel.

If you, my dear preacher brother, want it said, "he's a faithful minister," then don't keep back any part of God's revelation. Preach the Gospel. And let the Flesh-Chips fall where they may.

17 March 2011

FAITH *- the articles -*

The Biblical Church
A Two Part Series

Part One

The Real McCoy vs. McChurch

Modern churches are way too dependent on Professional Ministers. The early church didn't have 'em. None of the apostles ever held the job. In fact, Professional Ministers appear nowhere in the New Testament. It's surely not what our Lord had in mind when He said, "Upon this rock I will build my church."

Jesus' "church" (the Greek, *ekklesia*) refers to "the body of Christ," His believers. The word is similar to our concept of a town-hall meeting and is used about 100 times in the Greek of the New Testament to translate the Hebrew word *qualal*, an assembly.

The "church" is to be a Spirit-led setting where Kingdom business can be acted upon. But, in light of what *ekklesia* really entails, our popular conception of "church" is dangerously limited to coming to a building, singing, putting some money in a plate, hearing a sermon, and going home.

Take the Lord's Supper, for example. What began as believers remembering the Lord in a simple meal, morphed into a complicated liturgical "sacrament," which had to be officiated by a specially ordained Presbyter.

Today, most church-goers aren't active beyond their one-hour, drive-through weekly service. Almost universally, the modern church-institution is nothing more than a Clergy-centered, Spectator-Sport-McChurch, where we're fed McUnion and Grape-Juice, recite McCatechisms, come-clean through McFessions; where sinners are saved through 5-Point McAlter-calls and McTized in Holy Hot-Tubs. And all this is handled by the only Being qualified to do the job . . . the Professional Pastor/Priest.

All of this has resulted in a feeble flock, characterized by laity

FAITH - the articles -

malaise, a flaccid community of believers waiting for their Hired-Man to feed them and goad them into religious activities.

So why do we assume that the Professional System we function under is what we must work with and that the consequential wreckage just needs a Band-Aid to make it all better? Tradition! This is the fatal assumption that must be jettisoned.

We need to eliminate the connection of service in "the body of Christ" with a Profession. Something is very wrong when being a Pastor/Priest is a career choice. Especially, in view of the fact, that for every empty pulpit there are over 200 seminary applicants.

The people of God are Real, Organic, derived from Living matter, without artificial agents. We need to pray desperately that the giftedness of the whole *ekklesia* will again blossom in communities where our individual, redeemed, unorthodox-ed lives in Christ can flow as "living water" - not from a hired Specialist, but rather, from the Spirit of the Living God.

The root issue is that our practice of putting all our churchy-eggs in the pastoral basket (essentially trying to build "church" upon the presence and expression of one gift) is a mistake of mammoth proportions, and is without biblical warrant. We need to be radical, that is, go to the root, and cease the meaningless surface discussions that reinforce a hurtful system.

"The pulpit," suggested Pastor Paul Watts of Lower Ford Street Church, Coventry, UK, "stands for the authoritative Word of God, its public reading and preaching. The pew, through long usage, has become a symbol for the hearing and reception of that word." This is what "church" boils down to today: Pulpit & Pew.

If somebody pointed out that an area of our personal life needs more of Christ, we'd be very concerned. But people can go on year after year, stuck in a Pulpit & Pew routine, and never lift a finger to question the status quo. They know this way of doing things is not in the New Testament, but the religious machine is intimidating. Again, why do people have no hesitation in being watchful in their personal lives, but show no concern for what's missing in their Christ Body-Life with others?

Why not return to the biblical design where Christ is the Head and everyone has a role to work as a part of His body, both leaders and developing believers (1 Corinthians 12:4-12; 14:26)? The early church didn't have useless functions like Ushers, Special Music and Sunday

School - none of which has anything to do with the maturing of the saints (that proof is in the "fruit" pudding of today's church). The early church was more like a basic training camp where each individual was completely functional or training towards that end.

The participatory Real McCoy Christian community replacing the spectator McChurch could change what "church" is all about - especially in the minds of our young people, who are totally uninspired by our traditional model.

It should be noted that our modern office of Professional Clergy can be none too healthy for the mortals themselves. Christ never instituted an individual position to bear the burden of His flock's corporate salvation. When Paul chastised the church at Corinth, he never mentioned their Leaders as having failed in their responsibilities.

According to a NYT 2010 Pastor-Burn-Out survey: Some 1,500 pastors leave the ministry each month in the U.S. because of unique pressures associated with the job. About 80% of Seminary and Bible school graduates entering the ministry will leave the ministry within the first five years. 70% felt God called them to pastoral ministry, but after three years of ministry only 50% still felt called. 80% of pastors' spouses wish the pastor would choose another profession. 57% would leave if they had somewhere else to go.

But those numbers only tell half the story. The other half is in the Pew. The congregations themselves simply don't understand the nature of Ministry. So, when their Man-Of-The-Cloth breaks down or has a moral failure, congregations, without embellishment . . . kick 'em to the curb!

Pulpit & Pew McChurches have become everything in the Christian religion, yet there is nothing about them in the Writings we claim to be a revelation from the Lord to us, His Church. So whatta we do?

Next week: Welcome to the Revolution.

25 August 2011

The Biblical Church
Part Two

Welcome To The Revolution

Today, over 112 million Christians worldwide do not attend Brick & Mortar churches. Every year, one million Christians leave the Institutional-Denominational Church in the United States. Presently, the number of adult Christians meeting outside the Brick & Mortar Church in the USA is eleven million. This number is growing by the day. And the reason is simple. The people of God are sick-to-death of man-made Religion, Professional Preachers, and the unbiblical segregation of Pulpit & Pew. They want Church, not an Institutional Corporation.

God's way and law of fullness is an additive-free Life. In the Divine order, life produces its own organism, whether it be a vegetable, animal, human or spiritual. Everything comes from the inside. Function, order and fruit issue from this law of life within. It was solely on this principle that what we have in the New Testament came into being. Organized Institutional Christianity has entirely reversed this order.

I have thousands of people worldwide, who read my books, columns and internet ministry writings, weekly - and they're searching. Searching for a non-traditional Church that is born out of Spiritual Life instead of constructs of human Institutions, held together by religious programs, seminarians and Collars.

One dear brother, "Brother Jim" - whose ministry to Chinese orphans with birth defects has put him in an intimate relationship with the Chinese underground House Church - told me that there are no seminary graduates or paid ministers heading the Chinese Persecuted Church. This may seem strange to our Brick & Mortar ears, but, because of that arrangement, China has the fastest growing Christian population in the world. Why? Because the Chinese Believers have an intimate relationship with the Lord and with one another. Their worship is lived-out 24 hours a day in difficult circumstances, and non-believers, who witness their love for the Lord and for one another, want what they have, in spite of the danger.

Church life should be a grass-roots experience, which is marked by face-to-face community, every-member functioning, open-participatory meetings (opposed to Pastor & Pew services), non-hierarchical leadership, and the centrality and supremacy of Jesus Christ as the functional Leader and Head of the gathering. In its purest form, the Church is the fellowship of the Triune God brought to earth and experienced by Believing human beings.

If someone tries to create an apple in a laboratory by human ingenuity and organizational business skills, the lab-created apple would not be an honest-to-goodness apple. But, if someone plants an apple seed, it'll produce an apple tree that will produce a real substance necessary for growth, health, and life . . . an apple!

In the same way, when we sin-scarred mortals try to create a Church the same way we would start a business, we defy the principle of real Church Life. A Church is one that is naturally produced when a group of Believers, who have encountered Jesus Christ in reality, come together without external ecclesiastical props and worship together as one in the Lord. Each "gift" freely working, in order, without hindrance. With this freedom, the people of God embody the biblical teaching that the church is a spiritual organism, and not an institutional organization.

A church that is created by human organization, chain-of-command styled leadership, and institutional programs is not the Church. Simply, because it's always marked by a weekly order of worship officiated by a Professional Presbyter. These churches are controlled by a top-down, hierarchical organization and human social conventions, called "offices." It's been called "the traditional church," "the organized church," etc. Congregants watch a religious performance once or twice a week, and then retreat home to live their individual Christian lives. But the Church is not a theater with a script. It's a lifestyle - a spontaneous journey with the Lord Jesus and His disciples in close-knit community.

In the hierarchical Institutional Brick & Mortar and some Home churches, Christians are divided into Clergy & laity. Granted, some Institutional Churches have small group meetings outside their weekly church services, where members get a taste of community life. But this community life is not the driving force of their Institutional Church. A hierarchical leadership structure is in place in those small group gatherings, and someone is always "in charge," and the group is ultimately under the authority and restrictions of a Professional

Institution. Any Home-Group established as or from an Institution is a retrogression that kills Believing life.

If we believe that the simplicity of Christ is truth worth continuing, then we must resist our tendency toward Institutionalism with every fiber of our being. If believers were satisfied with Jesus Christ alone, institutions wouldn't have a chance of taking over.

Too often institutions are about the needs of the institution, not of the people. Jesus didn't come to start another Religious Institution with every candle and pulpit in its proper place. By giving His life in crucifixion, taking His life back in resurrection, returning to the Father by His ascension, and pouring out His Spirit on the day of Pentecost, He assured that His people would express His life in them as the Body of Christ on earth – organically, not as an Institution.

The people of God could learn a lot from support groups like AA. They do not own buildings and have virtually no overhead. Maybe the best thing that could happen to many churches is to have its building torn-down and to lose all its money. Then all that the people would have left would be God and each other.

The Church is one living, breathing, unconventional organism - many participants with one function. We're organic. That best describes the kinds of churches Diana and I, and many other Christians around the world have experienced, lived in, and enjoyed. And it's the kind of church I believe the Lord is raising up in this hour. Add to that, the church we find in the New Testament was above all things . . . organic and revolutionary.

Welcome To The Revolution.

1 September 2011

Ruling Piety & Devotion

One of my precious friends wondered why I had not made an effort to press forward concerning public piety - public school prayers, devotions and the like, to be precise - as governmental mandates. "Since this subject," he said, "is so pressing in our day." The issue is a large one, to be sure, but I can not command anyone's heart - no man has dominion over another man's faith. As significant as this subject may be, I am at best, only a man with an opinion. It is therefore each man's liberty, in the Body of Christ to address the issue as he - in clear truth - feels is right. "Happy is he that condemns not himself in that thing which he allows" (Romans 14:22). But here are some particulars I will attempt to address.

First of all it is very dangerous to ask a governmental agency, especially one reluctant to keep "In God we trust" on our money, to legislate spiritual behavior of any kind. If, for example, a recognized Atheist was asked to teach in your children's Sunday school concerning the redemption of the Lord, doubtless you would be the first to rise up in horror. Rightly so. Therefore to suggest that stipulated laws should be passed which would force public school teachers or public officials - who are in many cases humanistic at worst, agnostic at best - to lead our children in prayer or any religious observance is just a little incongruous.

Modern day Germany not only allows religion to be taught and prayers to be spoken in public schools, but Church and state officials work together to provide religious education to every school child who wants it. This is, in all probability, an outgrowth to converse Nazism after World War II.

Any German public school with ten or more children from the same religious tradition, is required, upon the request of the parents, to supply a special teacher which will give their mandated religious instruction to the students. That sounds worthwhile at face value, but Germany now faces an unexpected problem. Seven hundred thousand Islamic students in the public schools have now requested Islamic instruction. Although the German constitution states that all religious instruction in the public schools must be based on the Bible, the previously nonexistent situation has happened. The German schools are

FAITH - *the articles* -

now required (by law) to read the Koran (the Islamic Bible) as well as the Jewish and Christian Bible. Germany has a democratic government.

If we institute a law in a country such as ours - one with a democratic system - which would require Bible reading or prayer in our public schools and arenas, then passages from everyone's Bible would need to be read. Bureaucracies interpret the term, Bible , as a very broad-minded noun.

The Koran is the Islamic Bible. The Book of Mormon is avowed as, "another Testament of Jesus Christ," The Buddhists have a Bible. The Bhagavard-Gita, The Essential Kabbalah, The Essential Rumi, The Tibetan Book of the Dead, and the Tao Te Ching are all considered Bibles by their followers. Each of these Bibles - including the Hebrew and Christian Bible - would of necessity, be taught and their prayers mandated, if a law was passed which requires religion to be taught and prayers to be expressed in our public parks, schools and any government sponsored SportsPlex. The question then is, "Which bible?" Remember we live in a democracy. Everyone has a vote.

There is a movement which has formed in the past few years which would call for silent prayer to be observed in our public schoolrooms and public school functions, such as football games and the like. The men of this movement love to quote, "Now mine eyes shall be open, and mine ears attentive unto the prayer that is made in this place" (2 Chronicles 7:15). But silent prayer only opens the door to transcendental mediation and other various mystic thoughts (prayers) - giving cults the ability to enjoin themselves at the same time the Church is praying to our Father in Heaven. One of my teachers referred to this movement as "abominable silent prayer." I agree. Public silent prayer will, and does, cause confusion of the deepest sort - confusion of the mind and the spirit.

When we ask the federal government to legislate a responsibility which is ours - the Church's - the door is then opened to every kind of problem which will follow. I am grateful for the Christian influence which is present in these United States of America. But I hope every believer understands that when it comes to our children, Christian education, instruction of and participation in Christian learning or prayer is the responsibility of the parent, and not the onus of the government.

I do hope your children pray before you send them off to school each day. I hope Brooke and Alison prayed before they went off to school each day. But that hope and that pursuit is the responsibility of the parent, not the obligation of the government.

Martin Luther once said, "I can't get anything done if I don't spend at least two hours a day in prayer." Dear Martin didn't spend these two hours in public.

A Very Public Prayer

A Kansas minister named Joe Wright was asked to give the opening prayer for a session of the Kansas Senate - October 2000. He offered the senators a bit more than they'd bargained for and, in fact, some of them were so offended that they walked out. He prayed:

Heavenly Father, we come before you today to ask Your forgiveness
And to ask Your direction and guidance.
We know Your Word says, "Woe to those who call evil good"
But that is exactly what we have done.

We have lost our spiritual equilibrium
And reversed our values.
We confess that We have ridiculed
The absolute truth of Your Word
And called it Pluralism.

We have worshiped other gods
And called it multiculturalism.
We have endorsed perversion
And called it alternative lifestyle.

We have exploited the poor
And called it the lottery.

We have rewarded laziness
And called it welfare.

We have killed our unborn
And called it choice.

We have shot abortionists
And called it justifiable.

*We have neglected to discipline our children
And called it building self-esteem.*

*We have abused power
And called it political.*

*We have coveted our neighbors' possessions
And called it ambition.*

*We have polluted the air with profanity and pornography
And called it freedom of statement.*

*We have ridiculed the time-honored values of our forefathers
And called it enlightenment.*

*Search us, Oh, God, and let us know our hearts today;
Cleanse us from every sin and set us free.
Guide and bless these men and women
Who have been sent to direct us to the center of your Will,
And we ask it in the name of Your Son,
The living Savior, Jesus Christ.*

Amen.

Wrapping The Cross With Ole' Glory

"Judgment must begin at the house of God"
(1 Peter 4:17).

As a student of both the Bible and history, I am of the opinion we in America are living in times that are reminiscent of the days leading up to the rise of the Third Reich. If you, after reading my analysis, want to dismiss my conclusions as insipid and irrelevant, you are certainly free to do so. But before you shrug off my thesis, may I suggest you take into consideration the words of George Santayana, who said, "Those who do not remember the past are condemned to repeat it." If America is truly flirting with any semblance of a fallacious and fallen Reich, it is incumbent upon each and every true American Christian to renounce, reject, and repudiate such flirtations as early and vehemently as possible.

Many facets of the Third Reich could be analyzed, but my focus will be on the attitude and actions of the ministers and churches in Germany at the time of Hitler's rise. This is predicated upon the historical fact that any nation will rise or fall according to the attitudes and actions of its Christian leaders and churches. ". . . the time has come that Judgment must begin at the house of God" (1 Peter 4:17). Our nation can, and will outlast corrupt, self-indulgent politicians, intemperate, nefarious citizens and avaricious trade conglomerates, but it will not survive a cowardly, compromising Church. As the Church goes, so goes the nation.

The German churches were the primary institutions that reduced their country to penury. The German churches equipped Hitler with their moral and spiritual covering. The German churches and ministers allowed Hitler to seduce the nation. Some were no doubt deceived. Others ate the forbidden fruit with their eyes wide open. Either way, without their help, the Nazi Party could never have become such a vile autocratic beast.

What were the attitudes and actions of Germany's churches? How do they compare to America's churches today? Is there any similarity?

When Adolph Hitler began his ascent to power, most of Germany's Christians believed he was an answer to their prayers. In Erwin Lutzer's book, *Hitler's Cross: The Revealing Story Of How The Cross Of Christ Was Used As A Symbol Of The Nazi Agenda*, Chicago, IL, Moody Press (I recommend you read this book), he states, "many Christians replaced pictures of Christ in their homes with pictures of Hitler. They truly believed Hitler was 'God's man' for Germany. They believed that to resist Hitler was to resist God. . . they yearned for a leader who would do for them what democracy could not." (pg. 17)

Hitler had revived Germany's collapsed economy, eradicated the shame of Germany's defeat in WWI by reclaiming the Rhineland, created numerous trade schools that trained and equipped Germany's workers . . . He gave a vacation, so to speak, to the German people. Almost overnight Germany's vast unskilled labor force was replaced with highly skilled workers. As strange as it may seem to us now, under Hitler, Germany had virtually no unemployment (at first). Hitler brought crime under control. He built freeways and highways that were the envy of Europe. He literally brought the German people out of poverty and despair and made them a great and proud people once again. As a result, the German people, including German Christians, loved him!

Under the cover of prosperity and military might, Hitler began taking away the rights and liberties of the German people. Germany was a republic before Hitler came to power. The principles of individual freedom and constitutional government were precious to the German people. Over time, a short time at that, the German people (and church) gladly traded their liberty and freedoms for Hitler's promise of security and the good life.

Many churchmen wanted to believe that Hitler was on their side, and a few were actually convinced by Hitler's lies that he was on their side: "Even for those within Germany known to be critical of the regime, Hitler could in a face-to-face meeting create a positive impression. He was good at attuning to the sensitivities of his conversation-partner, could be charming, and often appeared reasonable and accommodating. As always, he was a skilled dissembler. On a one-to-one basis, he could pull the wool over the eyes of hardened critics. After a three-hour meeting with him at the Berghof in early November 1936, the influential Catholic Archbishop of Munich-Freising, Cardinal Faulhaber - a man of sharp acumen, who had often courageously criticized the Nazi attacks on the Catholic Church - went away convinced that Hitler was deeply religious" (Ian Kershaw, *Hitler 1936-45: Nemesis* pg. 29).

The fact that many Christians in Germany at that time were

nominal cultural Christians, who were indoctrinated into the Nazi world view, helps to "explain how the SS troops could perform monstrous acts of cruelty and yet return home for Christmas and attend church and still think of themselves as good Christians. They were not murderers, they were men who were building a race of supermen and helping the inferior people get on with their evolutionary journey" (Lutzer, Ibid. pg. 95).

At the time of Hitler's rise, there were approximately 14,000 evangelical churches in Germany. To win the support of those churches Hitler literally wrapped himself, the Nazi Flag and the Nazi Party around the Cross of Jesus Christ. This salient religious display convinced Germany's pastors and churches that the Nazi Party was God's party and Hitler was God's man. By the time Hitler consolidated his power and became Germany's Fuhrer, the Nazi Swastika was proudly displayed on the walls of Germany's churches, both Catholic and Protestant. In an attempt to impose administrative and cultural uniformity, many American churches now incorporate a similar presentation using Stars and Strips and Cross. Because of Nationalistic pride, which had replaced Christian purity, with few exceptions the German church looked the other way while Adolph Hitler implemented his "Final Solution" to his Jewish problem.

Sermons were preached supporting Hitler and the Nazi Party. Supporters of any other party or any other potential leader, were told, they were "fighting against God." Congregants who refused to swear loyalty to Hitler were denied last rites and Holy Communion by Catholic priests. Protestant pastors simply excommunicated church members and pastors who did not toe the Party/church line - quoting Romans 13 from the pulpit as scriptural justification for loyalty to Hitler.

> *Let every soul be subject unto the higher powers. For there is no power but of God; the powers that be are ordained of God. Whosoever, therefore, resists the power, resists the ordinance of God; and they that resist shall receive to themselves judgment. (damnation - KJV) Romans 13:1-2*

"Christ has come to us through Hitler . . . through his honesty, his faith and his idealism, the Redeemer found us." German pastor, Julius Leutherser (Lutzer, Ibid. pg. 101)

" . . . in Hitler's day being a good Christian involved being a good German nationalist. God and country were practically one and the

FAITH - the articles -

same." (Lutzer, Ibid. pg. 102)

Hitler knew exactly what he was doing. He needed the support of Germany's churches, so he played the role of Germany's Christian leader. Privately, however, he despised Germany's clergymen. He said, "The parsons will dig their own graves. They will betray their God to us. They will betray anything for the sake of their miserable jobs and incomes." (Lutzer, Ibid. pg. 104)

A major reason Hitler opposed Christianity was because Hitler saw Christianity and Science as diametrically opposed to each other (Larry Azar, *Twentieth Century In Crisis*, pg. 154). He concluded science would win, and the Christian church would eventually, in due time, be destroyed. Hitler even believed the German race created Science. Hitler was trying to use science - especially Darwinism - to create a utopia on Earth, and he made it absolutely clear that there would be "no place in this utopia for the Christian Churches" in his plans for the future of Germany. He realized that this was a long term goal and "was prepared to put off long-term ideological goals in favor of short-term advantage" (Kershaw, Ibid. pg. 238). Hitler had to fight one battle at a time - and elected to take on the fight with the churches in due time. The Christian church would be destroyed later, and for now it was needed. Only after the war would Germany be able to fully implement the "final solution" to the "Christian problem" (Kershaw, pg. 516). In the meantime, "calm should be restored . . . in relations with the Churches" (Kershaw, p. 39). But it was "'clear,' noted Dr. Paul Joseph Goebbels, himself numbering among the most aggressive anti-Church radicals, 'that after the war we have to find a general solution . . . There is, namely, an insoluble opposition between the Christian and a Germanic-heroic world-view'" (Kershaw, Ibid. pg. 449).

The churches' sin was not in inspiring Hitler to commit his many crimes, but in not stopping him - a similar sin that the churches are guilty of in the modern West today. The German churches' sin was less in commission, than in omission. "Nonetheless, most other institutions usually did far less to oppose Hitler than the Churches. Nor did Hitler wait until the war ended to begin destroying Christianity." (Eugen Gerstenmaier, "The Church Conspiratorial," pgs. 172-189, in Eric H. Boehm's *We Survived: Fourteen Histories Of The Hidden And Hunted In Nazi Germany*). Although the "resistance efforts of the clergy have been exaggerated, it is nonetheless no myth that after the first few years of Hitler's rule the Gestapo and the Nazi Party singled out the clergy for heavy doses of repression to guarantee their silence and their parishioners' obedience. Thousands of clergymen, both Catholic and Protestant, endured house searches, surveillance, Gestapo interrogations, jail and prison terms, fines, and worse" (Eric A. Johnson, *Nazi Terror: The Gestapo, Jews, And Ordinary Germans*, pg. 224).

Altogether, Hitler's killing machine murdered 6 million Jews, and 10 million Christians. [This was a little published fact that caused Jewish historian Max Dimont to declare "the world blinded itself to the murder of Christians" by Nazi Germany (Max I. Dimont, *Jews, God and History.*, pg. 391-392).] In Poland alone, 881 Catholic priests were annihilated (Azar, Ibid., pg. 154). In time, many more priests would end up in concentration camps.

Out of 14,000 German churches, all but 800 gave Hitler their unflinching loyalty. Among the clergy of the 800 uncompromising churches was the Christian patriot Dietrich Bonhoeffer, who was later assassinated by Hitler's henchmen. Virtually all of the 800 courageous pastors who refused to support Hitler were sent to concentration camps.

"Hitler was largely exempted from blame. Despite four years of fierce 'Church struggle,' the head of the Protestant Church in Bavaria, Bishop Meiser, publicly offered prayers for Hitler, thanking God 'for every success which, through your grace, you have so far granted him for the good of our people.' The negative features of daily life, most [people] imagined, were not of the Führer's making. They were the fault of his underlings, who frequently kept him in the dark about what was happening" (Kershaw, Ibid. pg. 28).

Were Christians imprisoned? Yes!

The concentration camp at Dachau held the largest number of Catholic priests - over 2,400 - in the Nazi camp system. They came from about 24 nations, and included parish priests and prelates, monks and friars, teachers and missionaries. Over one third of the priests in Dachau alone were killed (Johannes Lenz, *Untersuchungen über die künstliche Zündung von Licht_gen unter besonderer Berücksichtigung der Lichtobogen-Stromrichter nach Erwin Marx*). One Dachau survivor, Fr. Johannes Lenz, wrote an account of the Catholic holocaust. He claimed that the Catholic Church was the only steadfast fighter against the Nazis. Lenz tells the agony and martyrdom of the physical and mental tortures Dachau inmates experienced. Men and women, Catholic and Protestant alike, were murdered by the thousands in Dachau, and those who survived were considered "missionaries in Hell." The fact is, official Nazi workers taught both anti-Semitic and anti-Christian doctrines: "If one believes the anti-Semitic, one should also believe the anti-Christian, for both had a single purpose. Hitler's aim was to eradicate all religious organizations within the state and to foster a return to paganism" (Dimont, Ibid., pg. 397).

Are the actions of Nazi Germany's ministers and churches being repeated in the United States today? Have American Evangelicals wrapped the Cross of Christ in Ole' Glory? Does some of the American churches quote Romans 13 to justify their resolute support for unholy, unjust, prejudicial laws and taxes? Are some of the American people of God willing to surrender their freedoms and liberties so that the American government might protect them. Do some Christian pastors and congregations malign anyone who dares to challenge or question the President or the American Congress? The answers of those questions are up to you my dear Christian reader. But three facts I know: conservatives gave us an Adolf Hitler, liberals gave us a Vladimir Ilich Lenin and God the Father gave us His Son, Christ Jesus the Lord.

Don't Worry, Everything's Under Control

> "... *the exceeding greatness of His power towards us who believe,*
> *according to the working of His mighty power,*
> *which He wrought (skillfully worked) in Christ*
> *when He raised Him from the dead ...*
> *and has put all things under His feet"*
> *(Ephesians 1:19-22).*

Many Christians are greatly the losers, whose thoughts about Christ are confined to His manger at Bethlehem or His cross of Calvary. While none of us can be sufficiently thankful for Christ's death for our salvation and for the everlasting bliss which hinges thereon, we must bear in mind that His death at Golgotha, His resurrection from His sepulcher, His being carried up into Heaven, was not the termination of His history. He is now seated at the right hand of God, where He intercedes for His people. But that's not all, for ...

All things have been put "under His feet." And this "all" includes, not only all His friends by way of voluntary submission, but all His foes by forced subjugation, and all events by way of His immediate operation. It is not simply "all creatures" but "all things." Providence itself is now directed by the hand of Lord of glory: All history is shaped by His imperial hand! Every moment, every occurrence, both in heaven and in earth is ordered by the King of all Kings and Lord of all Lords. Christ Jesus is clothed with all authority and invested with universal dominion, and, as a surprise to some, He is now actually engaged in exercising the same. This fact ought to affect the hearts and lives of every Christian. But do most of us conduct ourselves in total submission and subjection to Him? As we see the blasphemous, immoral, corrupt, events around us, and the many enemies who oppose us, do we remember the force of His "Fear not little flock"? When we catch sight of the troubled waters of this world, are we conscious of the fact that our mighty Captain is at the helm of the ship.

All things have been put "under His feet." This expression refers to (as well as many other "things") Christ's triumph over His enemies. If you will remember after Joshua had gained such a remarkable victory over the five kings and the combined armies of the Canaanites, he said, "Open the mouth of the cave, and bring out those five kings unto me out of the cave." And they did so. And he said to his captains, "Come near, put your feet upon the necks of these kings." And they did so. And Joshua said to them, Fear not, nor be dismayed, be strong and of good courage: for thus shall the Lord do to all your enemies" (Joshua 10:22-25; cf. Isaiah 51:22-23). Psalm 110:1 touches on similar discourses: "until I make Your enemies Your footstool," i.e., crush and destroy. The Church is, as are "all things," under Christ's feet by way of subjection, but she is not His footstool by way of subjugation and degradation - that is the position of His and her enemies.

We need to consider and apprehend God's objective in subjecting "all things" to the Redeemer - not only as illustrating the principles of His moral government and the good which results to us from them: for "he (*anyone*) who humbles himself shall be exalted" (1 Peter 5:6-9; et al.); "Them (*anyone*) that honors Me I will honor" (1 Samuel 2:30). But we also need to consider and apprehend the bearing it should have upon our character and conduct.

The salvation of the Church was the direct design of the whole of Christ's mediation work. For His Church, He voluntarily suffered humiliation and death; for the promotion of her interest, God exalted Christ and now He employs for her the selfsame benefits, which have been bestowed upon Him. Although He has been raised so high, He has neither lost His love for His sheep, nor relinquished His purpose concerning His people. By Him kings reign, and princes decree justice (Proverbs 8:15), yet He is exercising His dominion in subservience to His purpose of grace, disposing all affairs of the universe for the good of His Church. "All things work together for good to them that love God, to them who called according to His purpose" (Romans 8:28); "That the trial of your faith, being much more precious than goal that perishes, though it be tried by fire, might be found unto praise and honor and glory at the appearing of Jesus Christ" (1 Peter 1:7).

A lot of the time, we don't realize or remember that Christ is over men and angels, demons and Satan himself. This world is under the control, under the feet, in the hands of the One whose hands were nailed to the cross. He rules and overrules in "all things" for the good of His Church - in the deliberations of the senate, the conflict of armies, the history of the nations. Though many Neros, Charlemagnes, Napoleons, Hitlers, who for a brief season strut upon the stage of this world's drama, they are but puppets and serve the highest and ultimate interest of His people. When nations are in conflict and seem totally out of control, "the Lord has His way in the whirlwind and in the storm" (Nahum 1:3). There is nothing for us to be alarmed at. The ark of the covenant is in no danger. No weapon formed against us shall or will prosper (Isaiah 54:17). So don't worry, everything's under control. We have His promise!

Dr. Jay Worth Allen is a freelance writer for many publications (online & print), senior writer of Freed In Christ!, and president & co-founder of Dr. Jay & Miss Diana Ministries, Inc.

© 2010 Dr. Jay & Miss Diana Ministries, Inc
Used by permission. All rights reserved

This was the first article published in The County Journal
15 July 2010

FAITH *- the articles -*

The Trial Of Your Faith

Peter tells us, "the trial of your faith, being much more precious than of gold that perishes, through it be tried by fire, might be found unto praise and honor and glory at the appearing of Jesus Christ" (1 Peter 1:7). The words Peter uses here are wonderful. They speak of a goldsmith at work. Before the goldsmith could fashion the rough gold into the shape he desired, he first had to refine the gold. The gold must be unadulterated. Pure. He did this by testing and trying, by burning out the corruption, the unacceptable ingredients; removing the dross from the gold, leaving only the uncorrupted metal: the pure gold.

The goldsmith first placed the unrefined gold into a large mortar-like bowl. The mortar was placed over a searing fire to liquefy the metal. The fire segregated the dross from the gold. The goldsmith, during this long process, would periodically take a trial, a long spoon-like instrument, and dip it into the molten liquid. Placing a small drop of the refining gold onto a wooden plank, he would inspect the gold; testing for purity, hue, structure and clarity. This burning out of the corruption from the gold took hours. Drop by drop, testing and trying until the dross, the last bit of corruption, was removed and the gold was pure.

Do you know how the goldsmith knew when the corruption had been completely burned out of the gold? When, in his last test, the final drop of gold placed on the wooded plank, the only object he could see in the drop of gold, was his own reflection. No dross. No impurities. No corruption. Wonderful.

So the Lord tries us and tests us to bring us forth as pure gold. "Beloved, now are we the children of God, and it does not yet appear what we shall be, but we know that, when He shall appear, we shall be like Him; for we shall see Him as He is" (1 John 3:2). When the Lord sees us in that day, the only object He will see in us is His own reflection. Glory! We are made pure by the testing and trying of our faith by fire, by the goldsmithing of the Lord.

When the apostle Peter exhorted us to, "think it not strange concerning the fiery trial which is to try you, as though some strange thing happened unto you" (1 Peter 4:12), he was referring to experiences which we will meet in this life, and ones which, as his language denotes, are by no means exceptional. Each of us will face "fiery" trials. In this century, we may not experience the trials of being thrown to the lions, or "the spoiling of our goods," or living in caves, "destitute and afflicted." But during the last two centuries the Lord's people, and especially His servants, have faced "fiery" trials, which have come in a more subtle manner: The Lord's people have had to suffer the reproach of credulity and simple-mindedness, of being called "behind the times," because we refuse to believe agnostic scientists and their theories of "modern scholarship." Our sensitive natures can find such reproaches harder to bear than physical sufferings of past centuries. In this day, the test, the "fiery" trial, is to resist the seductions of an alluring world, to refuse any and all compromise.

Everyone who confesses the name of Christ will be tested - the true believer, as well as the false professor, in Christ will be tried and tested and proved. C. H. Spurgeon was right when he said, "Whether your religion be true or false, it will be tried; whether it be chaff or wheat the fan of the great Winnower will surly be brought into operation upon all that lies on the threshing floor. If thou hast dealings with God, thou hast to do with a 'consuming fire.' Whether thou be really or nominally a Christian, if thou comest near Christ He will try thee as silver is tried. Judgment must begin at the house of God, judgment will begin with you." It is the will of God that whosoever takes upon him the profession of His name shall be tried, tested, and proved. The Lord tested the rich young ruler (Mark 10:17-23). The Lord tests those who build their faith "upon the sand" - whose hope is based on a "faith in Christ," which produces no obedience to Him. To such professors He says, "Why call ye Me, Lord, Lord, and do not the things which I say?" (Luke 6:46). They are tried and tested and found wanting. The intellectual professor is tested by being constantly subjected to alterations of the Truth. The Pharisees were of this sort - relying on their intellect, their knowledge, their apprehension of formal truth. Intellectual professors admire Truth, but they will not die for it. When tested the intellectual will go with what seems more comfortable, more compatible to their own interest. New mythical experiences, so-called new found biblical facts or translations, inconstant intelligence is the fire which test the intellectual's faith. Intellectual knowledge of the truth is fluctuating, ephemeral. Truth is entertained as a transitory idea and found wanting.

Pilate was tested as an intellectual. He had a theoretical knowledge that it was contrary to the evidence to condemn Christ to death, but when the issue of his own interest with Cesar was raised, his practical judgment dictated him to save his own prestige. God allowed Adam and Eve to be tempted and tried by Satan. God tried Abraham when He charged him to take his dearly loved son and offer him up for a burnt offering on Mount Moriah. The Lord gave all that Job had, except his life, into the hands of Satan - to test and try his faith. God left Hezekiah to himself to try him and make known what was in his heart when the ambassadors of Babylon came to inquire of him what wonders the Lord had done in the land (2 Chronicles 32:31).

All who profess the name of Christ will be tried and tested and proved - whether they bear "good fruit" or "bad fruit" that we "might be found unto praise and honor and glory at the appearing of Jesus Christ."

5 August 2010

FAITH *- the articles -*

Thorns

"Of such an one will I glory: yet of myself I will not glory,
but in my infirmities. For though I would desire to glory,
I shall not be a fool; for I will say the truth:
but now I forbear, lest any man should think of me
above that which he sees me to be, or
that he hears of [not from] me"
(2 Corinthians 12:5-6).

Paul's words to the Corinthian Church are exquisitely lovely. He could have boasted about the high favor which God had shown him, but he did not. Had he gloried, it would not have been as a fool or empty boaster, but according to truth, to fact (see 2 Corinthians 12:2, 4). But Paul restrained himself because he desired that others not think too highly of him. He preferred that men should judge him by what they saw and heard and not lionize him by the special revelations God had given him. He would glory in his "infirmities," for weakness, sustained by grace, and that is all that any saint may boast in himself.

Paul continues, "And lest I should be exalted above measure through the abundance of the revelations, there was given to me a thorn in the flesh, the messenger of Satan to buffet me, lest I should be exalted above measure" (2 Corinthians 12:7). Having stated that he did not wish others to think of him more highly that they should, he now tells us what means God used to prevent him from doing so. Paul was in danger of being unduly euphoric by the extraordinary manifestation of the divine favor he had received. Which was understandable. The Lord knew this and graciously dealt accordingly, giving Paul that which kept him humble.

By nature Paul was just as proud and foolish as all other men. If his heart was kept lowly, it was not by his own unaided fidelity to the truth, but because of the faithfulness of his Master, who dealt so wisely with him.

We must distinguish between the cause and the occasion of pride: the former is the evil nature, or principle, from which it proceeds; the latter, the object on which it fastens and which it perverts to its use. The pride of life (1 John 2:16) can feed on anything and turn temporal mercies and even spiritual gifts and graces into poison. Pride was the main ingredient in the sin of our first parents. They aspired to be as God. There is pride in every sin, since it is the lifting up of the creature against the Creator. The Lord has shown us how He regards and abominates pride in Proverbs 6:16-19 where seven things are mentioned that the Lord hates. The list is headed with "a proud look!" The great work of grace is the subduing of our pride.

The heavenly revelations Paul received had no tendency whatsoever in themselves to produce or promote pride, but like all other things they were capable of being abused by indwelling sin. Therefore lest Paul should be spiritually proud, become vain and self-confident, regarding himself as a special favorite of Christ, there was given to him "a thorn in the flesh."

Since Paul termed this gift a "thorn," it would signify something that was painful. The words "in the flesh" would seem to indicate that it was a bodily affliction. That it remained with Paul is seen from his three requests that it might depart. That Satan aggravated it, appears from the next clause of the verse: "the messenger of Satan to buffet me."

As to what Paul's "thorn in the flesh" was, I will be frank to say that I have no idea. I've been eyewitness to godly teachers proclaiming, giving verse and chapter, that Paul's vexation was his eyes, ". . . he was three days without sight" (Acts 9:9); ". . . you would have plucked out your own eyes, and given them to me" (Galatians 4:15). I myself have taught (in times past) that Paul's "thorn in the flesh" speaks to his constant harassment from the Judaizers. Also giving chapter and verse, "You shall make no league with the inhabitants of the land . . . they shall be as thorns in your flesh" (Judges 2:2,3); (Galatians 1:6-9; 3:1-5), et cetera. Now, in all honesty and sincerity I have to say, I don't know.

Paul not only accepted this painful affliction as a gift from the Lord, but he also perceived the reason it was given him. This "thorn" came to humble him, which is usually God's chief design in His disciplinary dealings with us. In Paul's case the affliction was not for correction, but for prevention. Such may have been God's merciful design towards you: perhaps He turned a wealthy relative against you to will his money elsewhere, or perhaps He has withheld business prosperity from you lest you become proud. How effective Paul's "thorn" was appears from the fact that for fourteen years he had never mentioned his rapture into paradise and would not have done so now but for this exceptional circumstance.

We all have at least one "thorn" - a little lameness, a hobble, an uneven gait to keep us humble. My father told me he only trusted men who, "have a limp." Thorns, limps, reprimands, bridling, discipline of any kind are far from pleasant, and we desire their prompt removal. But the Lord wants us to see how His grace triumphs over nature, our hearts gladly acquiescing to the Lord's design. Paul's "thorn" did not cause him fret and fume; it caused him to pray! Can we avow the same?

FAITH *- the articles -*

After This Manner, Pray . . .

Prayers in the Bible may be described as those of humiliation, those of supplication, and those of adoration. The first are expressions of repentance, and confession of sin. The second are expressions of faith, wherein we request God to supply the needs of ourselves and others. The third are expressions of veneration and love, wherein we are occupied with the perfections of God Himself, and pour out our hearts in worship before Him. The last are *doxologies*, which consist in magnifying the divine Being, celebrating His excellence.

The Lord's disciples asked Him to teach them to pray (Matthew 6:9-13; Luke 11:1-4). And He did.

"After this manner, pray . . .

Our Father (Matthew 5:9), who art in heaven (Job 22:12),
Hallowed (Psalms 145:17) be Thy name (Malachi 1:11).
Thy kingdom (1 Corinthians 15:24) come (Matthew 3:2).
Thy will be done in earth, as it is in heaven (Matthew 26:39).
Give us this day our daily bread (Proverbs 30:8,9).
Forgive us our debts [trespasses] (Romans 3:23),
as we forgive our debtors [trespasses]
(Ephesians 4:32; Colossians 3:13).
And lead us not into temptation (James 1:14),
but deliver us from evil (the evil one).
For Thine is the kingdom, and the power,
and the glory, forever (1 Chronicles 29:11).
Amen (Psalms 106:4; Revelation 3:14)."

Christ has given us this prayer, and within this prayer, He has supplied a perfect model. In it He has taught us not only that it is our privilege to ask for those things which are needful for ourselves and fellow believers, but also to ascribe to God those excellences which pertain to Himself. The due consideration that He is our "Father which art in heaven" and the expression of the fervent desire, "Hallowed be Thy name" take precedence over presentation of our own requests. "Thine is the kingdom and the power and the glory" is to be heartily acknowledged, and a sense of the same should remain upon our souls at

FAITH - the articles -

the conclusion of our petitions. To praise and adore God for what He is in Himself is an essential part of our duty. We are required to respond to the call "Stand up and bless the Lord your God for ever and ever: and blessed be Thy glorious name, which is exalted above all blessing and praise" (Nehemiah 9:5 KJV).

Some Additional New Testament Prayers

Both of the following passages from 1 Timothy are of the nature of magnifying the Lord's divine Being. In them God is adored for what He is in Himself.

Prayer of Worship: (1 Timothy 1:17; 6:15-16).

"Now to the King eternal, immortal, invisible, the only wise God, be honor and glory for ever and ever. Amen" (1 Timothy 1:17).

"Which in His times He shall show, which is the blessed and only Potentate, the King of kings, and Lord of lords; who only has immortally, dwelling in the light which no man can approach unto; whom no man has seen, nor can see: to whom be honor and power everlasting. Amen. (1 Timothy 6:15-16).

That is the chief end of worship: not to benefit ourselves but to honor God. Many of our petitions begin and end with self, and therefore in no way honor God.

Prayer and Praise: Romans 1:8-12.

"Whoso offers praise glorifies Me" (Psalm 50:23) is His own declaration. Praise is to be offered to God, not because He needs it, but because He is entitled to it, and because it is a testimony to our reverence, faith, and love for Him.

Instruction in Prayer: Romans 15:5-7.
Prayer in Hope: Romans 15:13.
Prayer for Peace: Romans 15:33
Prayer for Insight: 16:25-27.
Prayer for Weaker Brothers: 1 Corinthians 1:4-7.
Prayer Considering Tribulation: 2 Corinthians 1:3-5
Prayer in Affliction: 2 Corinthians 12:7-10
Prayer for Benediction: 2 Corinthians 13:14
Prayer for Gratitude: Ephesians 1:3
Prayer for Faith and Knowledge: Ephesians 1:15-17
Prayer for Understanding: Ephesians 1:18
Prayer for Spiritual Apprehension: Ephesians 1:19-20.

Prayer for Appreciation of Christ's Triumph: Ephesians 1:20.
Prayer of Adoration: Ephesians 1:20-23.
Prayer for Inner Strength: Ephesians 3:14-16.
Prayer for Christ-Centeredness: Ephesians 3:17.
Prayer for Comprehension of God's Love: Ephesians 3:18-21.
Prayer of Doxology: Ephesians 3:20-21.
Prayer for Discerning Love: Philippians 1:8-10.
Prayer for Fruits of Righteousness: Philippians 1:11.
Prayer for a Worthy Walk: Colossians 1:9-10.
Prayer for Long-Suffering: Colossians 1:11-12.
Prayer for Joy and Thankfulness: Colossians 1:11-12.

"My brethren count it all joy when you fall into various temptations [or trails]" (James 1:2). We Christians are just as responsible to be joyous in adversity as in prosperity, when the devil rages against us as when he leaves us in peace for a season; and we will do so if our mind is properly employed and our heart delights itself in the Lord.

James does not exhort us to rejoice in the trails as such, but by an act of spiritual judgment to regard them as joyful. If we were possessed of more spiritual discernment, we should readily perceive that as the communication of saving grace to a lost soul is the greatest blessing which can be bestowed in this world, so the testing of that grace, exercised and brought forth to the glory of God, is the next greatest mercy. For that grace to approve itself to God in a manner well pleasing to Him, is a matter of vast significance and spiritual-weight. So, the genuineness of our faith being manifest by overcoming the world in esteeming the reproach of Christ's greatest riches rather than the "treasures of Egypt", by valuing the smile of God more than fearing the frowns of men, by firmly enduring persecution when others fall away (Matthew 13:21), brings much (or should bring much) comfort to our soul.

Prayer for Brotherly Love: 1 Thessalonians 3:11-13.
Prayer for Sanctification of the Young Saint: 1 Thessalonians 5:23-24.
Prayer for Persevering Grace Occasion and Importunity: 2 Thessalonians 1:11-12.
Prayer for Persevering Grace (Petition, Design, and Accomplishment): 2 Thessalonians 1:11-12.

There more differences of opinion among sermonizers and commentators on this prayer than on any other in the New Testament. It is not easy to make a translation of the Greek into simple and intelligible

English, as appears from the additions made in the Authorized Version, for the insertion of the italicized words quite alters the scope and meaning of its clauses. A good translation is: "Therefore we also pray always for you that our God would count you worthy of *this* calling, and fulfill all the good pleasure of *His* goodness, and the work of faith with power, that the name of our Lord Jesus Christ may be glorified in you, and you in Him, according to the grace of our God and the Lord Jesus Christ" (2 Thessalonians 1:11-12 NKJV). The best rendering I have found is *Bagster's Interlinear*, which is as close to and most literal of the original Greek as can be given: "For which also we pray always for you, that you may count worthy of the calling of our God, and may fulfill every good pleasure of goodness and work of faith and power, so that may be glorified the name of our Lord Jesus Christ in you, and you in Him, according to the grace of our God and of [the] Lord Jesus Christ."

Overall, the best translations of the Hebrew of the Old Testament is found in the *New International Version* (NIV) and the best translations of the Greek of the New Testament is found in *The New King James Version* (NKJV). The *New American Standard* (NAS) provides a good translation of both, but it's much too dry for my taste.

<u>Prayer for Comfort and Stability</u>: 2 Thessalonians 2:16-17.

<u>Prayer for Love towards God</u>: 2 Thessalonians 3:5.

<u>Prayer for Patience</u>: 2 Thessalonians 3:5.

"The Lord direct your hearts into the Love of God and into the patient waiting for Christ." The Greek verb here rendered "direct" occurs twice elsewhere in the New Testament: in 2 Thessalonians 3:11, and in Luke 1:79, where it is translated "to guide our feet into the way of peace." Literally the word signifies "to make thoroughly straight what has gone awry, to turn back or straighten what has become crooked." The Christian's heart is apt to return to its old bias and become warped: this prayer is for the righting of that fault. We are prone to allow our affections to wander from God and consequently make an idol of some creature; therefore we constantly need to beg Him to bind hearts to Himself, that our love may be unalterably fixed upon its true and only worthy Object. We all are prone to grow slack in the performance of duty, to become weary in doing good, especially when we meet with opposition and affliction; therefore we need to earnestly ask God for the grace of endurance, that our knees do not become feeble and that our hands do not hang down, but that we "hold fast the confidence and rejoicing of the hope firm to the end."

A Conspicuous Omission of Prayer

Much has been written about prayer in the New Testament (*as evidenced from the above*). Numerous books have been penned on the subject of what is usually called "The Lord's Prayer," which I consider more of a "Family Prayer." Browse through any Christian bookstore or seminary library, and you'll find a cornucopia of exegesis, analyses and commentaries on the high priestly prayer of Christ in John 17, but I can find only a handful of treatises on the prayers of the apostles. Strange indeed.

So I decided to investigate this conundrum for myself. As I began to survey the recorded prayers of the apostles, two things impressed me and surprised me at the same time:

First off, in the book of Acts, which supplies us with the most information about the apostles, not one prayer of theirs is recorded in its twenty-eight chapters. I suppose this omission is in full harmony with its character because the book of Acts is much more a historical, rather than a devotional book - consisting of what the Spirit did through the apostles, rather than what He did in them. Acts records the public actions of the Lord's ambassadors, rather than their private practices. The book of Acts does show these men to be men of prayer: *"We will give ourselves continually to prayer, and to the ministry of the word"* (Acts 6:4). And we see them engaged in this holy exercise: *"Peter put them all forth, and kneeled down and prayed"* (Acts 9:40); *"Peter went up on the housetop to pray"* (10:9); *"And when he had thus spoken, he knelt down and prayed with them all"* (20:36); *"And we knelt down on the shore, and prayed"* (21:5); *"Paul entered in, and prayed"* (28:8); yet we are not told what they said in any of these prayers. The nearest we come to a documented prayer is in Acts 8:15: *"Who when they were come down, prayed for them to receive the Holy Spirit,"* but what was said in this prayer is not recorded. The prayer of Acts 1:24 is a prayer of the hundred and twenty, and Acts 4:24-30 is a prayer of "their own company," neither of these are an individual apostle's prayer.

The second conspicuous omission - in all of the apostolic prayers - is that which occupies so much prominence in many Churches today. Not once do we find any of the apostles asking God to save the world or to pour out His Spirit on all flesh. Neither did the apostles pray for the conversion of a city in which a particular Christian church was located. They, as we should, conformed their prayers to the teaching of Christ, instead of the belching of men. *"I pray not for the world,"* He said, *"but for them which You have given Me"* (John 17:9). Now some may argue that He was praying for His immediate apostles or disciples, but He extended His prayer to His believing people to the end of time. *"Neither pray I for these alone,"* He continued, *"but for them also who shall believe on Me through their word"* (John 17:20). The Lord's prayer was not for the world, not for the Holy Spirit to be poured out on all flesh, not for the conversion of a city or a community or a particular street, not for unbelievers, but only for His believing people.

Before anyone's neck-hairs are raised in furry, I will admit that the apostles did exhort that prayers *"be made for all* (classes of) *men; for kings, and for all that are in authority"* (1 Timothy 2:1-2) - in this, most of us are woefully lax - yet this exhortation is not for these individual's salvation but, *"that we* (the Church) *may lead a quite and peaceable life in all godliness and honesty"* (v2).

As the sweetness of honey is best known by the eating, so the ambrosia of the divine and spiritual are realized in the portion in which we are actually and actively engaged in them. May we all garner prayerful skills from the object lessons of the prayers of the Lord and His apostles.

This portion published in The County Journal
10 March 2011

Doubt

The apostle Paul spoke of "unfeigned faith," which was demonstrated in the life of Timothy (2 Timothy 1:5). There he used the Greek word, *anupokitos*, which is used six times in the New Testament. Four times it is translated "unfeigned," once "without dissimulation" Romans 12:9, and once "without hypocrisy" James 3:17. Unfeigned love, faith and wisdom.

This "unfeigned faith," of which the word of God speaks so clearly, is a divine enablement which reveals God and His Kingdom to the believer. Although, today faith is usually projected as an energy which can force God to obey the commands of the practitioner. Thus, "faith" deifies man and humanizes God - inasmuch as man becomes the commander and God becomes the servant. Yet, the Word declares that Christ Jesus is the Lord, and we are His servants; He gives the orders, and we obey.

The two similes, which Christ employs when speaking of the believer, are very striking - and their order significant. He resembles us to "salt" to humble us. Salt is cheap, common, and insignificant. And He likens us to "light" to encourage us. Light is illuminating, conspicuous, shinning. How wonderful. But in order for any of us to "shine" we must first be "salted." We cannot hope to successfully apply salt to the consciences of others if we have never felt the bite of it on our own. We are to take "grace" seasoned with the "salt" of the Word and furnish clear direction to the brethren. Great! But, if "salt" is mixed with dust and rubbish it looses its pungency and efficacy; if the Word is mingled with profane levity or world-wise anecdotes its power can be (and often times is) nullified. It is "salt" (not sugar) we are to employ; something the world and the lightly-salted will be more inclined to spit out, rather than swallow. We must not expect faithful preaching and teaching to be acceptable and popular. It is contrary to nature for those whose consciences are pricked to be pleased with those who wield the prod.

We are living by faith. But living by faith does not mean doing without, or doing at all; it means doing His will. It is a walking with God into new territories, as Abraham did. It is obeying God when the

FAITH - *the articles* -

request seems incongruous to all known facts, as in Noah's life. It is learning to depend, rather than developing independence.

The opposite of faith is not unbelief, nor does unbelief begin with fear. The greatest enemy to our faith is not fear or unbelief, but rather, doubt. Unbelief and fear is expelled through our daily reading of the Word and our consistent prayers to the Father through the Holy Spirit. We are renewed in our faith daily through Christ Jesus. Hence, the great enemy of faith is doubt.

"And Jesus stretched forth His hand, and caught him, and said to him . . . you of little faith, why did you doubt?" The term, "little faith" comes from the compound, *oligo pistos* in the Greek and is found virtually nowhere except in the synoptic Gospels. It does not signify the total absence of faith - led by fear - but refers to a diminishing of that faith. The more Peter looked at the pressing problem, the smaller his faith became. He was set on a doubting course that offered him nothing but disaster. He was not in fear. If he had been in fear, or in the beginning of fear, the Lord would have used the word "fear," *phobos*, which is caused by being scared; *deilia*, which denotes cowardice and timidity and is never used in a good sense; or *eulabeia*, caution; reverence, godly fear as in Hebrews 5:7. But the Lord used the compound word *oligo pistos*, "little faith."

The Greek word Jesus used for doubt is *distazo*, which fundamentally means "to waver (in opinion), or to doubt." Paul wrote, "And he that doubts is dammed if he eats, because he eats not of faith; for whatsoever is not of faith is sin." The word used there is, *diakrino*, which means to withdraw from, to discriminate, hesitate: hence, to doubt, judge, stager, or waver. A reducing of faith does not begin with fear, but rather with our hesitating to obey the command given; ie, doubt enters in, not fear, not unbelief, but doubt.

Doubt, as it is used in the New Testament, is a wavering, a hesitancy, or a staggering in faith. It is not fear. It is not unbelief; it is more a poor handling of belief.

When we begin to withdraw from God's Word, when we start to discriminate between what we will read and what we will not - studying only the verses we have underlined and highlighted, or the verses our favorite preacher preaches from - and begin to hesitate in believing what God is saying within the entirety of the Bible ("rightly dividing the Word of truth," from Genesis to Revelation) - we are already involved in doubt. Doubt is uncertain about God's promises; doubt lacks confidence in the God of those promises and considers their fulfillment very unlikely. Doubt puts our experience over against God's Word and causes us to trust our reasoning more than the Word's reality. Doubt is the first tool Satan used against the human race: ". . . has God said?" Doubt is still mightily used against us today.

Doubt is not drawing back in apostasy, it is simply hesitating, reexamining, or questioning what has already been proven. It is not honest inquiry; it is a wavering in faith after faith has come. As such, doubt is one of the severest contrarieties to faith, for it dissipates faith after faith has been received. Peter didn't doubt until he had walked on the water for quite some distance. The other disciples to whom the word of faith was not addressed were not condemned for doubting because they were totally without faith for water-walking.

Doubt is extremely costly for us who have been given the gift of unfeigned faith. It prevents what God has purposed, and often forces the doubter to produce something as a substitute for the faith that had been given. See 2 Kings 18, 19.

When God speaks, faith flows, and we generally believe and obey. But in the action of obedience our minds begin to rationalize the situation, often producing doubts of such magnitude as to totally short-circuit our faith and make it of no effect. The old cliché is well worth remembering: "Never doubt in the darkness what you trusted in the light." The time for doubt checking is when God is speaking. Once we get into battle, it is too late to determine "has God said." Having put our hands to the plow it is far too late to look back. If obedience was an act of faith, doubt, which will stop faith's action, will produce disobedience, and great will be the penalty thereof.

One of the fatal characteristics of doubt is that it presumes that what we see, hear, feel, and taste in this world is the true and real, and what God speaks of in His spiritual kingdom is unreal. But if God says it is real, not only is it real, but by faith, "unfeigned faith," we can reach into His realm and make it become a living reality in our world of sense and space. One of my dear preacher friends, who is fond of acrostics loves to cite, "**F.A.I.T.H**: Forsaking All I Trust Him."

While it is most commendable that David could cry, "at what time I am afraid (Hebrew, *yare*: to be frightened), I will trust. . ." (Psalms 56:3), Isaiah projects a superior concept in saying, ". . . I will trust, and not be afraid (Hebrew, *pachad*: to be startled) . . ." (Isaiah 12:2). Neither of these saints were speaking of fear in opposition to belief, but rather belief in the midst of fear.

David was daunted because of the constant oppression he was receiving from the Philistines (1 Samuel 21:10-11). Yet, he did not become entangled in unbelief, but rather, he trusted - literally, 'leaned on' - the Lord in the midst of it.

If the thesis, "unbelief begins with fear" be true, then David, at the beginning of Psalm 56, opened the door to unbelief. And if that be so, then the remainder of the Psalm should speak of a very dark hour in the life if David - but it does not. The entirety of Psalm 56 speaks of David's trust in the Lord, not his fear or doubt in his surroundings. David never lost sight of the Lord's promise or power. David did seem to be becoming a little doubtful of his own ability to withstand the long and constant oppression he was receiving from the Philistines, which was hampering his belief - but even that did not disarm his faith, which would have been unbelief. So David ends this Psalm with, "You have delivered my soul from death, will not You deliver my feet from falling, that I may walk before God in the light of the living." This was a rhetorical statement - David trusted and was not afraid - he knew the Lord had and would continue to deliver.

Isaiah, on the other hand was in thanksgiving, not in fear or unbelief in Isaiah, chapter 12. His words speaks for themselves: "Behold God is my salvation; I will trust and not be afraid; for the Lord, is my strength and my song; He also is become my salvation." These are not the words of unbelief.

If we read a verse of scripture in context, we can build a mountain with the living stones of faith we find there. But if we read the same verse out of context, we will erect a brick wall of refusal, unbelief and a total reluctance to believe. In commenting on the words of David and Isaiah, Charles Spurgeon suggested that "all who get aboard heaven's train will arrive in heaven, but those who join David will ride third class, while Isaiah's will go first class."

In his book *An Exposition of Hebrews*, Arthur W. Pink (one of my favorites) declares:

> "Faith shuts its eyes to all that is seen, and opens its ears to all God has said. Faith is a convective power which overcomes carnal reasoning, carnal prejudices, and carnal excuses. It enlightens the judgment, molds the heart, moves the will, and reforms the life. It takes us off earthly things and worldly vanities, and occupies us

with spiritual and Divine realities. It emboldens against discouragements, laughs at difficulties, resists the Devil, and triumphs over temptations. It does so because it unites the soul to God and draws strength from Him. Thus faith is altogether a supernatural thing."

Since faith "is altogether a supernatural thing," there is no way that mixing our natural faith with it can enlarge, expand, augment, extent, or increase it in any way. Jesus told Nicodemus, "That which is born of the flesh is flesh; and that which is born of the Spirit is spirit," and someone has added, "never the twain shall meet."

Faith, divine "unfeigned faith," is not a spiritual muscle that enlarges with exercise; nor is it an intellect that expands by study and speech. Although, the more we walk in faith, the more faith we seem to have. Faith is a divine gift, a spiritual fruit, and a wholly supernatural, divine energy. It is not reproducible; it is only receivable. "Faith comes by hearing and hearing by the word of God." Not by planting a seed of faith and watching it grow. Our faith becomes more real to us when we practice it. Faith is not a plant in God's garden; it is an energy inherent in nature - God's nature. We cannot plant, cultivate, nurture, or reproduce faith (especially the faith given to others) any more than we can raise a harvest of divine holiness or mercy. They are given to us from God and must be treated as such. If we want our faith increased, we must believe and walk, not plant. "Faith comes by hearing and hearing by the word of God." If you want more faith, read more of His Word. Then you'll believe more steadfastly, walk more faithfully, and live more abundantly.

A life of faith is like walking a precipice while surrounded by a miracle. There are risks to living by faith, but the rewards far outweigh any risk. The key to success is to always keep Christ Jesus as the object of our faith. He has never failed. No doubt about it.

FAITH - the articles -

Puritans' Progress

In early May 2010, Diana and I lost our Nashville home, car, clothes, furniture, recording equipment, PA equipment, a number of musical instruments, plus a bunch of personal keep-sakes and accounting papers to the flood that ravaged Middle-Tennessee. But thanks to the grace of the Lord we have a roof over our heads in our building we own in Hardeman County, and we still receive some resources from our songs (which at this point is 120 days past due) and other writings and artistic pursuits, so we're not left in the dispirited shape of some.

That being said, the loss of home, furnishings, friends and income did give us a burst of the blues. And not the twelve-bar Robert Johnson kind, but the, "how bad the economy is blue funk despondency kinda blues . . . yada, yada, yada." We're not collective plebeians who go with simpleminded tips like, "start exercising to relieve stress" or "try to stay hopeful" - that new cyber-counseling kind of internet blog froth I hate. I'm reluctant to exercise in good times - no matter how liberating I'm told it would make me feel - so even a noble tête-à-tête on the subject was out. But, being an avid reader, I found, while looking through our massive collection of books, some encouragement, of what I feel is worthwhile encouragement for the millions of out-of-work, out of home and family mortals. This is encouragement which will hopefully not ring hollow, encouragement which won't leave those thigh-deep in hopelessness wondering where to turn for practical advice, encouragement which comes from an unexpected source: the Puritans.

Often misunderstood and perennially maligned, the Puritans - tested first by religious persecution and later by the elements in their primitive surroundings - grew not into the fuddy-duddy, party-poopers of modern history books, but into a tenacious and stalwart people. By sheer necessity, they developed one of the most highly defined and well-honed work ethics in history. If anyone knew a trick or two about surviving hard times, they did.

Defined primarily by their religious separation from the Church of England, the Puritans (not surprisingly) had a view of work in which God looms large. Living according to the Westminster Shorter

Catechism, which states that "Man's chief end is to glorify God and enjoy Him forever," the Puritans believed that all of life, including their work, was God's, and, as such, infused with purpose and meaning. They saw hardship not as a sign of failure, but as a path to growth and maturity, a mind-set that kept them from the kind of work-related despair seen in today's news.

Reformer and forefather of much Puritan theology, Martin Luther, in his doctrine of vocation, taught that God gave each individual an occupational "calling." Man's vocation was not seen as impersonal and random, but as from a loving and personal God who bestowed each individual with natural talents and desires for a particular occupation. This thought further deepened the Puritan's sense of purposefulness, fortifying him in difficult times.

Much like modern work is separated into white and blue collar, 17th century tradition held that sacred occupations (like preacher, priest, or monk) trumped secular ones (like farming, blacksmithing or homemaking). The Puritans, however, rejected such a distinction. Holding to "Whatever your hand finds to do, do it with your might" (Ecclesiastes 9:10), the Puritans sanctified the common, believing that all work, however lowly, if done for the glory of God, was good. Christ Himself "was not ashamed to labor; yea, and to use so simple an occupation," said Puritan Hugh Latimer. The farmer's plow became his altar, his tilling an act of service to God, every bit as holy and valuable as the priest's, reminding the unemployed that temporarily taking a step down in pay or status does not equate to failure.

Long before the days of therapists and career coaches, the Puritans learned how to cope with depression. They scorned idleness, believing it was indeed the devil's workshop, bogging down the body in inertia, and leading to brooding. Luther had promoted, a life of diligence, saying, "God . . . does not want me to sit at home, to loaf, to commit matters to God, and to wait 'till a fried chicken flies into my mouth." Long before endorphins were discovered, the Puritans knew that moving and tiring the body in manual labor (even if that labor is the unpaid kind that paints the house and organizes the garage) proved a talisman against a host of mental ills. This puritanical sweaty antidote although, does not consist of a tri-weekly sweat on a stationary bike at the local gym. It's productive, rather than theoretical effort, which produces the cure.

Contrary to the misconstrued Victorian concept of "Puritanism," an idea C.S. Lewis calls "the haunting fear that someone, somewhere, may be happy," the original Puritans, serious as they were, embraced not only hard work, but the pursuit of joy. Lewis, opposed to the misconstrued and inaccurate view of the Puritans, would agree with writer, Richard Bernard, who said, Christians "may be merry at their work, and merry at their meat." Thomas Gataker wrote that Satan was the one who would try to convince people that "in the kingdom of God there is nothing but sighing and groaning and fasting and prayer," but the truth was that "in his house there is . . . feasting and rejoicing." Lewis, further debunking the myth that Puritans never had fun, said "bishops, not beer, were their special aversion." The Puritans pursued joy, the very antithesis of depression, even in the midst of hardship, believing they were firmly in God's hand, not forgotten and never forsaken.

More than just an annual turkey fest, the Puritans gave America a pedagogy of work and an attitude toward life that upsets the modern notion that a person's occupation equals his value. The Puritans might advise the unemployed and the hopeless that a man's worth is to, "lay your service to God and to your fellow man, not in titles or financial portfolios." Rather than seeing life as a series of random events, the Puritan's belief in Providence imputed a profound sense of a loving God's purpose for every man, a purpose that left very little room for despair.

I do hope this little historical treatise helps any and all who are in job-loss, home-less, low-spirited despondency. It helped us. Realizing the Puritans went through starving days, lonely nights, loss of families, etc. and came out winning in the end because of their trust and belief in the Providence and grace of the living God, made both Diana and I all the more single-minded, unwavering and resolute to keep going. I hope you, my dear reader get this same unction.

FAITH *- the articles -*

God In Everything!

In 2 Samuel 15 & 16, we see David display a striking blending of light and shadow. This was David's darkest hour, yet in it, we see not only the shinning forth of some of his loveliest virtues, but we also see his friends and followers at their best.

David's favorite son, Absalom, and his chief counselor, Ahithophel, had turned-traitors, risen in rebellion, and through stealth and conspiracy, had usurped the Throne and the hearts of the people. So David, barefoot and hooded (2 Samuel 15:39), along with a few faithful friends, hightails it out of the city.

Now, how are we to view David here? As a scared puppy, or as a contrite penitent? I prefer the latter. David's refusal to stand his ground against Absalom's rebellion is not moral weakness, but spiritual strength. David saw the righteous retribution of God upon his sins against Bath-sheba and Uriah, and accordingly he humbled himself beneath God's mighty hand. David meekly bowed before the Lord's chastening rod, bringing "forth fruits worthy of repentance," which is as acceptable to God, as "the fruits of righteousness" in their season.

David's sins had found him out. So he bowed his head and humbly accepted His reproofs. He crossed the Kidron and ascended Olivet barefoot, in tears (2 Samuel 15:30), turning his face toward the wilderness . . . where he and his little following, while coming down into the valley leading to the Jordan, come face to face with, Shimei, a descendant of Saul, who starts throwing rocks and cursing David. Now David was not a man, naturally speaking, "to suffer fools gladly." But in this instance he endured with silence. Ablishai, one of his friends, wanted to kill the guy, but David told him, "No. The Lord has told him, 'Curse David'" (2 Samuel 16:10), which raises a language problem in the relationship of God to evil; but David was not guilty. He spoke to a solemn truth.

David saw God in everything, in every circumstance. To David it was not Shimei, but the Lord. Ablishai saw only a man, and like Peter, wanted to defend his beloved Master (John 18:11). Both Peter and Ablishai were living on the surface, looking at secondary causes. The Lord Jesus, living in total subjection to the Father, answered Peter, "The cup which My Father has given Me, shall I not drink it?" This gave the Lord power over everything, because He looked beyond the instrument of God, beyond the "cup," to the Hand, which filled it. Whether it was Judas, Caiaphas, or Pilate, He could see that it was, His "Father's cup", which is where we see David in his reaction to Shimei. He looked beyond man, up to God, and with bare feet and hooded head, bowed before Him saying, "The Lord has said to him, 'Curse David.'"

Are you there? Is the Church there? Is the Church, corporally and individually, reacting like David in the valley, or like Peter in the garden? Are we seeing God in everything? Or are we living on the surface, ensnared by seeing secondary causes, and not seeing God in everything? If we are . . . ergo, Satan gets the victory over us.

If we, the Church, could lay hold of the fact that every event, every happening, even those where the voice of God may not be heard, His hand not seen - it is His hand holding the "cup" from which we drink - what peace would surround us. Men and Matters in this life would become welcomed agents, instruments and ingredients in our "Father's cup." Our minds would be tranquil, our spirits calm, our hands restrained. We would give-voice with the sweet Psalmist, "My days are like a shadow that declines, and I am withered like grass. But You, O Lord, shall endure forever, and Your remembrance unto all generations . . . Bless the Lord, O my soul, and all that is within me, bless His holy name" (Psalms 102:11,12; 103:1).

May we all begin to see God in everything.

12 May 2011

So, You Wanna Be A Preacher . . .

In the early Jerusalem Church, a dispute arose against the church among the Grecians - Jews who followed the Grecian culture, as the result of Alexander the Great's conquest of the world - Jews, who were no longer kosher. These Hebrew Christians, who had adopted the Greek culture, felt their widows were being slighted when the Church was doling out its welfare program. And they complained to the apostles, who said, "Let us appoint seven men that are of good report, full of the Holy Spirit and wisdom, to take care of this ministry of administering the Church's welfare, in order that we might give ourselves continually to fasting and prayer." So they chose seven men for the task of waiting tables, caring for the widows, etc. - Deacons. But, the Holy Spirit had other plans. And, their faithfulness "in a few things" qualified them for the greater ministry that God had for them.

No one starts at the top in ministry. We all begin with little things, simple tasks. As Jesus said, "You have been faithful in a few things, now I will make you ruler of many." This is the process the Lord follows: faithfulness "in a few things."

I hear a lot of, "I want to get into the ministry." And I'll say, "Go to the Sunday School department, that's the best place to start. If you can learn to relate God's truth to children, then you can relate it to anybody." It's important that we get started in some small task in order that we might develop our own abilities, as well as test to see if this is what God has actually called us to.

In Acts 6, we see that one of the seven Deacons was a guy named Stephen, who was "full of wisdom, full of the Holy Spirit, and of a good report." But it wasn't long before Stephen got into trouble, not with the Church, but with some leaders from the synagogue of the Libertines. They called him out to stand before their Counsel, because the Lord was working mightily through his life with "great wonders." They didn't like what he was saying, but were unable to deal with the Spirit of wisdom by which he spoke. So they hired men to bear false witness against Stephen, which brings us to Acts 7.

In chapter 6, Stephen is accused of blaspheming God, of saying that the temple was going to be destroyed, and of blaspheming Moses. These

FAITH - the articles -

false charges were partially true. A partial truth or a partial lie is extremely difficult to combat. An outright lie is no problem. But partial truth/partial lie is difficult to combat, and this is what Stephen faced. He, no doubt, had declared that Jesus was establishing a New Order. And that God was found not just in the Temple, but that God was at that time, and is now dealing with men everywhere in their hearts and lives. So these false charges were partially true.

> "Then the priest said, 'Are these things so?' And he (Stephen) said, 'Men, and brethren, and fathers, hearken . . .' " (Acts 7:1,2).

In his address, Stephen showed them that the history of their fathers isn't as illustrious and glorious as they would like to believe. Their fathers, for envy, sold Joseph as a slave to Egypt, but God was with him, and delivered him out of all of his afflictions, and gave him favor and wisdom in the sight of Pharaoh, who made him the governor over Egypt and all of his house. This was Stephen's first example of a mistake that their fathers made of a God-ordained leader. His second example is Moses.

In Egypt, when Moses was forty years old, it came into his heart to visit his brothers. He felt, "Surely they will know that God put me in this position in order that I might deliver them." But instead they said, "Who made you a ruler and a judge over us?" So he fled, and was a stranger in the land of Midian. After forty years, God then sent Moses, whom they had rejected, to deliver His people from Egyptian bondage.

Stephen used the mistakes that their fathers made of recognizing God's ordained plans and rulers. There's a pattern here existing in this nation, to which Stephen was exposing: Your fathers rejected Joseph; God made him a ruler. Your fathers rejected Moses; God made him a ruler. You have rejected Jesus Christ; God has made Him the Ruler. Then Stephen looked up and said, "I see heavens opened and I see the Son of Man standing there on the right hand of God."

> "And they cried out with a loud voice, they stopped their ears, and they ran upon him with one accord, and they threw him out of the city, and they stoned Stephen, and he called upon God, saying, Lord Jesus, receive my spirit. And he kneeled down, and cried with a loud voice, Lord, lay not this sin to their charge. And when he had said this, he fell asleep" (Acts 7:57-60).

Stephen was called to the ministry. He was "faithful in a few things" - humbly serving the people of God. But we find in his martyrdom the true ministry the Lord had for this man.

So, do you still wanna be a preacher? Are you willing to be "faithful in a few things"? Do you feel called to the ministry? Are you willing to leave father, mother, wife, children, worldly possessions, "for the sake of the Gospel"? Are you willing to die for the sake of the Truth? These are the questions everyone must answer before they venture into the Eternal work of the Lord.

"Faithful is He who called you, who will also do it"
(1 Thessalonians 5:24).

23 June 2011

FAITH - *the articles* -

Islam
A Multi-Part Series

Wake Up Church! Islam's A Comin'

*". . . Then shall they deliver you up to be afflicted, and shall kill you;
and you shall be hated of all nations for my name's sake.
. . . But he that shall endure unto the end, the same shall be saved. . . ."
(Matthew 24:3-14).*

In late June, 2010, Michigan police arrested Christians for talking to Muslims.

Four Christians were arrested and jailed for talking to Muslims about Jesus, by order of police chief Ronald Haddad of Dearborn Michigan, who defended the arrests one week after the Sixth Circuit Court of Appeals ordered those same police to let Christian evangelist George Saieg preach openly at a Muslim festival there.

"We didn't distribute literature, or preach anything," said one of the four jailed evangelists. "We spoke only to those people who first approached us, we talked only about Jesus' love . . . and within minutes we were handcuffed and jailed." But Haddad was unrepentant. "We did make four arrests for disorderly conduct," Haddad said. "They did cause a stir" [with their free speech about Jesus]. Is talking quietly about Jesus now disorderly, just because some Muslims get angry?

"Allah Akbar!" shouted two Muslims as the Christians were taken away in handcuffs by police who also seized the Christians' video camera evidence and refused to return video footage of the arrests.

Live video is now on YouTube of another group of three evangelists being detained by the same police the very next day, because they distributed the Gospel of John on a public sidewalk outside the Muslim festival. This new video got 15,000 hits in 3 days, after the police told those being held that city policy states Christian literature is not allowed within 5 city blocks of the Muslim festival, creating a "banned-Bible zone" in violation of the First Amendment.

"The police are enforcing Sharia law in America," said one of the four arrested Christians, explaining that Muslim Sharia law is not just about putting Burkas on women, but also prohibits anyone from talking to Muslims about Jesus, and prevents listeners from escaping Islam by converting to any other religion.

Richard Thompson, President of the Thomas More Law Center, defends the Christians for the ministry called Acts 17, saying: "Contrary to the comments made by Police Chief Ron Haddad, our Constitution does not allow police to ban the right of free speech just because there are some hecklers. Not all police officers approve of the way their department treated these Christians." Richard Thompson also stated that, "Judge Paul Borman had affirmed the city's ban on handing out Christian material near the festival. It was last year when Dearborn police threatened Saieg with arrest if he handed out information on Christianity near the event." The city's ban was temporarily restrained by the Sixth Circuit, but the Police ignored the court, saying the TRO (*Temporary Restraining Order*) only applied to Saieg, not to any other Christians.

Arrested on charges of "Breach of the Peace" are: Negeen Mayel, Dr. Nabeel Qureshi, Paul Rezkalla, and David Wood. Thomas More Law Center reports Mayel, an eighteen year old female, whose parents emigrated from Afghanistan and a recent convert from Islam to Christianity, was also charged with failure to obey a police officer's orders, because she raised her voice while being physically violated. She was approximately 100 feet away and videotaping a discussion with some Muslims when her camera was seized.

We, the Church, must get our heads out of the temporal and into the sacred, before we are hauled off to camps for the "narrow-minded intolerant."

Note: Dr. Jay was one of the founders, along with Dr. Ralph Winter, director of The Center For World Missions, in birthing Perspectives, a college course dedicated solely to getting the Gospel into Islam and Islamic countries. This class has gone into many countries and thousands of people have been liberated from the bondage of Islamic teachings due directly from the fruit of this course.

At the time of this book's printing, the YouTube video referenced in this article could be viewed online at the following url:

http://www.youtube.com/v/Smw9QuH1xkA&hl=en_US&fs=1&

Islam
Part One

One If By Land! Two If By Sea!

It was just after dawn in Memphis when the first bomb hit New York City, and as usual, I was writing advertising copy. But not for long. Sports cars and sunny beaches suddenly seemed irrelevant, compared to the sea of destruction and utter devastation coming out of New York television newscasts.

Even the Golf Channel was broadcasting war news. It was the worst disaster in the history of the United States, including Pearl Harbor, the San Francisco earthquake, and probably the battle of Antietam in 1862, when 23,000 American soldiers were slaughtered in one day.

The battle of the World Trade Center lasted about 99 minutes and cost 3,000 lives within the span of two hours - anything that kills a legion of trained firefighters in two hours is a first class disaster.

And it wasn't even Bombs that caused this massive damage. No nuclear missiles were launched from any foreign soil, no enemy bombers flew over New York, Pennsylvania or Washington to rain death on innocent Americans. No. It was four commercial jetliners.

They were the first flights of the day from American and United Airlines, piloted by skilled and loyal U.S. citizens, and there was nothing suspicious about them when they took off from Newark, Logan, and Dulles on routine, cross-country flights to the West Coast with fully loaded fuel tanks, which would soon explode on impact and utterly destroy the world famous Twin Towers of downtown Manhattan's World Trade Center. Boom! Boom! Just like that.

The towers are gone now, reduced to bloody rubble, along with all hopes for Peace in Our Time, in the U.S. or any other country. Make no mistake about it: we are At War now - with somebody - and we will stay At War with this strange and mysterious Enemy for the rest of our lives . . . unless they are stopped.

But who is this unconventional Enemy? This eccentric, mystifying movement working inside America today? Its name is Islam and its objective is to convert the world's peoples into Muslims and transform

FAITH - *the articles* -

the United States into an Islamic nation.

Islam's goal is not terrorism. Their ultimate goal is to establish a global Islamic state over the entire world. If they can accomplish this in a peaceful manner, that's fine. But they are decreed by a holy punitive Code to establish this global Islamic state on the rubble of every civilization, every constitution, every government, every religion, every people, who oppose them and their Prophet.

Imam Siraj Wahhaj (born Jeffrey Kearse, in Brooklyn, New York) - the first imam (Muslim clergy) to offer a Muslim prayer in the U.S. House of Representatives - believes that if Muslims unite, they could elect their own leader as president, "Take my word," he stated, "if 6 to 8 million Muslims unite in America, the country will come to us."

Ahmad Nawfal, a well-known Jordanian speaker, says that if fundamentalist Muslims stand up, "it will be very easy for us to preside over this world once again."

At a Muslim convention held in San Jose, just one month after the atrocities of Sept. 11, 2001, one of the delegates declared: *"By the year 2020, we should have an American Muslim president of the United States."*

Americans need to wake up to the fact that all religions are not alike. America was founded on Christianity. That's all well and good. But Christianity, as it happens, is the only religion built around, and because of God's love. *"God so loved the world, that He gave . . . "* (John 3:16) and following.

Islam is a religion built on forced conversion and conquest. Islam is a religion of the sword. Islam does not put a value on love or forgiveness. The Shi'ia have still not forgiven the Sunni for the death of Hussein at the Battle of Karbala in 680 A.D.

The teachings of Islam are not some hale and hearty, feel-good guidelines thought up by a few desert-dwelling nomads. They are binding laws with severe punishments attached - from public floggings to chopping off of body parts and on through to executions by beheading. Islam is far more than a religion; it is a comprehensive way of life. The Qur'an and the Hadith (Mohammed's sayings), Islam's holy books, contain the religious, social, civil, commercial, military, and legal codes to which Muslims must conform.

Islam dictates whom one should worship, how to dress, what to eat, how to answer the call of nature, how to invest money, how to have sex, when to beat one's wife, when one must kill, and the cause for which one should die.

Islam claims well over a billion followers worldwide, whose holy Warriors chase their enemies like a pack of vicious stray dogs - trying to kill you, but you don't know why. This iron-fisted faith has invaded America's shores, protected by our freedom of religion, and is fanning out like a veiled 7th Century plague. Islam has taken advantage of the fact that the American majority knows very little of Islamic language and history. The most alarming fact about Islam is that if it is allowed to become powerful enough, "We the People" will lose our choice to either accept it or reject it. The only options left will be either to bow the knee to Allah or suffer butchery by the judicial authority of a sword.

Next week: Qur'an 101.

9 September 2010

Islam
Addendum

Don't Burn Books!

I'll go on record as being totally against burning the Qur'an! And I'm not alone. Countless major Christian organizations spoke against torching the Qur'an - the Catholic Church, the Southern Baptist, etc. But there's a big difference between arguing against burning Qur'ans and actually promoting Islam itself.

Last week a bunch on the Religious Left came out defending and even advocating the spread of Islam. And I have to admit that the, up-in-arms, book-burning scene did remind me of Ray Bradbury's, *Fahrenheit 451* - a frightening vision of the future, where firemen don't put out fires . . . they start them in order to burn books. Which is scary in itself, but somehow these so-called Christian lightweights have decided Islamic evangelism is the right response.

The Massachusetts Bible Society declared they would hand out two Qur'an's for every one burned. Yes, an organization supposedly committed to Christianity is now committed to spread Islam.

A South Carolina church gave a bunch of Qur'ans to a mosque in Charleston. In Raleigh, N.C., one Christian church put together an interfaith gathering to read excerpts of the Qur'an in their church building. Yep, right in the heart of the Bible-belt - Christians spreading Islam. Do they see the likelihood of it one day being the Qur'an-belt? Do they think giving out and reading passages from a false-religion book is part of the Great Commission? I'm not sure how you can make that argument theologically.

> *"Then Jesus came to them and said, 'All authority in heaven and on earth has been given to me. Therefore go and make disciples of all nations, baptizing them in the name of the Father and of the Son and of the Holy Spirit, and teaching them to obey everything I have commanded you. And surely I am with you always, to the very end of the age" (Matthew 28:18-20).*

That commission is for Christians to spread the gospel: Christ was crucified and resurrected for our sins that we might have eternal life. When the Lord's disciples entered other nations with pagan gods, they didn't promote those gods. Instead, they let those nations know that they were missing the truth of the One, true God. To spread any other religion is to deny the gospel and Jesus Christ Himself!

No matter how ashamed we might be of Christians going bananas and burning books, our response should never to be ashamed of the gospel. By promoting Islam instead of the Christianity, those religious loonies are showing nothing more than shame and self-loathing of themselves and Christ Jesus and His people!

There are other examples of Christians all but giving up their faith to promote Islam in our nation these days. However, it is possible to be against a false religion and still stand up for Christ! Because, if we do not stand for Christ Jesus and His Church, we might eventually become a nation of people bowing toward Mecca.

16 September 2010

The above article was written in response to the widely publicized "International Burn a Qur'an Day" planned by Rev. Terry Jones of Gainesville, Florida on the ninth anniversary of the September 11, 2001, attacks on U.S. soil by radical Muslims.

Islam
Part Two

Qur'an 101

The Warrior is loose, the Zealot, the Extremist, running fast and loud on the TV News, ridding low in the saddle, hotfootin' it through the heartland at ninety miles an hour down the center stripe of America's religious freedom . . . Billy the Kids in Jubba jackets and kufiyas, monster Jinns with fiery tongues, no quarter asked and none given; the ill omen of our time is here. Wake up America, Islam's at our door!

America's climate is perfect for these holy Warriors, as well as convertibles, swimming pools, blondes and abulia. Most Muslims are harmless, weekend-type worshipers, no more dangerous than skiers, skin-divers or Southern Baptists. But ever since the middle of the 7th century, the world has been plagued by gangs of wild men waving sabers, roaming the byways in groups of thousands and stopping whenever they get thirsty or road-cramped to suck up any and all commerce and peoples they encounter. They are Islamic Jihad Holy Warriors! And they want the world! The hell-broth of publicity over plans to build a thirteen-storey mosque near Ground Zero has, once again, concentrated attention on the fact and nature of Islam - the Jihad Warriors are getting what they want.

In the ranks of the modern Jihadists, there were those who insisted that the Islamic outlaw scene (so needed for victory) went way off the hump in the early-nineties, when the original faces of Islam began drifting off to Western marriages, mortgages and time payments. And that had to be stopped! So they blew up the World Trade Center.

But why all this ruckus? Why roughhouse the infidel, when we could all live in peace? Because the Qur'an tells 'um so!

Most good Westerners have never seen a Qur'an, still fewer have read the thing. So let's start with a little Qur'an 101, to help the unlearned become educated and the more knowledgeable better convey the facts.

First off, according to Islamic teaching, the Qur'an (their bible) came down as a series of celestial revelations from Allah (their god) through the Archangel Gabriel to the Prophet Muhammad, who then laid down the law to his followers. Muhammad's acolytes memorized fragments of his teachings and wrote them down on whatever was at hand, which were later compiled into book form (the Qur'an) under the rule of the third Caliph (chief civil and religious leader), Uthman, some years after Muhammad's death.

The Qur'an is about as long as the Christian New Testament, comprising 114 *Suras* (chapters or sections) and is in no Western-eyed order. According to Islamic doctrine, it was around 610 AD in a cave near the city of Mecca (southwest Saudi Arabia) that Muhammad received his first revelation. Over the next twelve or so years, other revelations came to Muhammad for the inhabitants of Mecca, ordering them to forsake their pagan ways and turn in worship to the one Allah. The revelations that came later in Muhammad's career, after his emigration to Medina, reshaped Islam from a relatively benign form of monotheism into an expansionary, military-political ideology that America is just now catching a glimpse of.

As an example of the Qur'an's lock-horns ideology, Sura 9:5, commonly referred to as the "Verse of the Sword", states:

"Then when the Sacred Months (the 1st, 7th, 11th, and 12th months of the Islamic calendar) *have passed, then kill the Mushrikun* (unbelievers) *wherever you find them, and capture them and besiege them, and prepare for them each and every ambush. But if they repent and perform As-Salat* (Iqamat-as-Salat - the Islamic ritual prayers), *and give Zakat* (alms), *then leave their way free. Verily, Allah is Oft-Forgiving, Most Merciful."*

Looking for labels, it is hard to call a fundamental Islamist anything but a pious mercenary. Most are urban outlaws with nomadic ethics and a new, improvised style of self-preservation. Their image of themselves derives mainly from folklore, mythology and "Lawrence of Arabia" movies and two-fisted Mid-East TV shows that have taught them most of what they know about how societies should live. Very few, middle-of-the-road Mid-East Muslims, read books, and in most cases their education ended in early adolescence. What little they know of mankind's history has come from Shi'a Ayatollah's and Sunni Sheikh's irate tirades . . . so if they see themselves in terms of the past, it's because they can't grasp the terms of the present, much less, the future. They are sons of the poor man and the drifter. As people, they are like millions of other people: unschooled and ill-informed. So when an unimpeachable Islamic Cleric declares that a thief's hands are to be chopped-off, no one objects.

> *"As to the thief, male or female, cut off his or her hands: A punishment, by way of example, from Allah for their crime: and Allah is exalted in power"* (Sura 5:38).

This punishment was carried out in August 2010 by the Chieftains of Iran.

Is Islam, as its adherents claim, a "religion of peace," a bringer of benefits to mankind, a harbinger of a better world, a faith which, according to President Obama, accentuates "the dignity of all human beings"? Or, on the contrary, is it something entirely different, not so much a religion as a political ideology, grounded in rabble-rousing, seditious arsenals of mish-mashed jambalaya texts from ancient Warriors and Warlords; the theological opinions of Islamic ideologues and jurists from primeval times to the present, who want nothing more than to imprison the world?

Next week: The Islamic woman's fate in the mystical musings of Muhammad's manual.

16 September 2010

Islam
Part Three

The Ladies Of Islam

The Islamists are very proud of their U. S. News exposure, though the cover stories of late feature some of their most obscure and least typical looking Zealot members. Given the chance to present their viewers with a really unnerving tableau, the News Media instead goes with Feisal Abdul Rauf, a guy who looks and talks like Ben Bernanke's long lost brother. Feisal may be photogenic, but to foster him off as a typical Islamist Warrior is like re-shooting "Mad Max" with Bill Murray playing the lead instead of Mel Gibson. Feisal ain't the honest-to-Allah face of Islam.

The Qur'an, in defiance to The New York Times, commands its loyal male henchmen to wage war in the name of Allah against all non-Muslims. Decked out, not in Giorgio Armani but rather Bedouin head-scarfs, screaming bloody murder through unshaved kissers. Like savage commandos in the grip of a Book of myths, they are ordered to bring all un-believers to their knees! And if the Angel of Death happens to appear during a holy turf war, the virile Mohammedan is guaranteed more virgins in paradise than he can shake his sword at.

Okay, that's great for the red-blooded Islamic guys, but what about the ladies of Islam? What's their fate in the mystical mind of Muhammad?

According to Islam: Men are superior to women, and a wife is the possession of her husband: *"Fair in the eyes of men is the love of things they covet: Women and sons; heaped-up hoards of gold and silver; horses. . . "* (Sura 3:14). But, if a dog or a woman touches a Muslim man's prayer mat he must, without further ado, wash himself.

Islam teaches that it is acceptable for a modern Islamic husband to beat the living daylights out of his wife and abstain from sexual relations with her, if she refuses to make herself beautiful for him; if she refused to meet her husband's sexual demands; or, if she happens to leave the house without his permission. *". . . As to those women on whose part you fear disloyalty and ill-conduct, admonish them, refuse to share their beds, beat*

FAITH - the articles -

them" (Sura 4:34).

An Islamic woman cannot pray during her monthly cycle as she is considered unclean.

Islam considers the wife a sex object. *"Your wives are as a tilth (a field to be ploughed) unto you, so approach your tilth when or how you will"* (Sura 2:23).

A Muslim husband may divorce his wife by oral pronouncement. However, the Qur'an does not offer the same right to the wife. *"It may be, if he divorced you that Allah will give him in exchange consorts better than you . . ."* (Sura 66:5).

A woman's body is "Awrah" (pudenda) according to the Hadiths (Muhammad's sayings): *"It is natural that the sighting of a woman's body arouses men and creates an uncontrollable sexual urge. This urge is specially very acute in Muslim men due to their higher sexual potency. Allah gives all Muslim men a higher libido."*

Because of this unstoppable Islamic perk in the Muslim male, if a woman is raped, she is considered guilty of adultery, unless she can provide four adult Muslim male witnesses, who watched the attack, and, who will testify that the sex was actually forced on her and that she was not a willing partner. If she has only female witnesses, she is out of luck. Her punishment is stoning to death if she is married, or one hundred (100) lashes if she is single.

Recently, a 19 year old girl was gang raped repeatedly by six men in Saudi Arabia and was given a punishment of 200 lashes and six months in prison (the punishment was increased because she was raped by more than one sexually proficient Muslim male).

Sex with captured women or slave girls is given the green light in Islam (Suras 4.24, 4.3, 23.6, 33.50, 70.30). So, if a 19 year old rape victim is imprisoned, or any other woman is incarcerated for any other reason, she qualifies as a captured woman and sex with her becomes *Halal* (religiously acceptable): an Islamic fringe benefit for prison officials and guards who must work long hours at low pay.

Islamic women are to always veil themselves when they are outside of their homes. In certain situations, it's mandatory, even when in their own homes: *"And say to the believing women that they should lower their gaze and guard their modesty; that they should not display their beauty and ornaments except what appear thereof; that they should draw their veils over their bosoms and not display their beauty . . ."* (Sura 24:31) *"O prophet! Tell your wives and daughters, and the believing women, that they should cast their outer garments over their persons"* (Sura 33:59).

Islam teaches that the Qur'an is the Constitution. Allah is the author of the Law and the State is the agent to implement Allah's laws. In Islam, there is no separation between Church and State (Sura 12:40).

The farther away Islam roams from their own turf, the more likely they are to cause panic. Islam is growing rapidly in America. Locally you can run across Islamic-veiled women walking the isles of our local Wal-mart. It's just a matter of time before Islam will become the religion of the majority. America will then be labeled an "Islamic country." It will be ruled by the "Qur'an" and the "Hadith," or what Muslims call the "Sharia" law (the Islamic code of ethics). Then all of our beautiful, blonde California gals can stay home and tend to their chores like good Islamic housewives should: draped in a hijab and burqa to completely cover their head, face and body, of course.

Next week: Next week: The Fruit of Muhammad's Loins.

30 September 2010

Islam
Part Four

The Fruit Of Muhammad's Loins

Of all the habits and predilections that society finds alarming, the Islamists' high regard for the time-honored concept of "an eye for an eye" is one that frightens people the most. Their Men, Women and Children are all considered Jihadi, Outlaws, societal Outsiders who try not to do anything halfway, and Outcasts, who deal in extremes, are bound to cause trouble, whether they mean to or not. This, along with their belief in total retaliation for any offense or insult to their Sharia Law or Prophet, is what makes the Islamist such a problem for Modern Civilization and so morbidly fascinating to the News Media. Their claim that they don't start trouble is probably true in their eyes, but their idea of provocation is dangerously broad, and one of their main difficulties is that almost nobody seems to understands them. Yet they have a simple rule of thumb; in any argument a fellow Islamist is always right. To disagree with Islam is wrong - and to persist in being wrong is an open challenge.

Despite everything the Media-psychiatrists and leftist-Freudians have to say about the Islamist, they are tough, mean and potentially vicious as a pack of wild boar. Anyone who would strap an IED to a twelve year old kid, and send them out to blow-up a restaurant full of nonbelievers is dangerous. There's no talking to them. In this league of Muhammad's disciples, sportsmanship is for old liberals and young fools.

It's mind boggling to see how much of the News Media maintains that Islamic Law is not really that different than the U.S. Constitution. But they're also convinced that Lady Ga Ga is a singer. Islamic Sharia law has brought nothing to the World's table except slavery, bloodshed and destruction. And children are hit the hardest.

In the last couple of weeks a few less-recognized News Media began reporting about an attack on a Somalian Christian family by a group of berserk Islamic Jihadi. On July 21, 2010 Al-Shabaab Incendiaries broke into the home of Osman Abdullah Fataho and shot him Dead in front of his wife and four children: 5-year-old Ali; 7-year-old Fatuma; 10-year-old Sharif and 15 year-old Nur. Their fatherly remains was once a Muslim, who converted to Christianity and was a leader in an underground Christian Church. The Al-Shabaab let his wife go with a swift pistol-whip, but told her that they were "keeping the kids."

But why? Why would the Al-Shabaab keep the kids of the father they just shot in Cold Blood? Because of Islam's goal: reeducate, propagandize and force conversion of all peoples to Islam. And the younger the better; and then train them as terrorists to enforce Sharia Law.

Outlaw Islam and Sharia Law is growing worldwide - with children being added to their army of terror daily. These innocent sons and daughters of butchered Christians are being used as Gunnery Shields and Suicide Bombers to take out any, and all peoples who aren't on the side of Allah. All in the name of this so-called Peaceful religion, Islam. And none of this is new.

Muslims have been using the sway of terror throughout history in dealing with infidels - anyone who does not adhere completely to the teachings of the Muhammad.

In Southern Sudan, Muslims have destroyed whole villages, killing around 2 million Christians and Animists. Sudan leaders were crucified in front of their own people. Boys and girls were kidnapped and sold into slavery. All because they would not convert to Islam.

After embracing Islam, Idi Amin of Uganda slaughtered 300,000 Ugandans, most of whom were Christians. All in the name of a made-up god, Allah!

In Nigeria, Christians are beaten, imprisoned and killed. Converting to Islam is seen as an easy way out. Whether they believe it or not.

In the lands where Christianity was born, Jordan, the West Bank, Syria and Turkey, Christianity is vanishing. If this trend continues, Christianity will completely disappear from the area within a few years.

In 1974, the army of Muslim Turkey invaded the northern part of Cyprus, pushing some 200,000 Christian Cypriots toward the south.

At the beginning of the 20th century, Muslim Turks massacred more than 1.5 million Armenian Christians for no apparent reason, other than, they were Christians.

FAITH - the articles -

Are you alarmed? Are you alarmed enough? I hope you are. I had the privilege some years ago, while working with Dr. Ralph Winters, president of the Center for World Missions, to assist in writing a college mission course called, *Prospectives*. Our basic objective was to get the Gospel of Christ Jesus into the Muslim world. Those of us who have studied Islam and its brutal, barbaric, cold-blooded history know how bad it can get. Those who have lived under Islam know how bad it can get, and have fled their mother countries to take refuge in America. My uneasiness, my fear, is the thought that America could fall under Islamic rule. And if that happens, our children, our grandchildren, our neighbors, our Churches will have to flee America and seek refuge . . . but where? If that time comes, will there be any place in the world left to run?

14 October 2010

Israel: The Land God Promised

On June 3, 2009, the American president, Barack Hussein Obama, while addressing the Muslim world from Cairo, stated: "Israel has been depriving the Palestinians of their homeland for 60 years."

Since many of us may not remember our history, I'd like to clarify the background of his statement and argument. But first, we must ask three specific questions:

<u>Number One</u>: *When did Israel become a state?*
<u>The Answer</u>: In 1312 B.C.

<u>Number Two</u>: *Why is this land called Palestine?*
<u>The Answer</u>: In 63 B.C., Roman troops invaded Judah and named the land *Palaestina*, for Philistia. *Palaestina* (Syrian Latin) – our English word, Palestine – was named because of its location between Egypt and southwest Asia.

<u>Number Three</u>: *When was the state of Israel the Palestinian homeland?*
<u>The Answer</u>: Never! Palestine has been a center of conflict for thousands of years. Many peoples have invaded the region, yet there has never been an independent state of Palestine or a Palestinian homeland.

A Brief History of Palaestina

Amorites, Canaanites, and other Semitic peoples entered the area about 2000 B.C. (Genesis 10, *et alli*). The area became known as the Land of Canaan (Genesis 9:25-27; Exodus 23:31). Sometime between, about 1800 B.C. and 1500 B.C., a Semitic people called *Hebrews* (Genesis 14:13; 40:15)[2] left Mesopotamia and settled in Canaan, where they became

---

[2] see also Genesis 10:25; 11:16-17.

known as Israelites – named from their father, Jacob, later named Israel (Genesis 32:28)[3] by the Lord. In the 1200's B.C., Moses led the Israelites out of Egypt[4], and they returned to Canaan [5]. The Israelites practiced a religion centered on the belief in one God. Other peoples in Canaan worshiped many gods.

For about 200 years, the Israelites fought the other peoples of Canaan and the neighboring areas. One of their strongest enemies, the Philistines, controlled the southwestern coast of Canaan, an area which came to be referred to as Philistia.

Until about 1029 B.C., the Israelites were loosely organized into 12 tribes. The constant warfare with neighboring peoples led the Israelites to choose a king, Saul[6], as their leader. Saul's successor, David [7], unified the nation to form the Kingdom of Israel, about 1000 B.C. David established his capital in Jerusalem[8]. His son, Solomon, succeeded him as king and built[9] the first Temple for the worship of God. Israel remained united until Solomon's death about 928 B.C. The northern tribes of Israel then split away from the tribes in the south. The northern state continued to be called Israel. The southern state, called Judah, kept Jerusalem as its capital. The word Jew, which came to be used for all Israelites, comes from the name Judah.

During the 700's B.C., the Assyrians, a people who lived in what is now Iraq, extended their rule westward to the Mediterranean Sea. They conquered Israel in 722 or 721 B.C. After about 100 years, the Babylonians began to take over the Assyrian Empire. They conquered Judah in 587 or 586 B.C. and destroyed Solomon's Temple in Jerusalem. They enslaved many Jews and forced them to live in exile in Babylonia. About 50 years later, the Persian king Cyrus conquered Babylonia. Cyrus allowed a group of Jews from Babylonia to rebuild and settle in Jerusalem.

The Persians ruled most of the Middle East, including the southwestern coast of Canaan (or "Philistia" - again - the area that 467 years later would be called Palestine), from about 530 to 331 B.C. Alexander the Great then conquered the Persian Empire.

---

[3] Israel / Literally: he who strives with God; God strives; God rules.
[4] Exodus, Leviticus, Numbers, and Deuteronomy in their entirety.
[5] Joshua and Judges in their entirety.
[6] 1 Samuel 10
[7] 1 Samuel 16: 1 through 2 Samuel 2:4
[8] 1 Chronicles 11:4-9
[9] 1 Kings 5:1 through 8:66; 2 Chronicles 2:1 through 7:10

Israel: The Land God Promised

After Alexander's death in 323 B.C., his generals divided his empire. One of these generals, Seleucus[10], founded a dynasty (series of rulers) that gained control of much of Philistia by around 200 B.C. At first the new rulers called *Seleucids* allowed the practice of Judaism. But later, one of the kings, Antiochus IV, tried to prohibit it. In 167 B.C., the Jews revolted under the leadership of the Maccabeans and drove the Seleucids out of the Cannanic area of "Philistia". The Jews reestablished an independent kingdom called Judah.

In 63 B.C., as previously stated, Roman troops invaded Judah, and it came under Roman control. The Romans called the area Judea. Jesus Christ was born in Bethlehem in the early years of Roman rule. Roman rulers put down Jewish revolts in A.D. 66, 70 and A.D. 132. In A.D. 135, the Romans drove the Jews out of Jerusalem.

Most of the Jews fled from Judea, including the southwestern coast of Canaan, now called "Palestine" by their Roman conquerors. But Jewish communities continued to exist in Galilee, the northernmost part of Palestine. Palestine was governed by the Roman Empire until the A.D. 300's and then by the Byzantine Empire. In time, Christianity spread to most of Palestine.

During the A.D. 600's, Muslim Arab armies moved north from Arabia to conquer most of the Middle East, including Palestine. Muslim powers controlled the region until the early 1900's. The rulers allowed Christians and Jews to keep their religions. However, most of the local population gradually accepted Islam and the Arab-Islamic culture of their rulers.

In the 1000's, the Seljuks, a Turkish people, began to take over Palestine. They gained control of Jerusalem in 1071. Seljuk rule of Palestine lasted less than 30 years. Christian crusaders from Europe wanted to regain the land where their religion began. The Crusades started in 1096. The Christians captured Jerusalem in 1099. They held the city until 1187, when the Muslim ruler Saladin attacked Palestine and took control of Jerusalem.

In the mid-1200's, Mamelukes based in Egypt established an empire that in time included Palestine. Arab Muslims made up most of Palestine's population. Beginning in the late 1300's, Jews from Spain and

---

[10] Seleucus Nicator, one of Alexander the Great's generals, founded a dynasty called Seleucids that ruled over Syria and a great part of western Asia from 311 to 65 B.C. Its capital was at Antioch.

other Mediterranean lands settled in Jerusalem and other parts of Palestine. The Ottoman Empire defeated the Mamelukes in 1516, and Palestine became part of the Ottoman Empire. The Jewish population slowly increased, and by 1880, about 24,000 Jews were living in Palestine.

Beginning in the late 1800's, oppression of Jews in Eastern Europe set off a mass emigration of Jewish refugees. Some Jews formed a movement called Zionism, which sought to make Palestine an independent Jewish nation. The Zionists established farm colonies in Palestine. At the same time, Palestine's Arab population grew rapidly. By 1914, the total population of Palestine stood at 700,000. About 615,000 people were Arabs, and 85,000 were Jews.

During World War I (1914-1918), the Ottoman Empire joined Germany and Austria-Hungary against the Allies. An Ottoman military government ruled Palestine. The United Kingdom and some of the European Allies planned to divide the Ottoman Empire among themselves after the war. The Sykes-Picot Agreement of 1916 called for part of Palestine to be placed under a joint Allied government. The United Kingdom offered to back Arab demands for postwar independence from the Ottomans in return for Arab support for the Allies. In 1916, some Arabs revolted against the Ottomans in the belief that the United Kingdom would help establish Arab independence in the Middle East. The Arabs later claimed that Palestine was included in the area promised to them, but the British denied this.

In 1917, in an attempt to gain Jewish support for its war effort, the United Kingdom issued the Balfour Declaration. The declaration stated the United Kingdom's support for the creation of a Jewish national home in Palestine, without violating the civil and religious rights of the existing non-Jewish communities.

After the war, the League of Nations divided much of the Ottoman Empire into Mandated territory. In 1920, the United Kingdom received a provisional mandate over Palestine, which would extend west and east of the Jordan River. The British were to help the Jews *re*-build a national home and promote the creation of self-governing institutions. In 1922, the League declared that the boundary of Palestine would be limited to the area west of the river. The area east of the river, called Transjordan (now Jordan), was made a separate British mandate. The two mandates took effect in 1923.

The terms of the Palestine mandate were not clear, and various

Israel: The Land God Promised

parties interpreted it differently. Many Zionists believed that the United Kingdom did not do enough to promote a Jewish national home. They especially opposed restrictions set by the British on Jewish immigration and land purchases. The British hoped to establish self-governing institutions, as required by the mandate. But their proposals for such institutions were unacceptable to the Arabs, and so none were created.

The Arabs opposed the idea of a Jewish national home. They feared that the British were handing Palestine over to the Zionists by allowing too many Jews to immigrate to Palestine. During this period, a Palestinian Arab national movement first appeared. On several occasions, riots and demonstrations were mounted by the Arabs to protest British policies and Zionist activities.

In the early 1930's, over 100,000 Jewish refugees came to Palestine from Nazi Germany and Poland. This development alarmed the Palestinian Arabs. The Arabs organized a general uprising that almost paralyzed Palestine during the late 1930's. In 1939, the British began to drastically limit Jewish immigration and land purchases for the next five years. Any Jewish immigration after that would depend on Arab approval.

During World War II (1939-1945), many Palestinian Arabs and Jews joined the Allied forces. After the war, the Zionists used force to stop the United Kingdom from limiting Jewish immigration into Palestine. The Zionists wanted the British to allow immigration of several hundred thousand Jewish survivors of the Holocaust, the mass murder of European Jews and others by the Nazis.

The United Nations Special Commission on Palestine recommended that Palestine be divided into an Arab state and a Jewish state. The commission called for Jerusalem to be put under international control. The UN General Assembly adopted this plan on Nov. 29, 1947. The Jews accepted the UN decision, but the Arabs rejected it. Fighting broke out immediately.

On May 14, 1948, the Jews proclaimed the independent state of Israel, and the British withdrew from Palestine. The next day, neighboring Arab nations attacked Israel. When the fighting ended in 1949, Israel held territories beyond the boundaries set by the UN plan. The rest of the area assigned to the Arab state was occupied by Egypt and Jordan. Egypt held the Gaza Strip and Jordan held the West Bank. About 700,000 Arabs fled or were driven out of Israel and became

FAITH - *the articles* -

refugees in neighboring Arab countries.

The UN arranged a series of cease-fires between the Arabs and the Jews in 1948 and 1949. Full-scale wars broke out again in 1956 and 1967. By the time the UN cease-fire ended the 1967 war, Israel had occupied the Gaza Strip and the West Bank. Israel also held Egypt's Sinai Peninsula and Syria's Golan Heights. In October 1973, Egypt and Syria launched a war against Israel. Cease-fires ended most of the fighting within a month.

The 1967 war brought about a million Palestinian Arabs under Israeli rule. After the war, the fate of the Palestinians came to play a large role in the Arab-Israeli struggle. In time, the Palestine Liberation Organization (PLO) became recognized by all the Arab states as the representative of the Palestinian people. The PLO pledged to liberate Palestine. Israel strongly opposed the PLO because of its terrorist acts against Jews.

In 1978, Egypt and Israel signed the Camp David Accords, an agreement designed to settle their disputes. Israel withdrew from the Sinai Peninsula in 1982. The agreement included provisions for a five-year period of self-government for the residents of the Gaza Strip and the West Bank. This period was to be followed by a decision about the future status of these territories. But no arrangement for such self-government was made following the agreement.

Beginning in 1987, periods of violence occurred in the Gaza Strip and the West Bank as protests by Arabs swept through the regions. These actions became known as the first intifada[11], which means uprising in Arabic. Israeli troops killed a number of protesters. In 1993, 1995, and 1997, Israel and the PLO signed agreements that led to the withdrawal of Israeli troops from the Gaza Strip and most cities and towns of the West Bank. As the Israelis withdrew, Palestinians took control of these areas. In January 1996, Palestinians in the Gaza Strip and the Palestinian-controlled parts of the West Bank elected a legislature and a president to make laws and administer these areas.

In October 1998, Israel and the Palestinians signed another agreement. As a result of the accord, Israel turned over more land in the West Bank to Palestinian control, and it allowed a Palestinian airport in the Gaza Strip to open.

Peace talks between Israeli and Palestinian leaders continued in

---

[11] *intifada*: The origin is from an Arabic word denoting an uprising. Literally: a jumping up as a reaction to something - to be shaken; to shake oneself.

2000. However, the two sides were unable to agree on some key issues, especially those involving the final status of Jerusalem. In September 2000, Palestinians began to stage riots and demonstrations against Israeli security forces in Jerusalem, the Gaza Strip, and the West Bank. This violence came to be known as the second Palestinian intifada. Israel responded to the intifada with police crackdowns and military attacks in Palestinian areas. Hundreds of Palestinians and Israelis died in the violence.

So we see that Israel became a state in 1312 B.C, two millennia before Islam existed. Upon conquering the land in 1272 B.C., Jews ruled it for 1,000 years and maintained a continuous presence there for 3,300 years. The only Arab rule following conquest in 633 B.C. lasted 22 years. For over 3,300 years, Jerusalem was the Jewish capital and was never the capital of any Arab or Muslim entity. Even under the rule of Jordan, the existing Palestinian Arab state created by Britain, (East) Jerusalem was not made the capital and no Arab leader came to visit it. Jerusalem is mentioned 700 times in the Bible, but not once is it mentioned in the Quran. King David founded Jerusalem; Muhammad never set foot in it. In 1948, Arab leaders urged their people to leave, promising to cleanse the land of Jewish presence. Sixty-eight percent of them fled without ever setting eyes on an Israeli soldier. Arab refugees from Israel began calling themselves "Palestinians" in 1967, two decades after the creation of the "modern state" of Israel.

Seven hundred twenty-five thousand Palestinian Arabs living within the borders of Israel fled or were expelled in 1948. Today nearly 1 million Arabs live as citizens within the borders of the state Israel. It is rather strange to hear that today there are 4 million Arab refugees. Where do they come from? And why didn't affluent Arab leaders drenched in oil-money look after their own Arab people for 60 years? Because they have a Nazi-like lack of concern for their fellow men and enslave their women. They use those who live in the camps to pressure Israel – this is the dirty purpose of those camps.

There have been five wars against Israel by Arab nations all started by the Arabs. During the Jordanian occupation, countless Jewish holy sites were vandalized. The U.N. was silent when the Jordanians destroyed 58 synagogues in the old city of Jerusalem. It continued its silence while Jordan systematically desecrated the ancient Jewish cemetery on the Mount of Olives, and remained silent when Jordan enforced apartheid laws preventing Jews from accessing the Temple Mount and the Western Wall. Out of 175 United Nations Security Council resolutions up to 1990, 97 were against Israel; out of 690 General Assembly Resolutions, 429 were against Israel.

Former Prime Minister Olmert, as well as President Peres - misjudging the motives of their enemies - both seem to think that delivering more and more Israeli land to the Arabs will lead to peace. But this initiative will lead to putting the Jewish state in extreme danger.

The conference in Annapolis in November 2007 was a waste of money. No wonder Arab leaders urge a strong U.S. role in Israel/Palestinian peace talks. Hearing then President Bush talk about "occupied territories," it is easy to see that he has accepted their diabolical reasoning. Who are they to undo God's promises to the Jewish people?

A survey conducted by the Midgam Institutes reveals that 73 percent of the Israeli population refuses any concession on Jerusalem that is not approved by a referendum. In addition, 70 percent of respondents believe that Jerusalem cannot be the capital of both countries at once, according to Guysen International News. Another poll undertaken shortly before Olmert's departure to Annapolis sponsored by the Israel Policy Center for Promoting Parliamentary Democracy and Jewish values in Israeli Public life oppose handing strategic territory to the Arab Palestinians.

Our Founding American Fathers were crystal clear that a free society can only exist with responsible and moral people. That is true for any society. The Israeli government has to deal with liars and terrorists. According to Guysen International News, the Mufti of Jerusalem, Ikrema Sabri, stated recently during an interview by the Jerusalem Post, "There has never been a temple on the Mosque Esplanada." He thinks we should not talk about the "Temple Mount," but instead, talk about the "Al Aqsa" mosque. I am pretty sure that most, if not all, Arabs at the Annapolis Conference not only believe the same and therefore are committed to a lie, but are determined to liquidate the basis of Western Civilization in their midst, the thousands of years old Israeli heartland. Western leaders, including George W., Bush and Barack Hussein Obama, state that they are Christians, but in their political dealings deny our roots and capitulate to the aggressive Islamic lies.

And what about the brilliant Israeli proposition of Benno Elon, chairman of the National Union Party and a member of the Knesset

Foreign Affairs and Defense Committee? He describes the Israeli borders set by God in his booklet "Israel, Arabs, and the Middle East" when God gave the Land of Promise as a gift to Abraham and his descendents. Nowhere in the Bible is there any indication that God canceled His promises.

The God-given borders of the land belonging to Abraham's descendants through Isaac are from "the River" of Egypt (the Nile, or smaller wadi in Eastern Sinai) to The River (the biblical name for the Euphrates). These two border descriptions have never been fully occupied by the Jewish nation, but they stretch from Eastern Egypt past Damascus all the way into western Iraq.

To deny this is to deny God, who gave it.

FAITH - *the articles* -

Eradicating Christianity

Just days ago in Egypt, throngs of Islamist butchers, estimated at 3,000, fired rifles and hurled Molotov cocktails at Coptic Christian Churches, homes, and businesses in the Imbaba region near Cairo: twelve Christians were killed by rooftop snipers - 232 injured; three Christian Churches were set aflame to cries of "Allahu Akbar," while Coptic Christian homes were looted and torched.

Egyptian Islamic authorities did little to stop the rampage. According to eyewitnesses, the Islamic Mob opened fire around 5:30 p.m., but the Military didn't arrive till 10 p.m., providing ample time for the Islamic Horde to terrorize the Christians. One priest said he, "called everyone, but no one bothered to come. I mourn all those young people who died," naively adding, "We now must ask for international protection."

Noting that this attack is unprecedented in scope, Muslim liberal writer, Nabil Sharaf el Din said, "The army is either incapable [of stopping anti-Christian violence] or is an accomplice to the Salafis [fanatical Islam]."

So what triggered this latest bit of Salafi savagery - or, as Main Street Media (MSM) calls it, "sectarian strife?" Islamists claim that a Christian girl converted to Islam and the Christian Church responded by abducting her and torturing her into renouncing Islam. Hence, their wild rampage was, in their eyes, a "rescue" effort.

This issue of Christian women supposedly converting to Islam only to be kidnapped by Christians is the Islamists' latest excuse to make Egyptian Christian life a living hell. This justification is especially ironic, since the well-documented reality in Egypt is the opposite: Muslims regularly kidnap and force Christian women to convert to Islam. Indeed, days before the Rampage, thousands of Islamists marched in front of St. Mark Cathedral, Coptic Pope Shenouda's residence, demanding the "release" of two wives of the Christian clergy, whom the Muhammadan Madmen insist had converted to Islam only because they had been abducted and tormented by the Church to convert to Christianity.

Last week the Christians in Algeria, who are bordered in the northeast by Islamic, Tunisia, in the east by Islamic, Libya, in the west by

FAITH - the articles -

Islamic, Morocco, in the southwest by Islamic, Western Sahara Mauritania, and Islamic, Mali, the southeast by Islamic, Niger, sent appeals to Christians world-wide for urgent prayer after the Algerian Islamic Police ordered the "closure of all Christian Churches across Algeria . . . once and for all."

The Algerian Christian Churches received a notice, dated 22 May 2011, from the Islamic High Police Commissioner informing them that a decision had been made to Shut-Down all Christian places of worship throughout the country that are not Designated for religious purposes.

This mandated Shut-Down is problematic for Algerian Christians, because most Algerian Christian Church buildings have not been officially Designated for religious purposes. Why? Because it is impossible for Christians to obtain registration from the Islamic Authorities, who passed a Law strategically designed to restrict all Religious Activity of non-Muslims.

Islam's aim is Eradicating Christianity from the face of the Earth!

The Algerian High Commissioner threatened "severe consequences and punishments," for Christian violation of these orders, which is the typical sway of terror Islam has been using throughout history in dealing with infidels - anyone who does not adhere completely to the teachings of Muhammad.

Using Algeria's blasphemy law - that by its very nature, can be used to prosecute anyone who does not adhere to the religion of Islam - last week, officials sentenced Siagh Krimo, an Algerian Christian, to five years imprisonment after simply sharing his Christian faith with a neighbor.

In Islam the Qur'an (Muhammad's writing) is the Constitution. Allah (Islam's god) is the author of the Constitutional Law (Shari), and the State is the agent to implement Allah's Law, as chronicled by their prophet Muhammad. In Islam, there is no separation between Church and State (Qur'an, Surah 12:40). Conversion from Islam to Christianity, according to Islamic Shari Law, is punishable by Beheading.

Islam is a Religion of the Sword!

The Algeria Christian Church grew to be very strong in North Africa in the first six centuries after Christ's resurrection, producing such famous figures as Augustine. Sadly, after the Arab-Muslim invasions, the Christian Church was eliminated entirely and disappeared for over a thousand years.

Since its independence from France in 1962, Algeria has been a secular state with 99% of its of 35.7 million population being Sunni Muslim. Of the 1% left, 60,000 are Christians, and almost all of them are converts from Islam. That small Band Of The Faithful enjoyed six years of relative religious freedom following the end of their civil war in 2000. But in the past six years, the Islamic Authorities have been steadily clamping down and closing Christian Church activities - using Islamic Shari Laws, Regulations and Wild Rampage as the means.

These riots, fires, murders, clampdowns & closures are the latest and most worrying development in what appears to be a systematic campaign by Islamic Authorities to Eradicate Christianity in all of the Mid-East . . . and then the World!

While we, the American Church, debate sprinkle or dunk Baptism, wine or grape-juice Communion, sugar or chocolate glazed donuts for Church fellowships, our Mid-East Christian Brothers & Sisters are being slaughtered by rabid Islamic Mobs . . . just for believing the Truth.

God help us.

2 June 2011

FAITH - *the articles* -

God Judges to Restore

It is ever the purpose of God to cause us to experience sufficiently of what this world has to offer to make us long for that which is to come.

When God's people, Israel, committed sin and iniquity the Lord sent them judgment with a view of restoration. "And they committed harlotries in Egypt; they committed harlotries in their youth; there were their breast pressed, and there they bruised the breasts of their virginity . . . Oholah (Israel), the elder, and Oholibah (Judah) her sister; they were Mine . . . Oholah played the harlot . . . she doted on her lovers, on the Assyrians . . . with all their idols she defiled herself. Wherefore I have delivered her into the hands of her lovers, into the hand of the Assyrians . . . her sister Oholibah saw this, she was more corrupt in her inordinate love then she, and in her harlotries more than her sister . . . I saw that she was defiled, that they took one way, and that she increased her harlotries. . . as soon as she saw them (Chaldeans, Babylonians) with her eyes, she doted upon them . . . and the Babylonians came into her bed of love, and defiled her with their harlotries, and she was polluted with them, and her mind was alienated from them . . . Behold, I will raise up thy lovers against you, from whom your mind is alienated, and I will bring them against you on every side . . . I will do these things unto you, because you have played the harlot with other nations, and because you are polluted with their idols" - which is spiritual adultery - (Ezekiel 23).

The Lord judged His people, Israel, because of their sins; He raised up their lovers - other nations, other religions - as judgment on His people; to war against them. But why? Why did the Lord raise up the other nations to war against His people, bringing judgment on His people? To restore them. To let His people live - for a time in their sin - with their lovers. The Lord raised up the other nations to war against His people to demonstrate to them the traditions of the other nations, other gods - the practice of slavery - and then, to restore them to the traditions of God - the tradition of peace, safety and security. "Thus will I make thy lewdness to cease from you, and your harlotry brought from the land of Egypt, so that you shall not lift up your eyes unto them, nor remember Egypt any more"(v27). It is ever the purpose of God to cause us to experience sufficiently of what this world has to offer to make us long for that which is to come.

When Israel repented, the Lord brought restoration. "For thus said the Lord God; Behold, I, even I, will both search my sheep, and seek them out . . . and I will make them and the places round about My hill a blessing, and I will cause the shower to come down in its season; there shall be showers of blessing . . . and they shall be safe in the land, and shall know that I am the Lord, when I have broken the bars of their yoke, and delivered them out of the hand of those who enslaved them" (Ezekiel 34:11,26,27). God's judgments on His people are always with a view of restoration. A wonderful New Covenant example of judgment to restoration is found in Paul's letters to the Corinthians.

"It is reported commonly that there is fornication among you, and such fornication as is not so much named among the Gentiles, that one should have his father's wife. And you are puffed up, and have not rather mourned, that he that has done this deed might be taken away from among you . . . to deliver such an one unto Satan for the destruction of the flesh, that the spirit may be saved in the day of the Lord Jesus" (1 Corinthians 5:1-5).

The Lord brings judgment on His people - individually and collectively - because of our sins. He raised up our lovers - the lust of our flesh, the pride of our life, the lust of our eyes - as judgment on His people; to war against us; against our flesh. "For the destruction of the flesh . . . that the spirit might be saved." The Corinthian man (individually and the Church collectively) God judged to bring them back to Himself - to restore them. He judged the fornicating Corinthian Church-man and the prideful Corinthian Church. They were all judged because of their sin.

The Corinthian Church man sinned (sexually) with his father's wife. The Corinthian Church sinned in their pride - fabricating their walk, hiding their sin, turning a blind eye to the sin within the Church. The sin of the Corinthian man was evident in that he and the woman could be seen. The sin of the Corinthian Church was not so evident because it was hidden. Paul rebuked the Corinthian Church because of their pride. Because they were acting as "reigning kings," being "puffed up" and not functioning as ruling servants - as men under authority. "You have reigned as kings without us" (Paul was a sarcastic man at times) "and I would to God you did reign, that we also might reign with you" (1 Corinthians 4:8).

Reigning & Ruling

There is a considerable difference between reigning and ruling. We do not reign now, we rule now, because we have an authority over us and we rule by and because of His reign - His authority. We will, in that day reign with Him because He will give us, in that day something to reign over - "on the earth." "And has made us unto God a kingdom of priests, and we shall reign on the earth" (Revelation 5:10). We will reign then, not now. Don't get the cart before the horse.

Someone who reigns makes the rules. Someone who rules follows the one who is reigning. A reigning king appoints lords, dukes, etc., to rule in his kingdom. But a reigning earthly king will never appoint another king to reign over his kingdom, because the direction of authority will become eschewed. There is one Head and one body. The Bible calls us (at this time) co-workers, not co-reigners. The Lord makes the rules and we, His people follow them. If we, the Church, go about acting like little reigning kings, making our own rules, neglecting the word of God in certain areas, harping on the words in others, we will become "puffed up" in our own deceit. "Those who follow lying vanities, forsake their own mercy" (Jonah 2:8), which is what happened to the Church in Corinth. They had become "vain in their imaginations." They were "puffed up" with pride - inflated egos - proud. They had become self-appointed judges of what was right and wrong conduct in the body of Christ. "The Father judges no man, but has committed all judgment unto the Son." The Lord Jesus is The Judge of conduct within His body. He is the reigning One. We, as individual members of His body, are now ruling under His reign.

The Lord is reigning and we are following His reign in our place of ruling. "For He must reign, till He has put all enemies under His feet" (1 Corinthians 15:25). "... *till He has* ..." What is the last enemy that will be put under His feet? "And death and hades were cast into the lake of fire. This is the second death" (Revelation 20:14). When death and hades are tossed away, we will then reign with Him - not before.

"The Lord shall send the rod of thy strength out of Zion; rule thou in the midst of your enemies" (Psalm 110:2 AV). We are now ruling in the midst of our enemies. He is now reigning over His enemies. And, in that day, when He puts all of His enemies under His feet - casting them into the lake of fire - He "shall reign forever and ever." In that day, "the

Son of man shall come in His glory, and all the holy angels with Him, then shall He sit upon the throne of His glory" (Matthew 25:31). And in that day we shall reign with Him. "To him that overcomes will I grant to sit with Me in My throne, even as I also overcame, and am set down with My Father in His throne" (Revelation 3:21).

"Little Kings"

If we, the church, do not follow His reign, but rather begin performing like little kings by our own man-made feigned reigning; acting as if we have been given authority over entities and elements of which only the Lord has the authority, He will judge us - with a view of restoration. For even "Michael, the archangel, when contending with the devil he disputed about the body of Moses, dared not bring against him a railing accusation, but said, 'The Lord rebuke you'" (Jude 9). Why didn't Michael rebuke the devil? Because He was *under* authority (he was ruling), he was not *the* authority. So he said, "the Lord rebuke you!"

The Corinthians had become "puffed up," "having men's persons in admiration because of advantage." "Walking after their own lust; and their mouths speaking great swelling words" (Jude 16). We are His sheep. He is our shepherd. And He will rebuke the devil, correct the wrongs - and - when needed, judge us with a view of restoration.

Again, why does the Lord judge His people? To allow His people time to live in their sin - with their lovers - for the destruction of the flesh - to demonstrate to us the traditions of the other nations, other gods, our flesh, as the practice of slavery - to then restore us, His people, to the traditions of God - the tradition of peace. It is ever the purpose of God to cause us to experience sufficiently of what this world has to offer to make us long for that which is to come.

The particular judgment - "It is reported commonly that there is fornication among you" - which Paul addressed in 1 Corinthians 5, was a judgment of destruction to restoration. Paul told the Corinthian Church, "to deliver such an one unto Satan for the destruction of the flesh." This, "destruction" is from the Greek, *olethros*, which denotes something that is of no use; something which must be destroyed, taken out of the way. Paul's "destruction," is not a destruction which will send the believer to hell, but rather, a judgment which destroys or brings death to the flesh, so that the spirit might be saved in "the day of the Lord Jesus." Paul did not ask the church to pray for this brother, who was copulating with his father's wife, but directed them to kick the guy out of the church, remove him from their fellowship.

Sin is old leaven and the old leaven must be removed, because the church is now, in Christ, "unleavened." "Purge out, therefore the old leaven, that you may be a new lump, as you are unleavened. For even Christ, our Passover, is sacrificed for us." As soon as the leaven is removed, the Church can "keep the feast, not with the old leaven, neither with the leaven of malice and wickedness, but with the unleavened bread of sincerity and truth" - but not before. First, get the fornicating brother out of the Church!

There is no place for fornicators – sexually active unmarried men with women, men with men, women with women, etc. - within the Church of Jesus Christ. Fornication is a sin. We are told "not to company with fornicators" within the Church - brothers and sisters within the Church, not individuals we know in the world, because "then must you go out of the world." Paul's declaration was not a judgment of annihilation, but rather, a judgment of destruction - the Corinthian Church man's body was ruined because of continual fornication and was unsuitable or unable to fulfill its original purpose. All judgments are not necessarily God sending someone to hell, but rather, more than likely, they are judgments which deal with the believer's position. "For who the Lord loves He chastens, and scourges every son whom He receives" (Hebrews 12:6).

When I am asked to pray for a brother's deliverance from sins such as adultery, fornication, pornography and the like, I refuse. Because those are sins which must be destroyed, terminated, eliminated from the believer's life. No amount of prayer will help until the sinning brother has removed the sin from himself. This is a judgment of "destruction" - judgment of the flesh. The sin is the "lust of the flesh, lust of the eyes," no amount of prayer for deliverance can stop the psyche. "And she was polluted with them, and her mind was alienated . . . with her eyes, she doted upon them." If the sin is stopped, I will gladly pray and fellowship with my brother again. But not until the sin is removed. We need to judge and not hold back because of sentimentality or fear.

Restoration

The Lord's judgments are always - for the believer - with a view of restoration. "Sufficient to such a man is this punishment, which was inflicted by the many. So that on the contrary you ought rather to forgive him, and comfort him, lest perhaps such a one should be swallowed up with overmuch sorrow. Wherefore, I beseech you that you would confirm your love towards him" (2 Corinthians 2:6,7,8). Paul extorts the Corinthian Church to restore the man who was fornicating with his father's wife because he had repented; to bring the formally sinning believer back into the place of fellowship. The man had repented and was now "in danger of being swallowed up."

When a believer sins, God will send judgment. When a believer repents, God will send peace and restoration. And we, as fellow believing sinners should "restore such a one" back to a place of fellowship. God is "not willing that any should perish, but that all should come to repentance" (1 Peter 3:9). "As sons" the Lord chastens us "for our profit, that we might be partakers of His Holiness" because "afterwards it yields the peaceable fruit of righteousness unto them who are exercised by it" (Hebrews 12:7-11).

It is ever the purpose of God to cause us to experience sufficiently of what this world has to offer to make us long for that which is to come.

Joshua Judges Ruth
A Six Part Series

Joshua Judges Ruth
Part One

History is prophetic, in that, it outlines the method of God, and the principles of human life.

The book of Joshua speaks from two irrefutable truths: "Jehovah is a Man of war" (Exodus 15:3), and, "The just shall live by his faith" (Habakkuk 2:4).

The truth revealed in the song on the banks of the Red Sea, is never lost sight of throughout the whole Bible, "Jehovah is a Man of war." In the prophecy of Habakkuk, the truth which appears as a principle in Genesis is crystallized into a explicit statement, "The just shall live by his faith." The book of Joshua illustrates these two truths, revealing the intimate relationship between them.

Joshua is criticized, in some circles, as being out of harmony with the truth revealed in the New Covenant. Criticism with which I disagree. On the contrary, Joshua, rightly read, interprets the Truth, concerning Jehovah, which we, in the New Covenant, sometimes find difficult to understand.

The concept of, "Jehovah is a Man of war," runs through the whole Bible. From the clear statement at the Red Sea, through the history of the Hebrew people, on through the New Covenant. The people of God, Israel, were commanded to physically battle, under the direct authority of Jehovah. Strange concept to modern eyes, but it is celebrated by many Old Testament writers: "Jehovah, strong and mighty; Jehovah mighty in battle" (Psalm 24:8). "By fire and by His sword will Jehovah plead with all flesh; and those slain by the Lord will be many" (Isaiah 66:16).

This concept runs through the New Testament in spiritual, and, when appropriate, physical fervor, as well. It is manifested in the anger of Jesus (John 2), and in Revelation 19, when material symbolism and spiritual truth merge. "I saw heaven opened; and behold, a white horse, and He that sat thereon, called Faithful and True; and in righteousness He does judge and make war . . . And out of His mouth proceeds a sharp sword, that with it He should smite the nations, and He shall rule them with a rod of iron; and He treads the winepress of the fierceness of the wrath of Almighty God."

God is perpetually at war with sin - which explains the extermination of the Canaanites.

In Genesis, Abraham was told that the Hebrews would suffer hardship in a strange land for four hundred years, and then be brought back into the land to possess it. Then God noted, "The iniquity of the Amorite is not yet full." So, as the Lord is, "the God of patience" (Romans 15:5), 400 years goes by, and the Amorite iniquity was "full." And, as the Hebrews are about to enter back into the Land, He warns them, "Defile not yourselves in any of these things, for in all these the nations are defiled which I cast out from before you . . . therefore do I visit the iniquity thereof upon it, and the land vomits out her inhabitants." This was a direct order: the Canaanites were to be exterminated because of their evil, absolute immorality & atrocious cruelty. Canaan must be purged. Surgery must be performed. And it was surgery, not murder. The iniquitous cancer had to be surgically removed, so that the Land might Live - which explains why the Hebrews ousted the corrupt, cancerous peoples of the land of Canaan.

Remember, this surgery was done after long probation. Canaan had witnessed righteous teachings and warnings for at least 400 years.

Melchizedek, king of righteousness and king of Salem, lived in Canaan. Abraham had dwelt there. Solemn warning had been given in the destruction of Sodom and Gomorrah. But these people, blind to the light and deaf to the voice of these warnings, had persisted in sin until they became completely immoral & cruel. For the sake of succeeding generations and the surrounding nations, it was necessary to remove the cancer, and give opportunity to Life.

God is seen in Joshua as a war-like One proceeding to battle, not for capricious purposes, but in order to remove corruption in the larger interests of all Mankind - a conflict as between truth & liberty and lying & licentiousness. One or the other must go down in the struggle, and God moved forward as a warlike One, using the Hebrews as His scourge to purify the land, and to plant in that little strip, a people who, whatever their faults were, would become the depository of the Truth which would permeate the world, and give men everywhere the opportunity for Life.

God was not merely clearing a land in order to find a home for people for whom He had set His heart. Solemn warnings were given to the Israelites by word and deed, as well. If they turned to the sins of the people they had exterminated, they in their turn would be cast out too. That's what happened. In fact they did turn, in spite of the Law, in spite of the leading of God, to the abominations which they found in the land, failed to bear the testimony which they were created to bear, and consequently today are a people "scattered and peeled."

God is the terrible foe of sin, refusing to make truce with it. His method & rule is expressed by His righteousness, driven by His love. Just suppose the Canaanites had been allowed to remain; suppose there had never been a people who were to receive the oracles of Revelation, what would our history be now? By that purging, by those drastic measures of wrath against iniquity, God gave the human race its opportunity for Life, as He prepared the way for the coming of the One in whom His love & righteousness was to be incarnate, and perfectly manifest.

Next week: The other truth, "the just shall live by faith."

6 October 2011

Joshua Judges Ruth
Part Two

"The just shall live by faith" (Habakkuk 2:4).

God's opportunity is created by the attitude of His people towards Him, and by the attitude of God towards His people.

The book of Joshua perfectly illustrates this principle. In it we see, Israel's conception of the supremacy of God, their conviction of the righteousness of God, their confidence in the mercy of God, and their conformity to the will of God. God is to man what man is to God. "The just shall live by faith."

This truth emerged in Genesis, was clearly expressed by Habakkuk, and enforced by three New Testament references. The power of the righteous life is faith. It is by faith in God that the righteous live. The letter to the Hebrews renders the passage, "My righteous one shall live by faith." That is, we, His people, shall live, individually & collectively, the righteous life by faith. The power of righteousness is faith. The book of Joshua is an interpretation of that fact. The writer of the letter to the Hebrews declares, "By faith the walls of Jericho fell down," and that statement touches the keystone of the victories of Joshua. The first strategic battle was won at Jericho. Beyond that, the whole Promised Land stretched out before Israel. That history, of the conquest of the Promised Land by the people of God Israel, teaches us, His Church, how and why, "The just shall live by faith." Faith is the acceptance of God's standard of holiness, the abandonment to the government of God's will, the achievement in the strength of God's might .

We must first accept God's standard of holiness. In the beginning words of Joshua, there are warnings of dangers & difficulties which awaited Israel, and promptings that they remain Pure & Strong. In Joshua's last discourse the same standard is evident: " The just shall live by faith" - Faith, which does not ask for mercy, while being slipshod about holiness. Faith, which finds its anchor in the holiness of God.

Faith is the underlying secret of the strength and victories in Joshua. And the strength and victories in His Church, today. Faith is abandonment to the government of God's will. This was revealed in the story of the taking of Jericho.

At first glance, nothing could be more foolish than attempting to take a walled-city by marching & blowing rams' horns. But the eloquence of the story is rather an illustration of a heroic people with the ability to march seven days round a city, without striking a blow, after having won a battle by the sword on the other side of Jordan. They were not foolish! They were heroes! And they're given to us to translate our faith into flesh and blood, incarnations or historical mirrors, of our own struggle to abandon our faith to the government of God's will.

When the walls trembled at the blast of the rams' horns & the march of feet around them, they knew, and we know, that these people were being taught that God operates for the accomplishment of His purposes through the obedient and heroic faith of anyone who will obey Him - however foolhardy their action may appear in the eyes of men.

Similarly, during the 1800's English Revivals, Wesley & Whitefield, while riding through the countryside would sing, *"Fools and madmen let us be, yet is our sure trust in Thee."* That's heroic faith: Faith to be willing to do things at which the wisdom of the world scoffs - if God commands. By faith, God's victories are won, and in no other.

Faith is success in the strength of God's might. All the victories of righteousness testify to this fact.

Today "Jehovah is a Man of war." He is the foe of sin in personal, social, civic, and national life. At this moment He is moving forward in unabated, undeviating, unceasing hostility to sin. I thank God that He will not make peace with sin in my heart. I have tried to evade some issue with Him, to plead the excuse, "The fathers have eaten sour grapes, and the children's teeth are set on edge," to use the difficulty of my circumstance, to plead my infirmity. But God, as a Man of war, has refused to make truce with my sin or accept my white flag. He will only except my abandonment of sin . . . because He loves me. The moment anyone can prove that God will excuse sin, is the moment I cease to believe in His love. He is the foe of sin in me, in America, in the world. Just because His methods today are not exactly His methods of the past, let us never forget, that every army that marches is under His control. He still readies Cyrus, as in the days of old. He is still fierce & furious in His anger against sin, wherever it manifests itself.

Today, as in ancient days, "My righteous one shall live by faith." Individually.

FAITH - *the articles* -

If we are to have a victorious righteous life we must win it by faith . . . Accepting God's standard of holiness, abandoning our life to the government of God's will. Only then will we achieve personal victory.

This is equally true collectively.

To exercise a righteous influence, to produce the result of righteous conditions, we must collectively have faith in God. Blot the Lord out of our political strategy, refuse to have His name mentioned in our public designs, and confusion & failure will be written across our endeavors. It is only as God is recognized in His holiness, and obeyed in His laws, that righteous conditions can be obtained in personal, public, or political life.

Next: "Righteousness exalts a nation, but sin is a reproach to any people."

13 October 2011

Joshua Judges Ruth
Part Three

The book of Judges tells the story of the journey of God's people from Joshua through Samson. Within its 21 chapters, two ever-abiding Truths are laid-bare: "Righteousness exalts a nation, but sin is a reproach to any people" (Proverbs 14:34) and "Jehovah executes righteous acts, and judgments for all that are oppressed" (Psalm 103:6).

The book of Judges confirms to the People of God, in every age, how sin degenerates the morals of any nation or people ... revealing the cause, the course, and the curse of deterioration.

The cause of deterioration is always religious apostasy. Its course is always political disorganization. And its curse is always social chaos and crime.

The first development of religious apostasy comes when the People of God tolerate the presence of anything that is out of harmony with the holiness of God. That's the first evidence of religious apostasy ... always is. Religious apostasy never begins with intellectual query. I have great respect for anyone who is face to face with intellectual doubt. They're hunters, gathers, seekers ... Let 'em alone. They'll find the way out.

Religious apostasy begins with tolerance. Compromise. And compromise is followed by the veneration & approval of the activity or ideology tolerated, until compromise becomes conformity. And because of conformity, the People of God begin to bow down and erect alters to unrighteousness ... "Wherefore, come out from among them, and be separate, says the Lord, and touch not the unclean thing" (2 Corinthians 6:15-17).

Religious apostasy is always the first movement in religious & national deterioration, and is unavoidably followed by political disorganization. This manifested itself in the case of Israel almost immediately after the death of Joshua (Judges 2:10-13). The people of God ceased to act as one people. They began to live in their own small territories and fight for their own selfish ends. Civil war almost wiped-out the tribe of Benjamin. The people of God, as a People, were broken up into factions, and consequently, became weak and suffered defeat.

Their curse was displayed in civil lawlessness. Crime was

everywhere, and stubbornness marked the people's heart. One of the most startling details in the book of Judges is the speed with which Israel forgot their deliverance from Egypt, the taking of Jericho, the victory on the other side of the Jordan, etc. They were blind - unable to see the present activity of God, and totally incapable of recognizing His hand of judgment on the Nation & His people. Blindness and religious apostasy are related to each other, as effect is to cause.

Israel's folly was highlighted by their limited vision & pure selfishness. For any nation to have Laws & Policies, which forsake God's Laws & Principles, is to be blind indeed. The outcome of such blindness is selfishness. The people of God, Israel, (as the people of God, today), sought only their own personal increase of power, status, and wealth . . . and forgot God.

Finally, the inevitable outcome of the people of God's compromise, tolerance & forsaking God, is immorality and social chaos.

The book of Judges proves, beyond a shadow of doubt, that God does directly and definitely, punish sin. And, the book of Judges also reveals the method & purpose of that punishment.

Israel's punishment was the result of their own sin. As they lowered themselves to cut-rate, immoral ideals of religion, they were compelled to bend to the rule of the people to whose immorality they had stooped. The immorality which they should have driven out of the Land, they instead tolerated & admired. And thus, the immorality of the people they conformed themselves to, became their tyrants. And God brought upon His people the scourge of an immoral & unrighteous people . . . because His people had embraced unrighteousness.

I've painted a bleak, heart-breaking picture here, but bless God . . . there's more to this story. The prevailing activity of God is revealed throughout the book of Judges in three expressions: punishment, mercy & deliverance.

The punishment of God was, and is uncompromising & severe. During the years before Gideon was raised up, the People of God, with so great a birthright, were compelled to take refuge in caves, hiding their Birthright for fear. Yes, but there is another word to be uttered. Not only was their punishment uncompromising & severe, it was remedial. God always judges His people with a view of restoration. God's aim is always to bring His people back to a consciousness of sin and of Himself.

Through all His processes, Jehovah is seen in the book of Judges as watching and waiting in mercy for His people, hearing them the moment they cry to Him, and answering them immediately with deliverance. His deliverance at the right time, by the right man, to the right issue.

Next week: God's judges in the book of Judges.

20 October 2011

Joshua Judges Ruth
Part Four

The apex in the book of Judges is God delivering His people the moment they cried to Him, answering them immediately, at the right time, by the right man, to the right issue.

I don't want to dwell on the right moment here, because we've already seen how the Lord acted immediately, when His people turned back to Him. What I want us to catch sight of is how God's deliverance was shaped by the right man, to the right issue.

In Judges 3, the writer paints an eerie word-picture of the pagan nations the Lord left in the Land to test His people. The Philistines, the Canaanites, the Sidonians, etc., were there "to know whether they (Israel) would hearken to the commandments of the Lord" (Judges 3:4 KJV). Which they didn't.

So the Lord raised up Othniel, a judge whose story is a simple one. "The Spirit of the Lord came on him . . . and he went out to war . . . and his hand prevailed . . . and the Land had rest forty years" (Judges 3:10-11).

But, "the children of Israel did evil again . . . and the Lord strengthened Eglon against Israel."

So the Lord raised up a righteous, left-handed judge Ehud, then Shamgar . . . a rough, rugged hero, fitted for his time, delivering and correcting the people. Then there was the wonderful alliance between Deborah and Barak in an age short on enthusiasm & enterprise. Deborah was a woman of song, foresight & prestige. Barak was a strategist and adviser. Without Barak, Deborah would have kindled enthusiasm, but accomplished little. Barak, without Deborah, would have done zilch. Together the Land had rest forty years.

But, "the children of Israel did evil again . . ." So the Lord raised-up Gideon, in Israel's most strenuous hour, who proved his heroism by his fear. Never criticize Gideon for demanding proof on proof. He was a man afraid of himself, but sure of God. Gideon was a man who's faith in Jehovah's words was so complete that he lead an attack on a vast barbarian horde with three hundred men, armed with lamps, pitchers & trumpets. And won!

The story of Jephthah is full of power. I always feel sorry for

Jephthah. He was a man with iron in his soul, born out of wedlock, despised by his legitimate brethren. A man who became both pirate & outlaw. Unlike Johnny Depp's corsair, who comically channeled the ghost of a pre-dead Keith Richards, Jephthah remained an honest, rugged Israelite, full of faith & strength. When God wanted a leader in the days of anarchy, disorder, and outlaws, He took Jephthah, and made him the instrument of deliverance.

Samson's tale is full of sadness, revealing a nation utterly deteriorated, and a man unable to deliver: "he shall begin to save Israel," yet, he never succeeded. One of the most tragic statements in the Bible is written of him, "He knew not that the Lord was departed from him" (Judges 16:20). But don't look down on Samson. That same word may come to you, it may come to me, if we play with evil when we should be fighting the Lord's battles.

Where did God find these people? Where does He find His people today? "They who wear soft raiment are in kings' palaces." When God wants a prophet, He takes a herdsman; when needs a leader, He finds a shepherd; when apostles are called for, He picks fishermen.

Why did God raise-up these Deliverers? It is summed up in, "Every man did that which was right in his own eyes" (Judges 21:25). What does that mean? Religious apostasy, political disorganization, and social chaos. The book of Ruth follows Judges. How does it end? With David the king. What is its issue? The coming of the King, Jesus! The King who brings an end to religious apostasy, political disorganization, and social chaos in Israel & the world! So the line runs from Judges, through the *idyllium* of the kings, to the coming of the King.

The book of Judges is full of teaching for the Church, and for this nation. It gives a warning as true today, as yesterday. It reveals the process of deterioration: religious apostasy, which brings political disorganization, and produces social chaos. All social failure is rooted in religious apostasy. The process of restoration must begin with the cause, which changes the course, and removes the curse. When I'm asked to deal with social propaganda, I say, "No!" That's a waste of my time & energy. It's meddling with ineffectual scraps. As Christians we should cry, "Back to God! Back to God!" That's the only cry that will bring, first His people, then a nation, back to political emancipation and social order.

There is a message of hope in the activity of God. He is forever moving towards His ultimate goal. His methods remain the same. He still punishes by war, catastrophe, and poverty. Take up any newspaper, watch any TV, what do we see? The nemesis of impure man-made methods. God is making men their own executioners. Yet, He is forever ready to pardon. If His people, and this nation would be turned back to Him, He would visit us again with His own salvation & prosperity.

Finally, remember, when the punishment has done its work, and the discipline has brought a sense of wrong in the heart of His people . . . He brings deliverance. We cannot produce it. But we need to be careful not to stone it when it comes, simply because it may not appear where we're looking.

Next week: the Kinsman-Redeemer.

27 October 2011

Joshua Judges Ruth
Part Five

Never measure the value of a book by its size. The little booklet, entitled Ruth, is one of the rarest and most beautiful idylls in literature. But to catch its message, it is necessary to have a well-defined outline of the picture it represents.

The background of Ruth is clear, "And it came to pass in the days when the judges judged." Ruth chronicles troubled, stormy, and difficult times. Ruth takes place in the midst of religious apostasy, political disorganization, and social chaos - which is the beauty of Ruth. God never leaves Himself without witness. Even in the darkest days, His light has never been totally extinguished.

The foreground presents the persons of Elimelech, Naomi, Mahlon, Chilion, Ruth & Orpah living in a alien land (Ruth 1). The conditions are famine, emigration, and sorrows. We see the return of only one Israelite, Naomi, to the Promised Land, accompanied by a stranger from another nation, Ruth. And finally, we read of the wooing and the wedding of that stranger, by Boaz, a faithful Kinsman-Redeemer.

Two figures stand out in bold solace, Ruth and Boaz. Their illustration is strong, clear, definite - yet full of light and shade. To read the book of Ruth is to read of Ruth and Boaz. Ultimately, their union constitutes an ever present high-way for God, through the trials & trust of His people, for Him to accomplish His eternal purpose.

There are two permanent lessons in this book. First, God is sufficient for trusting souls. And secondly, trusting souls are instruments of God.

Ruth was a Moabite, who's ethnic origin, according to the law of Moses, should never have allowed her to enter the congregation of the covenant Israelites. While this book confirms that no such restrictions exists when faith in God is exercised, we can't lose sight of the difficulty Ruth faced. The more she came into contact with the Hebrews, the more she would have sensed the great chasm between the two. The only Hebrews she'd known had left the Land because of famine. From them she knew only the jeopardy & sadness of those who had remained in the land. Ruth, along with Naomi, her deceased husband's Israeli mother, had entered into a Land of poverty, into a people, who in all probability were hostile to them both. Yet Ruth, because of her unimpeachable character, flourished - surrounded by circumstances designed to crush her.

Boaz was a man of privilege in times of degeneracy. A hard place to live, for a man of faith. It's easier to live a godly life among worldly men & women than in the midst of worldly Church-Folk. Boaz was a man of wealth, who was able to secure whatever he needed for his material existence. A condition perilous to a life of faith. It's hard to live an out-and-out Christian life confined in ease and luxury.

Ruth was a woman capable of love, set-apart by modesty, exceptional gentleness and courage. A woman in all the grace and beauty of womanhood. Boaz was a man of integrity, of courtesy, tender passion and courage. A man in all the strength and glory of manhood.

In Ruth & Boaz, we see the sufficiency of God for those who trust Him.

Ruth was a woman unrestricted. A woman who made her own choice against the prejudices of her Moab nationality, against the persuasion of Naomi, transferring herself, her citizenship, and her faith to Jehovah. Saying to Naomi, "Where you go, I will go; and where you lodge, I will lodge: your people shall be my people, and your God my God" (Ruth 1:16). A bold move for a non-Israeli woman.

Ruth remained loyal to her choice. She turned her back on the land of her birth, her associations and acquaintances, and followed Naomi until she put the Jordan waters between herself and Moab.

Boaz was steadfastly loyal to God. In a time when men took the name of God upon their lips, while their heart was far from Him, stood a man absolutely loyal: A man of Truth in the midst of pretense. A man who showed his relation to God in his relation to his fellow men. A man who took personal oversight of all his affairs, yet he lived a life so godly as to be able to greet his workmen in terms which revealed his relationship to God. Boaz was a man of caution and of courage - two things which are never far apart. Caution is the very soul of courage. Courage is the true expression of caution.

The grace of Ruth, and the strength of Boaz lay in the fact that they both lived upon the principle of simple faith in God.

Faithful souls like these are instruments through which God is able to move towards the accomplishment of His purposes. The story of the ultimate values of the faith of Ruth and Boaz is told in the ending of this little book: From Boaz and Ruth, to Obed, to Jesse, to David, to the birth of the Redeemer. Throughout the book of Ruth, we see the very footsteps of Almighty God. Boaz the Hebrew, and Ruth the Moabitess, in union, became the highway for God's ultimate realization of His purpose.

Next week the conclusion: The Redeemer.

3 November 2011

Joshua Judges Ruth
Part Six

Ruth's message is simple: circumstances will not Make, nor Mar, a saint. The book itself is a weavers tale of the difficulties in the life of the wealthy, yet faithful, Boaz, and the impoverished, yet faithful, Ruth.

The difficulties of privilege in the case of Boaz, and the difficulties of limitation in the case of Ruth both speak, in tandem, to the language of Faith. How? Because God is the absolute flora & fauna, the background & backdrop of all human life. Because God is the inheritance, the dominant influence by which all poverty is cancelled, and all wealth is made nickel & dime. So I'll repeat my first proposition. Circumstances will not Make, nor Mar a saint. If we cannot begin our Faith in the land of Moab, we will never be Faithful in the land of Judah. If a man cannot be Faithful as a wealthy man, though he lose his wealth, poverty will not make him a man of Faith. If we cannot be Faithful in poverty, wealth, if it comes, will in all probability ruin us.

As a sequence to my first proposition, I'll add a second. The principle of victory is Faith.

"Faith is the assurance of things hoped for, the proving of things not seen" (Hebrews 11:1). Faith is the principle that takes hold of God, and appropriates His resources. Faith takes hold of what we need in God, and enables God to take hold of what He needs in us. From this truth we learn something of God's laws of Faith.

Faith is an open mind, a personal decision, a direct application of the things believed in every-day life. Faith is a persistent courage in the face of difficulty. Faith is not a sentiment we sing. Faith is an attitude of life, based upon the conviction of our soul.

Any life that surrenders and follows Him in Faith is of great value to God. The book of Ruth beautifully portrays and teaches this truth. Yet, the value in a life of Faith will never be known, until we pass within the Veil. The sequence with which the book of Ruth closes proves this point: Obed, Jesse, David . . . Boaz & Ruth had passed, and David, the king for whom the nation was waiting, had come. Yet, the sequence does not end with David. As we read later, when the prophet Micah broke into a striking prophetic song: "You, Bethlehem Ephrathah, though you be little among the thousands of Judah, yet out of you shall

One come forth unto Me that is to be ruler in Israel" (Micah 5:2). Far down the centuries there came a star at midnight, angelic songs were sung, and in the direct line of the man Boaz, of Judah, and the woman Ruth, of Moab, to Bethlehem came Christ the King of Kings!

Ruth & Boaz could not see the future. They did not live to see the harvest of their Faith, but God found a foothold in their Faith. That is the principle of which we need to be reminded. We talk about results. But if our results can be statistically written and seen by all, then our results are dismal failures. "Faith is the assurance of things hoped for, the proving of things not seen."

Paul was a saint restrained - in "affliction" and "prison." It is impossible to read Paul's letters without being conscious of a certain amount of restlessness in his appeals to, "remember my bonds." A man who saw Faith's horizon, who was forever conscious of the Gospel, who wrote, "I am debtor . . . I am ready," was a man in the end, restrained, contenting himself with writing letters. But today those letters are of greater value than all his work. Did he know his letters would be gathered together, and would constitute the great exposition of our evangelical Faith for all centuries? I doubt that thought ever entered Paul's mind.

The English missionary Robert Morrison (1782-1834) wrote, as young man, "This day I entered with Mr. Laidler to learn Latin. I paid ten shillings and sixpence, and am to pay one guinea per quarter, I know not what may be the end. God only knows." That ten shillings and sixpence was the beginning of Robert's linguistic education, which made him a translator of the Bible, and opened the way for much of the English evangelical work done in China during the 19th century. Little did he know . . . "Faith is the proving of things not seen."

We should take comfort in the life of Boaz & Ruth. Knowing that the life we live for God today will one day bear Fruit. Our life may be lived in a big city, or a small town - small, unknown, never published, never heard from a pulpit, never noticed either in the religious or irreligious sphere, and yet we may be, without ever knowing, God's foothold for His future work, which if we were told, we could hardly believe. The one cry of our heart, according to this book of Ruth, should be a cry for out-and-out abandonment to Him, in order that by our Faith, the Lord will win the victories for Himself alone.

10 November 2011

FAITH - *the articles* -

Go Show Yourself To Ahab
A Ten Part Series

Go Show Yourself To Ahab
Part One

The seventeenth chapter of First Kings introduces us to a very interesting character, Elijah the Tishbite - whatever Tishbite means. I don't know. There are conjectures as to its possible meaning - no one's really sure. A few learned commentators are convinced that Elijah was not really an Israelite, but that's speculation, no one knows for sure. But we do know that Elijah came from the area of Gilead, which today we'd call Trans-Jordan - an area across the Jordan in the land of Gad.

Elijah was sent to the apostate Northern Israeli Tribe at its lowest point. Ahab was king and his wicked wife, Jezebel, was at his side. Together, they had introduced Baal worship to Israel, broken down the altars of God, slain the prophets of God and all but eliminated the worship of God in the Northern Kingdom. It was at this dark period of history that Elijah appears on the scene.

Elijah's a very interesting character. Malachi foresees, before Jesus comes again, that Elijah will come and will turn the hearts of the children to their fathers (Malachi 4:5). God is going to send Elijah back to the nation, Israel, to bring a great revival to Israel before the Second Coming of Jesus Christ.

We know this because . . . When Zechariah the priest (Luke 1) was in the temple fulfilling his course of ministry, the angel Gabriel stood beside the altar and informed Zechariah that his wife Elisabeth in her old age was to bear a son. Saying, "And he shall go forth in the spirit and in the power of Elijah to turn the hearts of the children unto their fathers." The key there, is "the spirit and the power of Elijah."

In the first chapter of John, when John the Baptist was fulfilling his ministry, they came to John at the Jordan, and asked him, "Who gave you the authority to do these things? Are you Elijah?" And he said, "No." Well, "Are you that other prophet?" "No." "Then who are you?"

He said, "I'm the voice of one crying in the wilderness saying, Make straight the path of the Lord" (John 1:19-23).

John denied that he was Elijah. However, after his death, Jesus was talking about him and He said, "Of all men born of women there is not risen a greater prophet than John the Baptist, yet he who is least in the kingdom of heaven is greater than he" (Matthew 11:11).

The disciples said to the Lord, "You're giving John the Baptist credit for being one of the greatest prophets? How is it then that the Bible says Elijah must first come?" And Jesus said, "Elijah shall first come." In other words, the prophecy of Malachi will be fulfilled. Before Jesus comes again, Elijah will first come. But He said, "if you are able to receive it, this is Elijah," referring to John the Baptist.

The first part of Malachi 3:1 is quoted of John the Baptist (Matthew 11, Mark 1, Luke 7), but the next part, "the Lord, whom you seek . . ." is not found in the Gospel record. Why? Because the remainder of the passage is one of judgment, not grace. Malachi saw both advents, but he did not see the separating interval of the two. "My messenger" is John the Baptist, but the "Messenger of the covenant" is Christ Jesus the Lord, in both.

There are two aspects of the coming of Christ the Lord. His first coming was to give Himself as God planned, as a sacrifice for our sins. His Second Coming is to reign and to establish God's kingdom upon the earth. So we have two aspects to His coming, and two aspects to the prophecy of Elijah being the forerunner. Thus, John the Baptist, "in the spirit and in the power of Elijah" was the forerunner at His first coming, but Elijah, the man, will return to be the forerunner before Jesus comes again.

Some will no doubt say, "But Elijah did appear at Jesus' first coming. He was with Jesus on the Mount of Transfiguration. When the Lord went up to the mountain with His disciples, Peter, James and John, He was transfigured before them, and Elijah appeared there, with Moses, on the Mount of Transfiguration with the Lord." And they're right. But Elijah did not appear to the Nation of Israel as Malachi describes. In fact, the Lord told His disciples not to say a word about what they had witnessed on the Mount, until He had risen "from the dead" (Matthew 17)! No doubt, in Revelation 11, where John writes of the Lord sending the two witnesses to the nation Israel, one of the two witnesses will indeed be Elijah, and thus, will be the complete, two-fold fulfillment of the prophecy of Malachi 3:1-6.

So we see Elijah as a very interesting character, because he's interwoven. First Kings is the beginning of his career, but then he shows up on the Mount of Transfiguration with the Lord, and he's going to show up once more before the Lord comes again. Interwoven through scripture. Even today, because of the prophecy that Elijah will first come, when the Jews celebrate Passover they always set the empty chair and leave the door open. They're waiting for Elijah to come. The door is open. He's welcome, and they've got a chair set for him at the table and it's a sign of their anticipation of the Messiah's return - Elijah will come.

So Elijah, this very interesting "hairy man" (1 Kings 17:8,9) comes to the Northern Kingdom of Israel at one of its darkest periods of great spiritual decline.

Next: Elijah & Ahab.

17 November 2011

Go Show Yourself To Ahab
Part Two

In First Kings we're introduced to Elijah. A very interesting "hairy man" who appears to the Northern Kingdom of Israel at one of its darkest periods of spiritual decline. He turns-up at wicked king Ahab's door and says, "As the LORD God lives, before whom I stand, there is not going to be dew or rain for these years, until I say so!" (1 Kings 17:1).

Elijah appeared very dramatically, with a dramatic announcement and then dramatically . . . he disappears. He disappeared for three-and-a-half years. And for three-and-a-half years, there was a drought. Not a drop of rain & no dew, until the land became parched.

Elijah didn't vanish into thin air, as Ahab thought, he instead went to the brook Cherith, towards Gilead, from where he had come (1 Kings 17:1). There the Lord instructed him to drink its water, adding, "I'll feed you there." And He did. God commissioned a couple of ravens, who fed Elijah bread and meat each morning and evening (1 Kings 17:6).

Elijah stayed by the brook Cherith . . . until the brook dried up.

The Lord then commanded him to go to Zarephath, which is in the area of Lebanon today, saying, "There's a widow woman there who'll take care of you." So Elijah went to Zarephath, "and when he came to the gate of the city, behold, he saw this widow woman gathering sticks" (1 Kings 17:10). So Elijah says, "Would you bring me a drink of water? Oh, and while you're at it, how about bringing me some bread, too?"

Gazing-up at this "hairy man" she begins to pour out her heart saying, "I'm sorry, sir. I don't have any bread. In fact, I'm gathering a couple sticks to build a fire and I have just a little oil and a little flour left, enough to make a couple of pieces of bread for my son and we're going to eat those and then we're just going to die . . . we're depleted. Soon we'll have no flour, no oil. Nothing."

Elijah says, "First make me some bread. And then make it for you and your son. And according to the word of the Lord, the flour shall not cease, nor the oil until this drought is over."

So this widow lady made Elijah some bread. And surprise! There was still flour left in the barrel and oil in the jar. She kept feeding Elijah day after day. And during the entire drought, the flour or the oil didn't fail, there was always just enough to make one more loaf (1 Kings 17:8-16).

A miracle indeed. There's no taking away from, diminishing, or removing the miraculous aspect - God supplied miraculously. But it is interesting that the prophet said, "Make it for me first, and then for yourself." There is a spiritual aspect here - as far as giving to God the first-fruits of our lives. Jesus said, "Seek first the kingdom of God, and his righteousness; and all these other things will be added unto you" (Matthew 6:33).

That's the Key. That's our priority.

But, if we twist our priority, and start seeking other things first, then our life becomes so involved in seeking other things that we never have time for God. Our first priority is to seek our relationship with God, then everything else comes into balance. They'll just work out.

Our life exists on two plains: the vertical axis & the horizontal plain. The vertical is where our life revolves, and the horizontal plain, our outer area, is our relationship with other people. If the vertical axis of our life is correct, if our relationship with God is what it should be, then the horizontal plain of our life will be in balance. First God, then everything else.

However, if our vertical axis of our life is not correct, if our relationship with God isn't all that it should be, then the horizontal plain of our life is going to be out of kilter. And we'll find ourselves on a crazy topsy-turvy kind of existence, where we're continually trying to balance our life. We'll spend all of our time trying to get our life into balance and in the proper focus. But we never seem to quite make that happen. Just about the time we get one side in balance, the other side becomes out-of-whack. We're constantly working to get our life into balance, but never seeming to be able to do it. Because our relationship with God is not all that it should be.

If we spend our time trying to balance our life, we're only treating the symptoms. It's like trying to treat a brain tumor with aspirin. We sort of deaden the pain so we don't feel so bad. But we're only treating symptoms. We're not getting to the heart of the problem. Any doctor who only treats symptoms is a quack. Stay away from them. Anybody with half a brain wants a doctor that's going to find out what the cause is that's creating the symptoms. "Why are we getting dizzy? Why do we have this severe pressure in our head?" We want something more than aspirin.

People so often treat only the symptoms, trying to get their relationships to work. No! We become so busy in the horizontal plain trying to get it in balance, when in reality the solution is very simple. Get the vertical axis correct. "Seek first the kingdom of God and His righteousness."

Next, "Make me first the cake." So she did.

23 November 2011

Go Show Yourself To Ahab
Part Three

Here, in 1 Kings 17, we find Elijah, the Tishbite, has come upon a poor widow-lady gathering sticks to cook-up one last loaf of bread for herself and her son, to whom he says, "Would you bring me a drink of water? And while you're at it, how's about bringing me some bread, too? Oh, and don't worry about your flour & oil . . . they won't run out!"

So this widow-lady makes Elijah bread and, Bingo! . . . There was still flour left in the barrel and oil in the jar. She kept feeding Elijah day after day. And during this whole period of drought, the flour didn't fail, nor the oil, there was always just enough to make one more loaf (1 Kings 17:8-16).

If she had, first of all, gone in to make the cake for herself and her son, that'd been it. The barrel would have been empty of flour, and the oil would have been gone. They would have died. But she followed Elijah's instructions, "Make me first the cake and then for you and your son." She put the Lord first. When we get our priorities correct, God will take care of us, and all the other aspects of our life, too. The most important relationship that we have in all this world is our relationship with God, and nothing should come before that.

If we're going to work on any relationship at all, we should be working on our relationship with God above every other relationship, because when that relationship is correct, then the others will all fall into balance. If our relationship with God is out of kilter, then there is no way we're going to be able to balance our life. It will always be crazy, topsy-turvy. There is no way we can have a well-balanced life until our life is centered in God. That's the vertical axis upon which our life rotates.

Elijah set forth a principle with this lady for God to work. Put God first . . . and God will take care of you and your son. He'll take care of the seconds and the thirds and the fourths. But it's priority, it's simple, it's basic, and yet it's one of the most important truths that we need to learn in our whole experience of life: our relationship with God must supersede every other relationship, because our right relationship with God will see us through everything else.

So the little lady did as Elijah asked & God took care of the rest!

FAITH - *the articles* -

"The barrel of meal wasted not, neither did the cruse of oil fail, according to the word of the LORD, which he spoke by Elijah. Now it came to pass, that the son of this woman became very sick," so sick, that he quit breathing. "And she said to Elijah, What have I to do with you, O you man of God? Are you come to call my sin to remembrance, and to slay my son?" (1 Kings 17:16-18).

It is interesting that she thought the death of her son was somehow related to her own sin.

"And Elijah said unto her, Give me your son. And he took him out of her bosom, and he carried him up into a loft," [where he was staying, next to her house] "and he laid him on his own bed. And he cried unto the LORD, and said, 'O LORD my God, have you brought this evil upon this woman that I'm staying with in slaying her son?' And he stretched himself out on the child three times, and he cried unto the LORD, and said, 'O LORD my God, I pray you, let this child's soul (or consciousness) come into him again.' And the LORD heard the voice of Elijah; and the soul of the child came to him again, and he revived. And Elijah took the child, and brought him down to his mother and presented him to her: and he said, 'Look, your son is living.' And the woman said to Elijah, 'Now by this I know that you are a man of God, and the word of the LORD is in your mouth in truth'" (1 Kings 17:19-24).

"And it came to pass after many days, that the word of the LORD came to Elijah in the third year, saying, 'Go, show yourself to Ahab, and I will send rain upon the earth'" (1 Kings 18:1).

This is the important part of the story. "The word of the Lord came to Elijah saying, 'Go show yourself to Ahab. I'm going to send rain upon the earth.'" So Elijah has the promise from God that rain is going to come. Later on, we'll find Elijah on Mount Carmel praying, bowing himself and praying for God to send rain. And then we'll find him sending his servant out seven times to the Mediterranean to look for clouds. His prayer and his sending his servant out is related to the Lord's promise, "I will send rain." In other words, his prayer was premised upon the fact that he had heard from the Lord and already received the promise of God.

Prayers that are based upon God's promises and God's word, we can be sure are going to be answered. So we have the promise of God. Elijah heard the word of the Lord and on the basis of his hearing ears came his prayer.

1 December 2011

Go Show Yourself To Ahab
Part Four

"The word of the Lord came to Elijah saying, 'Go show yourself to Ahab. I'm going to send rain upon the earth.'" So Elijah sets-out to show himself to Ahab, in the area of Samaria, the Northern Kingdom, where they'd been without rain for three years. (1 Kings 18:2).

Meanwhile, "Ahab had called Obadiah, who was the governor over his house."

"Who's Obadiah?," you ask. Well, he's almost completely unknown apart from the meaning of his name: Servant or Worshiper of the Lord. Among all the prophets, he's the briefest in number of words - his prophecy occupies only one page in our Bible - yet in the grace of mysteries, he is their equal. The last words of his prophecy sums up the character of this man, "The kingdom shall be Jehovah's" (Obadiah 1:21).

During the time that Jezebel was cutting off all of the prophets of God, Obadiah took a hundred prophets, hid them in two caves, fifty in each cave, and fed them daily (1 Kings 18:3-4).

Obadiah was a man who feared God, not the king . . . or the queen.

"Ahab said to Obadiah, 'Now you go this way through the land and see if you can find any pools of water, where there might be some green grass around them so we can feed our mules and horses and keep them alive, that we don't lose all of our animals'" (1 Kings 18:5).

"So they divided the land between them to pass through it: Ahab went one way by himself, and Obadiah went another way by himself" (1 Kings 18:6).

As Obadiah was out looking for water, Elijah came to meet him. Obadiah, knowing Elijah's distinctive nature, fell on his face and said, "'Is that you, my lord Elijah?' And Elijah said, 'I am. Go and tell your lord, King Ahab that I am here'" (1 Kings 18:7, 8).

"Hey, what have I done to hurt you?" Obadiah parries. "You want me to go tell Ahab you're here? Fine & dandy. But, as soon as I do, the Spirit of the Lord will snatch you off someplace. So if I go to Ahab and say, 'Come on over here, Elijah's going to meet you,' and I bring him, I know that the Lord, will likely have carted you off someplace else and he'll kill me. I'm a family man and I don't mean you any harm.

FAITH - *the articles* -

Why would you ask me to do something like that?"

Elijah, dispelling Obadiah's angst, said, "I will surely be here and I will meet him. Now go and tell your lord, Behold, Elijah's here." So Obadiah found Ahab and told him, "Elijah's over here" (1 Kings 18:9-17).

Ahab, now, face to face with Elijah says, "Are you the one that has troubled Israel?" (1 Kings 18:17).

Ahab, like most people who live wicked lives, when the fruit of their wickedness comes, they blame God or His men for their calamities, as though God, or His men, actually owe them something.

But Elijah's not a man to take the blame.

"I haven't troubled Israel, but you, and your father's house have forsaken the commandments of the LORD, and you've followed Baalim. Now therefore send, and gather me together all Israel to mount Carmel, and bring in the prophets of Baal, all four hundred and fifty of them, and the prophets of the groves, the four hundred prophets of Ashtoreth, that you've been supporting."

"So Ahab sent unto all the children of Israel, and gathered the prophets together to mount Carmel. And Elijah came unto the people, and said, 'How long will you falter between two opinions? If the LORD is God, follow him, but if Baal, then follow him.' And the people didn't answer a word. Then said Elijah unto the people, 'I, even I only, remain a prophet of the LORD, but Baal's prophets are four hundred and fifty men. Now give us two bullocks, and let them take the choice, whatever bullock they want, and cut it in pieces, and lay it on wood, and don't put any fire under it, and I will dress the other bullock, and lay it on wood, and put no fire under, and let them call on the name of their gods, and I will call upon the name of Jehovah, and the God that answers by fire, let him be God.' And all the people said, [fair enough] 'It is well spoken'" (1 Kings 18:18-24).

So Elijah tells the prophets of Baal, "look, there's a lot of you guys, so choose one of the bullocks first, dress it, but don't put any fire under it and call on the name of your god." And they took the bullock which was given them, and they dressed it, and called on the name of Baal from morning until noon, saying, "O Baal, hear us." But there was no voice, nor any that answered. So they leaped upon the altar. Now it came to pass at noon, that Elijah decided to mock them saying, "Maybe you guys ought to be crying louder, look, he's a god, unless maybe he's in conversation, or maybe he's on vacation, or he could be asleep, maybe you need to wake him up. Why don't you just scream a little louder?" (1

Kings 18:25-27).

"So they cried all the louder. They cut themselves in great religious zeal with knives and lancets, till blood was gushing out all over them" (1 Kings 18:28). Leaping on the altar. Crying for Baal to send fire. And of course, nothing happened.

"Now about the time of the evening sacrifice, there was neither a voice to answer, nor any that regarded their cries. So Elijah said to all the people, 'Come on over here now near me'" (1 Kings 18:29, 30).

Next: Elijah repairs the altar of the LORD.

8 December 2011

Go Show Yourself To Ahab
Part Five

In 1 Kings 18, the prophets of Baal, after an afternoon of unsuccessful attempts to get their god to do anything, had started to cry louder and cut themselves in great religious zeal with lancets, till the blood was gushing out all over them. Crying for Baal to send fire. And of course, nothing happened.

"Now about the time of the evening sacrifice, there was neither a voice to answer, nor any that regarded their cries." So Elijah said to all the people, "Come on over here now near me." So the people came near to him. And he repaired the altar of the LORD that was broken down - taking twelve stones, according to the number of the tribes of Israel - building the altar in the name of the LORD. He then dug a trench around the altar, enough to contain about two measures of seed, he put wood in order on the altar, cut up the bullock in pieces, laid them on the wood, and told the people to, "Fill four barrels with water, and pour it on the burnt sacrifice, and the wood." Okay. "Now, do it a second time." Then, "Do it a third time." So that the water ran all over the altar, and filled the trench.

Around the time of the evening sacrifice, Elijah said, "Jehovah, God of Abraham, Isaac, and of Israel, let it be known this day that You are the God in Israel, and that I am your servant, and that I have done all of these things at Your word. Hear me, O LORD, hear me, that this people may know that You are Jehovah God, and that You have turned their heart back again." And the fire of the LORD fell, consuming the burnt sacrifice, the wood, the stones, the dust, and licked up all the water that was in the trench. When the people saw this, they fell on their faces, and said, "Jehovah, He is the God. Jehovah, He is God." Elijah said, "Take the prophets of Baal, don't let any of them escape." So they took all the false prophets to the brook Kishon, which is in the valley beneath Mount Carmel flowing out of Megiddo into the Mediterranean and there Elijah killed all 850 of them. Elijah turned to king Ahab and said, "Get up, and eat and drink, for there is a sound of an abundance of rain." So Ahab went to eat and to drink.

Meanwhile, Elijah went up to the top of Mount Carmel, and cast himself down on the earth, and put his face between his knees, and he said to his servant, "Go up and look toward the Mediterranean." And he went up, and looked, and said, "There is nothing." Elijah said, "Go again." Seven times he sent him. And it came to pass the seventh time, that his servant said, "Behold, there's arising a little cloud out of the sea, about the size of a man's hand." And Elijah said, "Go up, and say to Ahab, 'Prepare your chariot, and get down, in order that the rain doesn't stop you.'"

As Ahab rode off to Jezreel - at the other end of the valley of Megiddo - "It came to pass, that the heaven was black with clouds and wind, and there was a great rain." (1 Kings 18:29-45)

God answered by fire, and then sent rain in answer to Elijah's prayer. The confidence in Elijah's prayer came from the fact of his listening ear. This is always true. Real confidence in prayer comes from the fact that we have heard from the Lord. The listening ear is an important detail in prayer. So often we're so overwhelmed with our particular problems & situations that we rush into God and start blurting out the whole scene, rather than coming in and waiting for God to speak. Never thinking . . . maybe He's got something to tell me.

Some of you are likely thinking, "God does not speak to men today as He did in days of old." I disagree, and I'll give you a true statement: Men are not listening today as they once did. If men will listen, God will speak.

With many people, prayer is only thought of in terms of a monologue. Real prayer should be a dialogue. We should be speaking to God, and then we should be listening to God - to hear His instructions & directions. Our time of quiet, listening before the Lord is very important. We should sit down, relax and be quiet before the Lord so that He might have an opportunity to speak to us. Then we speak to Him again & so on. We wait for Him to answer.

Every morning I like to spend time reading, praying & listening . . . praying & listening again, that I might get directions, instructions and guidance from the Lord for each new day. It's always an exciting experience when God responds to my prayers and begins to give me direction and answers. When I listen, God will speak.

You may be saying, "God never responds to me." Or, "God doesn't say anything to me." Well, maybe you're not giving Him a chance? Are you really listening? Are you really waiting for His response? Well, are you?

Anyway, after all the commotion had died down, Ahab runs home to tell his wife Jezebel what Elijah did, and how he'd killed all her prophets. So Jezebel sent a messenger to Elijah saying, "Let the gods do to me, and even more also, if I don't make your life like the life of those prophets by tomorrow this time." When Elijah got the message, he hightailed it off to Beersheba . . . (1 Kings 19:1-3).

Next: There came a still, small voice.

15 December 2011

Go Show Yourself To Ahab
Part Six

Ahab, if you'll recall, has just informed his wife, Jezebel, that Elijah's killed all her prophets. Jezebel, in turn, has expressed her intention to kill Elijah. Elijah, upon hearing this news, hightails it off to Beersheba - which is about eighty-five miles south of Jezreel - leaving his servant there probably so bushed he couldn't go on any further (1 Kings 19:1-3). Elijah then journeys another day into the wilderness, sits down under a juniper tree, and asks God to kill him.

"Now, O LORD, I've had it, take away my life, slay me, I'm through" (1 Kings 19:4).

Elijah was speaking out of a distraught condition. We've all been there. We want God to end it. We're upset and say things we don't really mean. We run-off at the mouth - not really engaging our brains. Then afterwards we're sorry.

Anyway, Elijah's had it. "Lord, slay me. I'm through. Just kill me, Lord."

This is an odd situation. If Elijah really wanted to die, why didn't he just stay in Jezreel? Jezebel would have gladly killed him, herself. That was the whole purpose of his flight - to get away from Jezebel. The fact that he ran-off, proves that he wanted to survive.

So Elijah, now in the wilderness, at wits' end, decides to take a nap under a juniper tree. When he wakes-up, an angel had prepared him a meal.

"Arise and eat. Because you're gonna go a long way on this food" (1 Kings 19:5).

Angel's food. Good stuff. Very nutritious. Elijah journeyed another forty days on the strength of that one meal, until he came to Mount Horeb, the mountain of God (1 Kings 19:8).

Horeb, is way down south in the Sinai . . . way down. Elijah's really fleeing from Jezebel now, down in the barren wilderness of Mount Sinai or Mount Horeb - both names given to this Mount - the mountain where Moses met the Lord. There Elijah finds a cave to lay-low for a while . . . And the word of the LORD came to him, "What are you doing here, Elijah?" (1 Kings 19:9).

Elijah, it seems, didn't really understand the question. The question was, "What are you doing here, Elijah?" But Elijah gives Him the Why, not the What.

"I've been very jealous for the LORD God of hosts! Israel has turned against God. They've forsaken His covenant, broken down His altars, slain His prophets, & I'm the only one left, and they're looking to kill me" (1 Kings 19:10).

How much worse can things get? Israel's in total apostasy. They've forsaken the Lord, broken down His altars, killed His prophets. Only one prophet left and they're seeking to kill him. That was Elijah's overstatement of the case, because he's so upset, distraught & discouraged.

That's one thing about discouragement & despair, it causes us to overstate our case - making it look much worse than it really is. We get discouraged & despondent. We don't want anyone to cheer us up. We just want tea & sympathy. "This is bad. Really bad. No one's ever had it this bad." And we overstate our case, just as Elijah was overstating the problems in Israel. "They've killed all of Your prophets and I, only I, am left, and they're looking for me, to kill me. Lord, You don't have a single one but me left in Israel." So the Lord says, "That isn't quite right, Elijah, but you're upset and I understand."

Then the Lord tells Elijah, "come out of your cave and stand here on the mount." So Elijah comes out to the entrance of the cave. And a fierce wind came whipping through, tearing rocks lose, rolling them down the hillside. But God wasn't in the wind. Then came an earthquake, that shook the whole Mount. But God wasn't in the earthquake. Then came a raging fire. But God wasn't in the fire. Then came a still, small voice (1 Kings 19:11-12). And that was the voice of God.

We often miss the voice of God because we anticipate God speaking in a great, thunderous, mystic ways. And we miss His voice altogether.

When God speaks to us, we often think it should be something like, "Beep, beep, beep, turn right. Beep, beep, beep, go forward. Beep, beep, stop." People who think like this way, will often say, "God is leading me. I'm being led by the Spirit." Not so. In fact, when God speaks to us, when He begins leading our life, He does it in such natural ways, that generally, we're not even aware that God is doing anything, because it just seems so natural.

Don't expect God to speak in thunder & lightening. Why? Because it's awfully hard for us to hear, when our life is in the midst of a tempest or storm.

We need to get our hearts very quiet before God. We need to get away from the tempest, the storms, the shaking & the things around us that distract us, to be alone with God, to be in a place where we can really hear that still, small voice of God within as He guides us, as He assures us of His love, as He assures us of His purpose. We get strength and help from God when He speaks to us. And it's that still, small voice within we hear. That voice which is so natural, it seems as though it's coming from our own heart or mind. But in reality, it's God speaking. God planted that thought in our mind, with that still, small voice.

Back on the Mount, the Lord repeats the question, "What are you doing here, Elijah?" And Elijah repeats his Why answer. So the Lord gets specific with His upset prophet because in reality, Elijah's doing nothing.

Next: *God puts Elijah back to work.*

22 December 2011

Go Show Yourself To Ahab
Part Seven

Elijah, after all of his daring & bravery with the prophets of Baal, is doing what? Hiding in a cave on Mount Horeb. So the Lord questions him, "What are you doing here?" And Elijah tells Him why he's there (1 Kings 19:14). So the Lord repeats the question. And Elijah again tells Him Why he's there.

But the question was, "What are you doing here?" Not, "Why are you here?" So the Lord get specific with Elijah, because in reality, Elijah's doing nothing. God doesn't like His people to do nothing. So the Lord re-commissioned Elijah.

"Elijah, get out of here, and get on up to Damascus, and when you get there, anoint Hazael to be the king over Syria. And then get down and anoint Jehu to be the king over Samaria. And then anoint Elisha to take your place" (1 Kings 19:15-16).

God put Elijah back to work. God wants to put us all back to work. God wants to get us off our duffs and get back to doing something that's worthwhile for Him.

While He's at it, He corrects His prophet, "Elijah, you're exaggerating. For I have seven thousand men in Israel, whose knees have not bowed to Baal, whose lips have not kissed his image" (1 Kings 19:18).

Sound familiar? Haven't we all said, "I, only I am left." And God says, "No, no, you're not alone. I've got seven thousand more."

Anyway, Elijah leaves his cave, and finds Elisha plowing with his oxen. As Elijah passes by, he takes his mantle and he throws it on Elisha. And Elisha left his oxen and came running after Elijah. "Wait a minute, I pray you, let me go back and kiss my father and mother goodbye, and I will follow you." And Elijah said, "Go on back to your oxen, what have I done to you?" So Elisha went back and killed a yoke of oxen, boiled their flesh, gave it to the people, and then became the servant of Elijah (1 Kings 19:19-21).

Now Benhadad, the king of Syria, having gathered all of his host together to besiege Samaria, sent a messenger to Ahab saying, "Your silver and gold is mine. Your wives and your children, the best of everything you have, is mine." And Ahab answered, "My lord, O king, according to your saying, I am yours, and all that I have" (1 Kings 20:1-4).

But Benhadad wasn't satisfied.

"I will send my servants tomorrow, and they will search through your house, and the house of your servants, and it shall be, whatever is pleasant in their eyes, they shall put it in their hand, and take it away."

So Ahab call his elders, "Looks like this guy just wants a fight."

"Well, don't hearken to him, don't consent."

With his elders' backing, Ahab tells Benhadad, "All that you requested at the first we'll do. But that's all!" So Benhadad says, "The gods do so to me, and more also, if the dust of Samaria shall suffice for the handfuls for all the people that follow me" (1 Kings 20:5-10).

Ahab answers back, "Benhadad, better not count your chickens before they're hatched" (1 Kings 20:11).

When Benhadad heard this, as he was drinking with his kings, he says "Set yourselves in array."

Meanwhile, God's prophet comes to Ahab and says, "Thus saith the LORD, 'Have you seen this great multitude? Behold, I'm going to deliver it into your hand today, and you will know that I am the LORD.'"

Ahab says, "By whom?"

"Thus saith the LORD", says the prophet, "Even by the young men of the princes of the provinces."

But "who shall order the battle?"

"You will Ahab!"

So Ahab numbered the 232 young men of the princes from the provinces, and all of the children of Israel.

Now while old Benhadad was drinking himself drunk, some of his young men came to him, "There're men coming out of Samaria!" And he screams, "If they've come out for peace, take them alive! If they've come out for war, take them alive!" So his young men went out, and Israel slew them all with a great slaughter. Only Benhadad escaped.

After the victory, the prophet came to Ahab, "Go, strengthen yourself. At the end of the year this guy's going to be back" (1 Kings 20:12-22).

After their humiliating defeat, the Syrians were dumfounded. Consoling Benhadad, at his time of grief, they reasoned that, "Israel's gods are the gods of the hills and not the gods of the valleys. That's why they defeated us" (1 Kings 20:23).

They thought of gods in a localized sense. We should never think of God in a localized sense. God is omnipresent. He's everywhere at once. Therefore, it's wrong to think of God in a locality. Sometimes we think of God in a localized sense in heaven. And He seems very far off and remote because we don't know where heaven is. "It's out there in space, somewhere."

Or, we may think of God in the Church-House. Even in our prayers, we express that idea, "Lord, we are so thankful that we can come into Your presence, here, this day." Hey, we were in His presence when we left home. We were in His presence when we were driving to Church. We can't escape the presence of God. He is everywhere!

But the Syrians had a localized sense of God. All pagans see god locally, as, "the god of the hills." Next time fight in the valleys. There you'll be the victor.

So Benhadad gathered the forces of Syria together and he came up to Aphek to fight against Israel the second time.

"And the children of Israel went out against them. And the children of Israel pitched before them like two little flocks of kids" (1 Kings 20:27 KJV).

Israel was totally, hopelessly outnumbered . . .

Next: *"And there came a man of God."*

5 January 2012

Go Show Yourself To Ahab
Part Eight

At this point in the story, Benhadad has gathered the forces of Syria together to fight against Israel the second time.

"And the children of Israel pitched before them like two little flocks of kids," hopelessly outnumbered . . . "But the Syrians filled the country" (1 Kings 20:27).

"And there came a man of God, and spoke to the king of Israel, and said, 'Thus saith the LORD, Because the Syrians have said, The LORD is the God of the hills, but not the God of the valleys, therefore I'm going to deliver this great multitude into your hand, and you shall know that I am the LORD'" (1 Kings 20:28).

Now, the interesting thing here, is that, although wicked king Ahab had turned against God, God continued speaking to him. This is always true of God. Even though we may turn our back on God and go our own way, God continues to speak to us. God doesn't just forsake us and let us go . . . That's the way of God. God continues to speak to us, because He loves. He continually seeks to draw all mankind to Himself.

So the children of Israel came against the Syrians, in the valleys, and wiped them out and captured their king, Benhadad, who quickly told Ahab, "The cities, that my father took from your father, I'm going to restore them; and you shall make streets, and we'll make streets for you in Damascus, as my father made in Samaria."

Ahab, thinking this was a good idea, made a treaty with Benhadad, and sent him away.

Meanwhile, one of the sons of the prophets came up to his neighbor, "Smite me, I pray you." And the man refused.

"All right, because you've refused to smite me, you've not obeyed the voice of the LORD, so as soon as you depart from here, a lion is going to slay you."

And as soon as the man departed, a lion killed him.

So the prophet found another man, "Smite me." And the man whacked him good.

Then, the wounded prophet disguised himself and as soon as Ahab passed by, cries out, "Your servant went out into the midst of battle, and behold, a man turned aside, and brought a man unto me, and said, 'Keep this man, and if by any means he is missing, then we will require your life for him. And this man got away from me and now they want to kill me.'"

"You've pronounced your own judgment." Ahab bellows back. "You said that it was your life for his life and you let him get away. You've set your own judgment."

The prophet then rips-off his disguise, "Thus saith the LORD, Because you have let go out of your hand the man who I appointed to utter destruction, therefore your life shall go for his life, and your people for his people."

Ahab, knowing this was a word for him, returned to Samaria and began to live more carefully from that point on . . . "But he was heavily displeased" (1 Kings 20:34-43).

Now it came to pass after these things, that there was a fellow by the name of Naboth who had an excellent vineyard that butted-up to Ahab's property, down in the area of mount Gilboa. To no one's surprise, Ahab was desperate for that vineyard. So he spoke to his neighbor Naboth, "I'd like to buy your vineyard. Name your price."

"Hey, wait a minute!" Naboth contested. "This is my family's vineyard. If I sell it, I'll be selling my family's property. It's not for sale."

So Ahab, pouting, goes back to the palace.

"Why such a downed-face, my husband?" Jezebel asks.

"I want Naboth's vineyard. But he won't sell it!"

"Not to worry, my king, quit pouting! I'll get you that vineyard."

So queen Jezebel orders the men of the city to gather together, and hires a couple of guys to lie against Naboth saying, "We heard this man curse the king and curse God." Now the penalty for cursing God, was being stoned to death. So, with the two men bearing false witness against him, lying as they did, they killed Naboth . . . And of course, Jezebel took Naboth's vineyard and gave it as a present to her husband (1 Kings 21:1-16).

"And the word of the Lord came to Elijah saying, 'Arise, go and meet Ahab the king of Israel, which is in Samaria; he's in the vineyard of Naboth, he's gone down to possess it.' And you shall say to him, 'Thus saith the LORD, Have you killed, and taken possession? In the place where the dogs licked the blood of Naboth shall the dogs lick your blood.'"

So Elijah finds Ahab, and Ahab says, "'Have you found me, my enemy?' And Elijah answered, 'I have found you, because you have sold yourself to work evil in the sight of the LORD. Behold, I will bring evil upon you, and will take away your possession, and cut off from Ahab all of his descendants. And I will make your house like the house of Jeroboam the son of Nebat, and like Baasha'" (1 Kings 21:17-22).

In other words, "Ahab, your family dynasty is at an end. Kaput!"

Then Elijah turns to Jezebel, "The dogs shall eat Jezebel by the wall of Jezreel. And him that dies of Ahab in the city the dogs will eat; him who dies in the field the fowls of the air (or, vultures) will eat."

Here, the writer of 1 Kings adds, lest we forget, "There was none like unto Ahab, who did sell himself to work wickedness in the sight of the LORD, whose wife Jezebel stirred up."

"When Ahab heard Elijah's words, he began to really live more carefully, putting on sackcloth, fasting, and living very carefully" (1 Kings 21:23-27).

Next: *Elijah gives Ahab a final word.*

12 January 2012

Go Show Yourself To Ahab
Part Nine

It is impossible to read 1 Kings without being impressed by the severity of its note: "There was no king worse than Ahab." He "did very abominably in following idols, according to all the things that the Amorites had done before them, the people the LORD had cast out of the land."

But, when Ahab, evil & fiendish as he was, heard Elijah's words, "because you have sold yourself to work evil in the sight of the LORD. Behold, I will bring evil upon you, and will take away your possession, and cut off from Ahab all of his descendants. And I will make your house like the house of Jeroboam the son of Nebat, and like Baasha" (1 Kings 21:17-22) . . . Ahab began to really live more vigilant. "He put on sackcloth, fasted, and lived very carefully." So the LORD came to Elijah again , "These things will not happen in his days but in the days of his children" (1 Kings 21:26-29).

Ahab received clemency - and Israel had rest from war with Syria for three years.

In the third year, Jehoshaphat, who was the king of the southern tribes (Judah), came to visit Ahab. And Ahab said to his servants, "Ramoth in Gilead is ours, and we are still, and why not take it out of the hand of the king of Syria?"

Apparently, after three years of rest given by the LORD, Ahab's "sackcloth living" had come to an end - forgetting the mercy of the Lord. Paul was right. "Godly sorrow works repentance to salvation . . . but the sorrow of the world works death" (2 Corinthians 7:10).

"So Ahab said to Jehoshaphat, 'Will you go with me to battle at Ramoth-gilead?' And Jehoshaphat answered the king, 'I am as you are, my people as your people, my horses are as your horses. But, let's inquire of the Lord and see if we're to go to battle.'"

"So the king of Israel gathered his prophets together, 'Shall I go against Ramoth-gilead to battle, or shall I forbear?' And they said, 'Go up, for the Lord shall deliver it into the hand of the king.' Jehoshaphat, seeing that this might be a misstep, asked, 'Is there any other prophet that we can ask'" (1 Kings 22:1-7)?

"Ahab said, 'Well, there's this one guy, Micaiah, but that guy never gives me a decent prophecy. He's always saying something evil about me.' Jehoshaphat said, 'Oh, don't say that. Let's call him in and see what he has to say.'" In the meantime one of Ahab's prophets, "Zedekiah, made some iron horns and put them on his head and began running around with these iron horns on his head saying, 'Thus saith the LORD, With these shall you push the Syrians, until you have consumed them.' And all of Ahab's prophets said, 'Go up to Ramoth-gilead, and prosper. The LORD is going to deliver it into the king's hands.'"

Meanwhile, outside of the Palace, the messenger who went to get Micaiah said to him, "Now look, all the king's guys have given him good prophecies, so Micaiah, when you get in there, say something good, too. Don't lay a heavy one on him, you know" (1 Kings 22:11-13).

"As the LORD lives," Micaiah answered, "I'm going to tell him and I can only tell him what the LORD tells me to tell him. And what the Lord says, that's what I'm going to speak" (1 Kings 22:14).

So Ahab's messenger brought Micaiah into the king, and Ahab said, "Micaiah, shall we go against Ramoth-gilead or shall we forbear" (1 Kings 22: 15)?

Micaiah answered him in a very sardonic, sarcastic way: "Go, and prosper, for the LORD is going to deliver it into the hand of the king" (1 Kings 22:15).

Ahab, thinking that this guy was maybe trying to pull a fast-one said, "How many times have I told you, don't tell me anything that is not true in the name of the LORD" (1 Kings 22:16)?

"All right. You wanna know the truth? I saw all of Israel scattered on the hills, like sheep that have no shepherd. And the LORD said, 'These have no master, let them return every man to his house in peace'" (1 Kings 22:17).

In other words, Micaiah is prophesying Ahab's death: "The people are all scattered over the hills because their shepherd has been destroyed."

Ahab, looking at Jehoshaphat said, "Didn't I tell you that this guy would say something like this" (1 Kings 22:18)?

Then Micaiah continued, "Hear the word of the LORD: I saw the LORD sitting on his throne, and the host of heaven was standing by him on his right hand and on his left. And the LORD said, 'Who shall persuade Ahab, that he might go up and fall, (be killed), at Ramoth-gilead?' And one said on this manner, and another said on that manner.

And there came forth a spirit, and stood before the LORD, and said, 'I will persuade him.' And the LORD said, 'How?' And he said, 'I will go forth and be a lying spirit in the mouth of all of his prophets.' And the Lord said, 'That will work. Go ahead'" (1 Kings 22:19-22).

Micaiah's vision of heaven is very interesting. " I saw the LORD sitting on his throne, and the host of heaven was standing by him on his right hand and on his left." And the LORD said, "How are we going to get Ahab over to Ramoth-gilead that he might fall there?" And they began suggesting different things, until one spirit came up and said, "I've got an idea."

"What is it?"

"Well, I'll be a lying spirit in the mouth of all of his prophets."

The LORD said, "That will work. Go ahead."

Next: Why would God commission a lying spirit?

19 January 2012

Go Show Yourself To Ahab
Part Ten

Micaiah, in 1 Kings 22, saw an interesting vision of heaven: He "saw the LORD sitting on His throne, and the host of heaven was standing by Him." And the LORD said, "How are we going to get Ahab over to Ramoth-gilead that he might fall there?" So, one spirit says, "I've got an idea. I'll be a lying spirit in the mouth of all of Ahab's prophets."

The LORD said, "That will work. Go ahead."

Here we find something that is rarely considered, i.e., that Satan is a servant, serving God's purposes. That's why God has allowed him to exist. That's why God has allowed him freedom. Yes, he's acting in the sphere of his own free will, but yet, his controls are ultimately held by God. Satan is nothing but a glove on the hand of God. It's a tragic mistake to think of Satan as an opposite of God. There's no battle of, Good vs. Evil . . . in equal portions. There's God, and there's everything else! Satan is not an opposite of God.

God is an eternal, omnipotent, self-existent being, whereas Satan is a created being - in the rank of angels. If we're looking for an opposite of Satan, maybe we could look at Michael, or one of the archangels. There we'd find opposites. But in no way is Satan an opposite of God. Nowhere near. Satan exists under the total sphere of God, and though he is opposed to God, he is not an opposite of the eternal, omnipotent God in any sense of being.

Satan is definitely limited (by God) in his understanding, abilities, and powers. God says he can go so far, and no further. This was Satan's complaint to God in the case of Job. "You've put a hedge around that guy. I can't get to him." God puts limitations on what Satan can, and can not do. God allows Satan liberty within a limited sphere, to serve God's purposes. Thus, God can use, and often does use Satan or his emissaries to fulfill God's purposes - which is why God commissioned a lying spirit in 1 Kings.

God sent the lying spirit into Ahab's prophets (one spirit into all of them) to encourage Ahab to go against Ramoth-gilead and "fall." And it worked! Ahab believed 'em and orders God's true prophet, Micaiah, to be, "put in prison until I return in peace."

To which Micaiah replied, "If you return at all, then I'm not a prophet of God."

With Ahab's prophets' approval, he, and Jehoshaphat, king of Judah, head out to battle the Syrians. On the way, Ahab says to Jehoshaphat, "Hey, you take my chariot. I'm gonna put on some common garb and get into the battle myself."

So Ahab takes off his king's robes, gets into another chariot and rides-off . . . Ahab was thirsty for a little excitement.

In the meantime, the Syrian commander said to his fellows, "Now look, all we want is the king. Concentrate on Ahab. If we kill him the rest of the people will be so demoralized that that's all we'll have to do."

As the battle progresses, the Syrians see Jehoshaphat in Ahab's chariot, wearing Ahab's robe, and figure it's Ahab, and start to pursue him. Jehoshaphat, senses the problem and high-tails it off in the other direction.

When the Syrians finally catch-up to Jehoshaphat, they realize that it ain't Ahab.

And an interesting scripture occurs here. "A certain man drew a bow at a venture" (1 Kings 22:34).

In other words, he just let fly an arrow in the direction of their enemy. And, low & behold, the arrow hit Ahab.

The wounded Ahab turns to his driver and says, "Carry me out of the battle, because I am wounded."

Ahab, propped up in the chariot, his blood running out into the midst of the chariot dies - and was buried in Samaria. "And one washed the chariot in the pool of Samaria, and the dogs licked up his blood, and they washed his armor, according to the word of the LORD which he spoke. Now the rest of the acts of Ahab, all that he did, the ivory house that he had made, all of the cities which he built, they are written in the book of the chronicles of the kings of Israel (1 Kings 22:34-39).

So we come to the close of Ahab.

Interestingly, in the city of Megiddo, (one of the cities that Ahab rebuilt), there are about twenty different levels of cities - one built on top of the other. When one city was destroyed, they'd built a new city on top. Archaeologists have dug up twenty different civilizations on different levels of Megiddo.

The level that dates to Ahab's time, (next to the ruins of the temple of Baal that Ahab built), archaeologists found several hundred jars with the skeletons of babies that had been sacrificed by their parents to Baal - the worship Jezebel and Ahab introduced to the people. This is why

God wanted this horrible religious system utterly wiped out, because it involved the sacrifice, the human sacrifice of babies in the worship.

In this series, I've spent a lot of time in the northern kingdom, not because of Ahab, but because of Elijah. He's the central character of this story.

Back in the southern kingdom of Judah, Jehoshaphat reigned, walking in the ways of Asa his father (who was a fairly good king), doing that which was right in the eyes of the LORD. The remnant of the sodomites (homosexuals) which remained in the days of his father Asa, he took out of the land, but, the high places (for pagan worship) were not taken away" (1 Kings 22:42-47).

For the rest of that story . . . well, that's for another day.

Shalom.

26 January 2012

FAITH *- the articles -*

What makes a Man?

In my last weeks of High School, I was given some well meaning recommendations about what it meant to be a man: "Go to a good college." "Date a lot of girls." "Be tough and fight anybody who insults your girlfriend." "Don't show your feelings." "Drink lots of beer." "Get a good job, work hard and make lots of money." Et cetera.

I was a teenager at the time and my Soul-Mates and Kinfolk wanted me to be well equipped to go out into the world to become the man I was meant to be. My grandmother gave me a Bible and told me to, "Read this everyday . . . it will make you a man."

With all this wide-ranging counsel, I knew I was destined to fail.

As a adolescent, I didn't drink, do drugs or swear. I was one of two boys who didn't wear cowboy boots. I wasn't an Early Bloomer, so I shaved only once a week and was always embarrassed in the locker room. I never lettered in Sports. I made the Student Counsel by the eighth grade. I played first-chair clarinet in the school band and piano in a Bush League Garage Band. (To this day, I avoid anyone from my High School class; especially old football heroes.) I was a virgin and a Christian. The only thing that saved me from complete Geek-ness was the fact that I owned a car and had girlfriends, although my car was an older six-cylinder Chevy and none of my girlfriends were cheerleaders.

Today, I found an old picture of that boy. He is dressed in a cream colored sweater and jeans - not too lanky, hands on hips, the pose clearly adopted from some Rock-star poster. I can see hints in his clumsy adolescent body of the man he will become. In the awkwardness of his pose, I see him trying to be suave for the occasion and play the man, while he still feels himself to be a boy. I know he will feel boyish, not a man among men, well into his mature years.

It is his face which moved me. Open. Shinning. Filled with a strange power of innocence and strong dreams. His mask of sophistication hides a painful sensitivity he fears is a mark of inadequacy as a man. I don't see, but remember, the loneliness, the uncertainty, the feeling of being both proud and embarrassed by the secrete life the boy was living.

His clandestine life included many diversions not on any list of

FAITH - the articles -

requirements for being a man: writing & drawing; exploring the woods on his family farm; reading books, playing with ideas; imagining the woman of his dreams; wondering about the limits of his mind; loving his parents; going to Church; agonizing about poverty, injustice; wanting to do something meaningful - but what?

He did not know it, but hidden in his young heart was a craving to discover his own definition of manhood - he had already set out on a pilgrimage, a quest to find the Grail of being the man he was meant to be.

By my late twenties, my life was coming apart at the seams. College, after college, hadn't helped. Women hadn't helped. Money hadn't helped. By this time, I had Art Degrees & Writing Awards, toured with Rock-Stars, shared the Grand 'Ole Opry stage with Luminaries, and ingested enough drugs and alcohol to kill the nastiest Hell's Angel. I had lost that innocent boy, while trying to become a man. I was a mess.

One day I went to talk with someone I had known from my early Church years, an older, Godly-wise woman, a true witness, philosopher, someone acquainted with the darkness of the soul. Through a long morning we talked about life, love, God, drank coffee and prayed.

The last thing she said before I left was one of the most important bits of advice I ever got about manhood. "Jay," she said, "there are two questions a man must ask himself: The first is, 'Where am I going?' and the second is, 'Who will go with me?' If you ever get these questions in the wrong order you're in trouble."

When I left I knew my tide had turned. The rivulets of grief over my lost childhood, the ending of my life on the run, all flowed together and I found myself walking and weeping, knowing the time had finally come to sever the unbiblical cord that attached me to the false god of Success who was supposed to be my salvation. I called out to God, my Father. For the first time in years I was free. The innocence had returned and I was on the road to becoming a man. I was a prodigal, and I had come home to my Father.

The task of turning this reckless boy into a man began by the disruption of the bond between the world, the flesh, the Devil and the boy. In the natural we had been one in the flesh. To fashion me back into shape required a wounding of, and a sacrifice of my natural fleshly endowments. God had to begin to refashion me by a process of subtractions, judgments - chopping off here, trimming there. He had to prune me, shape me. As a stone in the quarry of the Lord, He began reshaping me with His mighty Chisel. This was not, and is not a fun time. But the work is necessary.

What makes a man? God. God alone makes a man. And I am convinced that we could each touch something universal, if we would speak personally to the silver of truth the Lord of Glory has refined from within each of our individual Believing lives.

Am I a man yet? Not really. But His refining continues.

14 October 2010.

FAITH - *the articles* -

More Reading

For a more in-depth study by the author on these subjects, the following references are available for online reading and/or download in *.pdf format at: http://www.drjaymissdiana.com/writingspage2.htm

The Doctrines of Grace Series
    See: Ch. 7 "The Counsel of His Own Will" *A Brief History of Redemption*, Dr. Jay Worth Allen, 2010.

One Baptism Series
    See: Chapter 9 "One Baptism" in *A Brief History of Redemption*, Dr. Jay Worth Allen, 2010.

Two Doors
    See: *Bless His Holy Name: God's Pattern For Worship, 2010*, Dr. Jay Worth Allen and Ch. 3 "What Shall The Righteous Do?" in *A Brief History of Redemption* Dr. Jay Worth Allen, 2010.

400 Years & Counting!
    See: "Deception By Appearance" on Eugene Peterson's *The Message* under the link: Freed In Christ!

The End-Times Apostate Church Series
    See: "Building The End-Times Apostate Church" and "The New American Religion" under the link: Freed In Christ!

    See also: Ch. 6 "If you can't lick-um, . . . join-um" in *A Brief History of Redemption* Dr. Jay Worth Allen, 2010.

The Biblical Church Series
    See: Ch. 3 "What Shall The Righteous Do?" in *A Brief History of Redemption* Dr. Jay Worth Allen, 2010.

Wrapping The Cross With Ole' Glory!
    See photos at the bottom of this article: "Wrapping The Cross With Ole' Glory" under the link: Freed In Christ!

www.ingramcontent.com/pod-product-compliance
Lightning Source LLC
Chambersburg PA
CBHW070721160426
43192CB00009B/1265